ALASKA'S SKYBOYS

Katherine Johnson Ringsmuth

ALASKA'S
Skyboys

Cowboy Pilots and the Myth of the Last Frontier

UNIVERSITY OF WASHINGTON PRESS
Seattle and London

© 2015 by the University of Washington Press
Printed and bound in United States of America
19 18 17 16 15   5 4 3 2 1

UNIVERSITY OF WASHINGTON PRESS
www.washington.edu/uwpress

LIBRARY OF CONGRESS CATALOGING-IN-PUBLICATION DATA
Ringsmuth, Katherine Johnson.
  Alaska skyboys : cowboy pilots and the myth of the last frontier /
Katherine Johnson Ringsmuth.
     pages cm
  Includes bibliographical references.
  ISBN 978-0-295-99508-3 (hardback : alk. paper)
1. Aeronautics—Alaska—History.
2. Bush pilots—Alaska.   I. Title.
  TL522.A4R56   2015
  629.13092'2798—dc23   2015011383

The paper used in this publication is acid-free and meets the minimum requirements of
American National Standard for Information Sciences—Permanence of Paper for Printed
Library Materials, ANSI Z39.48–1984.∞

For my husband, Eric, and my sons, Ben and Tom

CONTENTS

Alaska bush pilots were blazing new sky trails. Their landing fields were sand bars in rivers, beaches, small clearings anywhere, lakes, rivers and coastal waterways for planes on floats; the snow-covered tundra with planes on skis in winter. Of aids to aviation there were none: a moistened finger was held up to the breeze and the pilot took off.

—ERNEST GRUENING
The State of Alaska, 1954

ACKNOWLEDGMENTS

I AM NOT A PILOT. BUTTERFLIES FLUTTER IN MY STOMACH AND MY knuckles turn white when I board airplanes. Every muscle in my body goes tense. But I live in Alaska, where the number of pilot's licenses rival the number of driver's licenses. To swiftly go anywhere in this state, particularly Outside, we Alaskans have no choice but to fly. Therefore the first people I must recognize are the Wrangell Mountain pilots who made themselves available for interviews, provided photographs, and most important, kept me safe in the air while I flew from one remote airstrip to the next to conduct fieldwork. This select group includes Merle Smith's son, Kenny Smith; Kelly and Natalie Bay, owners of Wrangell Mountain Air; Martin Boniek, Wrangell Mountain Air pilot; Paul Claus, owner of Ultima Thule Lodge; Howard Knutson, former Cordova Airlines pilot; Gary Green, owner and sole pilot of McCarthy Air; and the elite helicopter crew flying for the National Park Service out of Gulkana, Alaska.

Others who contributed interviews were Susan Bramstead, former director of public relations for Alaska Airlines and former Cordova Airlines employee; James Edwards, longtime McCarthy resident and pilot; Charles "Bob" Lietzell, former Copper River Road surveyor; and Carl Benson and Charles "Buck" Wilson, scientists with the University of Alaska–Fairbanks's Geophysical Institute, both of whom worked on Mount Wrangell at the aptly named Wrangell Mountain Observatory. They provided beautiful photographs documenting their work on this active volcano as well as insights on how aviation supported their mountain-top operation.

Dave Helmso, a docent, mechanic, and independent pilot, provided his expertise of aviation history, particularly his rare knowledge of the historical aircraft. With his assistance in identifying the planes as well as the pilots to whom they belonged, I was able to directly link the aviators to the historical properties and flesh out the miners and businessmen who supported early aviation in eastern Alaska. Others who provided firsthand information include Ron Suttell, former Alaska Airlines employee; Paul White, a historical archeology professor at the University of Alaska–Anchorage; and Johanna Bouker, who, as a child, documented her experience at Nabesna in a journal while her father flew construction supplies to Northway, as part of the larger Lend-Lease operation during World War II. Archivist Jim Duran provided information from the Morrison-Kundsen collection at Boise State University. Research librarians at the Alaska Resource Library and Information Services found countless obscure aviation-related articles. Former Park Service historian Geoffrey Bleakley provided photos from his personal collection. I received unsurpassed support from Alaska cultural institutions, whose curatorial staff gave me full access to their archives and photograph collections. They include the Cordova Historical Museum, the Federal Aviation Administration in Anchorage, the Alaska Aviation Heritage Museum, and Wrangell–Saint Elias National Park and Preserve. Thanks must also go to Joanne Haines, who edited an early version of the manuscript.

Credit for this book must also be given to the National Park Service's Alaska Regional Office in Anchorage, where I was originally tasked to write a brief historical context of aviation in Wrangell–Saint Elias National Park and Preserve. The final document served as an appendix for a cultural landscape report of the McCarthy Airstrip and a multiple property nomination of aviation cabins and airstrips related to aviation for listing in the National Register of Historic Places. Because the nomination process determines significance of an area's built history, what was omitted was any discussion of the nineteenth-century characterization of aviation in Alaska. Therefore the narratives told throughout this book aim to place these "cowboyesque" pilots in historical context.

In addition to ground-truthing stories, many of the photographs provided by the aforementioned sources were exhibited at the Anchorage Museum in 2013, as a summer supplement to the *Arctic Flight* exhibition, which commemorated a century of Alaska aviation. Most of the photographs in the *Wrangell Mountain Skyboys* exhibit had never been viewed by the public. My appreciation goes to the Anchorage Museum and its director, Julie Decker, for giving me the opportunity to challenge visitors' preconceived notions of Alaska as the Last Frontier.

Finally, my deepest appreciation goes to Sunny Cook, Patricia Garrett, and the entire volunteer staff at the McCarthy-Kennicott Historical Museum for their constant support and enthusiasm for this project. The museum provided me access to a recently found photo album that provided key information about early flight in the Wrangells and invited me on several occasions to share my research with the local community. My aviation presentations always seemed to attract standing-room-only crowds—even on sunny days, when working pilots should have been out flying. This is a testament to the importance that residents place on their local history. Their sincere display of interest validated my time spent working on this project. I never left McCarthy without additional information, hearing a good tale, or gaining a new friend. So in the spirit of this Far North expression: "To the airmen of Alaska we say again, thank you and happy landings!"

ALASKA'S SKYBOYS

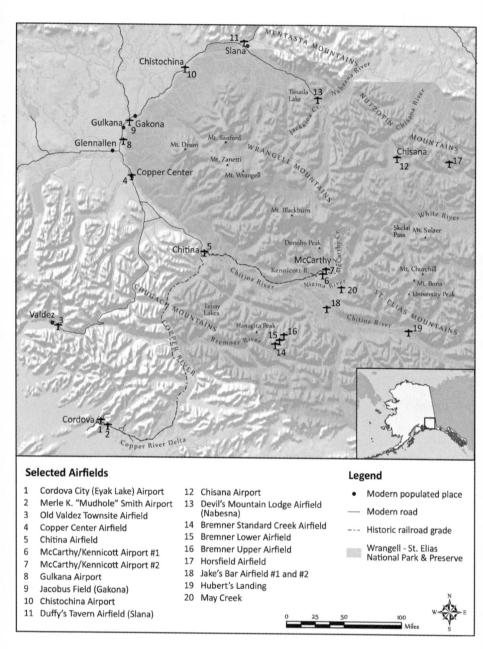

Selected Airfields

1 Cordova City (Eyak Lake) Airport
2 Merle K. "Mudhole" Smith Airport
3 Old Valdez Townsite Airfield
4 Copper Center Airfield
5 Chitina Airfield
6 McCarthy/Kennicott Airport #1
7 McCarthy/Kennicott Airport #2
8 Gulkana Airport
9 Jacobus Field (Gakona)
10 Chistochina Airport
11 Duffy's Tavern Airfield (Slana)

12 Chisana Airport
13 Devil's Mountain Lodge Airfield (Nabesna)
14 Bremner Standard Creek Airfield
15 Bremner Lower Airfield
16 Bremner Upper Airfield
17 Horsfield Airfield
18 Jake's Bar Airfield #1 and #2
19 Hubert's Landing
20 May Creek

Legend

● Modern populated place

—— Modern road

- - - Historic railroad grade

▨ Wrangell - St. Elias National Park & Preserve

0   25   50   100
Miles

Wrangell Mountains aviation landscape. Map by Barbara Bundy, 2014.

Introduction

WHY BUCK TAYLOR AND NOT BUCK ROGERS?

DURING THE PEAK OF WHAT *TIME* MAGAZINE COINED THE "AMERI-can Century," author and journalist Beth Day made two trips to Alaska in the mid-1950s to pen the story of the Last Frontier's famous flyers.[1] She spent several months interviewing pilots in Anchorage and flew with them across the territory. At that time, Alaskans, like Americans every-where, embraced airplanes as modern marvels. Test pilots like Chuck Yeager personified a new national hero. Since Charles Lindberg's trans-atlantic flight in 1927, these winged conquerors continued to push the boundaries between earth, sky, and space. In 1947, Yeager broke the sound barrier. That feat, bolstered by post–World War II military technology, ushered in a new era for the commercial sector commonly known as the jet age.

Instead of the 1920s- and 1930s-era biplanes constructed with fabric-covered wooden frames, the postwar vintage passenger planes—such as the cylindrical-shaped Douglas DC3, the Convair 240, or the Boeing 707—looked like rocket ships: they were sleek, all-metal, and aerodynamically designed. Supercharged turboprop engines lifted these behemoths into the atmosphere. Pressurized cabins, automated internal systems, and advanced radio and navigational equipment allowed jetliners to arrive at their des-tinations with speed, precision, and comfort. Jet aircraft represented an inevitable future—America was entering the space age—zooming toward what President John F. Kennedy termed America's New Frontier. By the mid-1950s the aviation industry represented the best of American inno-vation and technological know-how and, in many ways, epitomized the media's notion of the "American Century." And nowhere in the nation was the airplane more important than in Alaska. "Aviation and Alaska," as one historian put it, "were practically synonymous."[2] Air travel, by the time Alaska achieved statehood in 1959, dominated all methods of transportation. Alaskans flew more in proportion to their population than citizens from any other country in the world. In an age where the automobile symbolized the American dream, fewer than five thousand miles of highways crossed the northern territory, which spanned 586,412 square miles—approximately one-fifth the size of the Lower 48 states.[3] Undeterred, Alaskans made the airplane the automobile of the Far North.

Mechanical flight first captured Alaskans' attention when Captain James Martin flew over a Fairbanks ballpark on July 4, 1913. National interest in Alaska aviation came in 1920, when pilots of the U.S. Army's Black Wolf Squadron flew to Nome from New York and returned safely. The *New York Times* declared this first-of-its-kind mission to be the "most remarkable demonstration of the skill of our pilots, the efficiency of our mechanics, and the ingenuity of our designers and builders."[4] The decade's writers celebrated the new technology with a vocabulary distinctive of the times, employing such terms as "efficiency," "ingenuity," and "skill" to convey the grand achievement of modern flight and its inevitable progressive march forward. Within a span of four decades, Pan American, Pacific Northern, Northwest Orient, and Alaska Airlines all operated planes in Alaska, while two international lines, Scandinavian Airlines and Air France, made stops at Anchorage.[5]

Given Alaska's circumpolar proximity to Asia and Europe, the *New York Times* in 1958 anticipated that the industry of aviation was "Alaska's future." The paper predicted that the territory's largest city, Anchorage, and its international airport constructed in 1951, would continue to grow as a global aviation hub, noting that every year "others [airlines] are coming."[6] Alaska's territorial governor and soon to be U.S. senator, Ernest Gruening, observed in 1954 that Alaska provided the shortest course to Asia along the Great Circle Route. "For the first time in history," declared the governor, "Alaska's geographic position would prove to be an asset."[7] United Air Lines official Willis Camp agreed, writing in 1958, that "destiny of ideal location . . . will make Alaska a great air transportation center."[8] Both Gruening and Camp reasoned correctly that Alaska would serve as an air-bridge, linking North American passengers to destinations around the world by the end of the postwar period. And indeed, by

1962, the aviation industry considered Anchorage the "Crossroads of the Air World."[9]

At the same time aviation was changing the orientation of Alaska's position on the global map, its aviators were being memorialized in print. Most striking about the attention given to post–World War II aviators was a tendency to move away from the futuristic, science fiction–crazed atmosphere of the 1950s and focus on a more familiar past. Authors writing about bush pilots often addressed, but nevertheless downplayed, Alaska's advancement into the jet age and its central role in global aviation. This view—that Alaska was a far-flung frontier—was evident a few years earlier, when Congress debated Alaska's strategic role on the eve of World War II. At the time Americans, including their U.S. representatives, appeared to brush off Alaska politicians and their arguments for bolstering America's aviation front. Then, when the Japanese attacked Dutch Harbor and occupied the Alaskan islands of Attu and Kiska, this type of geographical and historical marginalization came, as Alaska's leadership had warned, at great peril. Instead of describing Alaska as a "Crossroad of Continents" that connected Alaska to people and places throughout the circumpolar North and the Pacific Rim—or as global events would quickly reveal, as a front line of the Cold War—the American mind continued to position Alaska as the final extension of a wilderness frontier, existing on the edge of North America. By the 1950s story after aviation story propelled "frontier Alaska" into the space age.

Perfectly illustrating this tendency was Beth Day and her widely popular and often praised 1957 aviation biography, *Glacier Pilot: The Story of Bob Reeve and the Flyers Who Pushed Back Alaska's Air Frontiers*. According to one aeronautic enthusiast, Day's book "caught the flavor of our last frontier in the fresh and salty language of the men who opened our great northern wilderness."[10] In many ways, Day was following the path of fellow author Jean Potter, who, in her 1945 groundbreaking classic *The Flying North*, famously wrote: "Alaskans are the flyingest people under the American flag and probably the flyingest people in the world."[11] Potter repeated her success in 1956 with *Flying Frontiersmen*, a profile of eight pilots from the Far North. Day's assignment a year later: go to Alaska and interview charismatic flyers.

Beth Day, a freelance writer and journalist, was no stranger to aviation. She had once worked as a staff writer for Douglas Aircraft Company, an aerospace manufacturer based in Long Beach, California, and maker of the Douglas Commercial (DC) series of commercial aircraft, often regarded as the most significant transport aircraft ever made. Her early writings, however, reflected a youthful market with strong interests in the American West. Titles such as *Will Rogers the Boy Roper* (1950), *Gene Rhodes, Cowboy* (1954), *America's First Cowgirl: Lucille Mulhall* (1955), and *Talk Like a Cowboy: A Dictionary of Real Western Lingo for Young Cowboys and Cowgirls* (1955) focused on cowboys and life on the open plains.[12]

In 1957 the New York book publishing giant Holt published Day's latest work, *Glacier Pilot*, to wide success. Readers, both young and old, embraced her tale of aviation coming of age in "the most unpredictable weather factory in the world."[13] The *Chicago Sunday Tribune, Christian Science Monitor,* and *New York Herald Tribune* each raved about the book that year.[14] A remark made by the book editor for the *New York Herald Tribune* even captured a longing for a boyhood make-believe, so brilliantly captured by Day: "One almost regrets that the times have changed," lamented the editor, "and that bush pilots now are regulated as much as the rest of us."[15] *Glacier Pilot* appeared to be the perfect vehicle in which Day expertly merged her writing experiences and interests. "The Alaskan bush pilots," she wrote, "are a hardy breed of independent, free-lance [*sic*] flyers who were conquering the Far North in their single-engine planes, without airports, navigational aides, or government subsidy. . . . Without help from anyone or anybody, they were making history on their own, charting the wilderness by learning to read the nameless mountains and rivers that run God knows where."[16]

Day's story of Alaska pilots remains a popular classic and the definitive biography of flyer Bob Reeve. The historical details of the account are exhaustive and comprehensive; in fact, much of the information found in subsequent chapters here came from Day's unrivaled work. But the devil is not in the details of Day's research, nor is it in the historical accuracy of the flyers' feats, but rather the way in which writers (even before *Glacier Pilot* came out and arguably ever since) have portrayed Alaska bush pilots and the orientation of their historical narratives. Like the book editor of the *New York Herald Tribune* wistfully expressed, these stories look to the past.

Instead of using a more timely figure for their prototype—such as the futuristic Buck Rogers, a hugely popular cultural icon, whose comic-strip stories paralleled the development of America's air and space technology—*Glacier Pilot* (and a host of titles afterward) evoked the swashbuckling cowboy of Buffalo Bill's Wild West shows, a fellow named Buck Taylor. Indeed, Day's historical figures presented in the book are steeped in a familiar tale of American prowess, freedom, and exceptionalism—the story of the Wild West. *Glacier Pilot* paints a portrait of the Alaskan bush pilot as an enduring symbol of Frontier Alaska—and to Americans everywhere, the Last Frontier.

Aviators Harold Gillam, Merle "Smitty" Smith, and, of course, Day's central hero Bob Reeve are presented as pathfinders—sky cowboys—blazing trails in fixed-wing biplanes; defiant, independent characters who could also constitute the cast of a Sam Peckinpah film. Day's bush pilots conquered a foreboding Last Frontier wilderness in the name of development, despite the personal risk. She positions them as central figures in the opening of Alaska, akin to the figurative Daniel Boone escorting settlers through the Cumberland Gap. Day depicts these pilots as laissez-faire entrepreneurs and "pioneers of civilization."[17] And like any gunfighter, these rough and tough flyers, especially pilots like Bob Reeve, were not afraid of a fight. They were, of course, all male. The occasional woman flew with "moxie." The most daring flyers opened Alaska's "empty land" to mineral development and carried to new heights mountaineers aiming to conquer the continent's highest unnamed peaks. Pilots aided exploration by transporting scientists to unknown regions and unlocked new territory to the Boone and Crockett trophy hunters. When Alaska became an air bridge to Russia, these cowboy pilots even became war heroes. "When the full story of the Alaska operation can be told in detail," declared a Morrison-Knudsen airfield construction contractor in 1944, "a saga as dramatic as the Oregon Trail, the building of transcontinental railroads, or any of the brilliant achievements upon which the spirit of America firmly rests will be written."[18]

Often omitted, however, from this last frontier narrative were topics that included the economic reality of flying in the early 1930s, the repercussions of aviation on Native communities in the 1940s, and the strategic business decision made by aviators to sell Alaska as the "Last Frontier" to promote tourism after World War II. Perhaps most glaringly missing is the role that the federal government played in subsidizing the growth of aviation in Alaska, and how Alaskans made aviators symbols of local resistance to the "Outside" even though aviation's own advances—technological innovation, airline establishment, and the selling of wilderness—had opened the floodgates. Perhaps Day's adoption of the cowboy motif to tell the story of Alaska's flyers should not be too surprising, for at the same time she had arrived in Alaska to interview pilots, adolescent youths across the nation were not only reading her scripted cowboy books but enthusiastically watching *Sky King*, a television show that centered on a former World War II pilot named Schuyler (pronounced "Skyler") King. He, along with his niece "Penny" and nephew "Clipper," used his airplane *Songbird* to round up local bad guys and protect the top-secret military installation near their Flying Crown Ranch in the fictitious town of Grover, Arizona, from being robbed, spied upon, or blown up by communists.[19]

The western imagery invoked by *Sky King* was just as powerful in the Far North. Even those who witnessed Alaska's rise into the jet age described northern aviation in terms of the Last Frontier. In the foreword to Oscar Winchell's biography, *Alaska's Flying Cowboy*, U.S. Senator Bob Bartlett (Alaska) remarked: "The early airplanes were mechanical marvels flown by resolute men who became folk heroes in their own time. . . . They were as truly pioneers as were the men who moved into the American West by horse and by ox team, and who drove the railroads to the shores of the Pacific."[20] In *The Last of the Bush Pilots*, Harmon Helmericks wrote: "The bush pilot of Alaska must . . . take his place alongside the stagecoach driver, the dispatch rider, riverboat man, voyageur, and the Pony Express man as a communications pioneer in the country's history."[21]

Contributing to the bush pilot's heroic persona was the magical machine with which angel-like flyers not only defied the laws of nature, but made it accessible in unprecedented ways. "No technology is more important in Alaska than that associated with aviation," wrote historian Roderick Nash. "The bush plane is Alaska's covered wagon."[22] In his romantically titled *Cowboys of the Sky*, writer Steven C. Levi exclaimed: "It was the airplane that brought Alaska into the twentieth century." Yet he describes such transformative and progressive change using nostalgic expressions. He calls the bush pilot "the unsung hero of the north," who, by overcoming mountains, glaciers, frigid temperatures and blinding blizzards, became "the stuff of legends." "These 'Cowboys of the Sky,'" insists Levi, "make Alaska what it still is today."[23] To Alaskans everywhere, aviation was a natural extension of the pioneering days of the gold rushes; indeed, Alaska's own manifest destiny.

Those inhabiting Levi's legendary Alaska would surely agree that it is an exceptional place. Most would describe bush pilots as self-reliant, individualistic, defiant, and daring individuals. The perception of bush pilots as modern-day cowboys of the North, who embody the frontier spirit of Alaska, remains a powerful narrative that resonates with most Americans. Day was not alone in her use of frontier imagery to define Alaska and its aviators. This universal perception requires little explanation, and even today serves as a trademark designed to sell not just reliable but *extraordinary* air service. "I have never encountered anything in aviation quite as unusual," remarked Alaska Airlines historian Robert Serling, "as an airline that technically, economically, operationally, and geographically has outgrown its name—and yet refuses to change it."

Popular culture's fusion of pilots and cowboys has created what might be described as a "skyboy narrative," used to express the historical significance of Alaska aviation to the general public and, perhaps more important, set it apart from the more modern story of aviation in the Lower 48. As one Alaska bush pilot explained: "I can't imagine Alaska without flying. It's part of the frontier spirit up here. Take away flying and it just wouldn't be Alaska anymore."[24] Still, it seems strange that everything from pop culture to corporate America identifies Alaska aviation with the quaintness of the nineteenth century, rather than celebrating pilots and planes as modern twentieth-century creations. To put it another way: Why Buck Taylor and not Buck Rogers?

* * *

Alaska Skyboys: Cowboy Pilots and the Myth of the Last Frontier is less about the details of flying and more about how the frontier narrative has shaped the way people understand Alaska's past. It aims to expose and explain how the frontier myth has moved through Alaska history by using aviation as an interpretive framework. Similar to David Courtwright's *Sky as Frontier: Adventure, Aviation, and Empire, Alaska Skyboys* argues that with the advent of the airplane, the skyways over Alaska's nearly impenetrable landscape similarly transformed into a new, dimensional frontier. Courtwright postulates that by the 1920s, the American frontier, particularly the nineteenth-century frontier, had in his words "become an irresistible metaphor for the country's growing presence in the air."[25]

By the 1930s Alaska's aviation scene matched Courtwright's definition of a type II frontier. Accordingly, farming characterized a type I frontier, but a type II frontier revolved around extractive economies, masculinity, and egalitarianism.[26] Life on a type II frontier could be deadly, but it was meritocratic. Credit in the form of social admiration was awarded to those who overcame great risk—risk that ultimately led to settlement. Like the miners who constituted the type II frontier of the California Gold Rush, the 1930s-era Alaska bush pilots stood shoulder to shoulder with the sourdough of the Klondike Gold Rush, becoming the new face of the Last Frontier. "Next to the Gold Rush miners of '98," declared aviation enthusiast Stephen E. Mills, "these men—pilots, mechanics and the farsighted entrepreneurs who supported them—did more than any other group to open Alaska to civilization. Many of these air pioneers . . . gave their lives blazing new trails in the sky and paving the way for the growth of the 49th State."[27] To a nation plagued by economic despair, Alaska and its heroic aviators were thrust into a powerful, twofold position: Bush pilots were seen as pioneers, instrumental for bringing reliable and safe air service to the Alaskan mainstream (type I), while simultaneously perceived in the popular imagination as mavericks, brave enough to blaze new trails and buck an over-controlling, bureaucratic system (type II).

Similar then to America's early aviators, Alaska bush pilots risked their lives for adventure, prestige, and work in a dangerous environment and independent social setting that was simultaneously congenial and competitive—and at times dangerous and even fatal.[28] Courtwright argues that aviation's frontier stage lasted only three decades, then was replaced by commercial growth and military reach that led the way to rationalized, routine flight. This paradigm can be applied to Alaska aviation as well, as Alaska's "age of frontier flight" gave way to the "age of the airlines" in the postwar years. But where the frontier permeation of aviation vanished from the Lower 48, it has managed to survive in Alaska. The question *Alaska Skyboys* hopes to address is why.

Finally, this book is not meant to be a comprehensive history of Alaska aviation. Alaska is continental in size. As aviation developed across the territory, it adapted to the unique environmental conditions featured within those places. Specific aircraft and individual pilots—especially after air routes were designated by the federal government—became local expressions of a specific region. Consequently, *Alaska Skyboys* does not try to tell the story of every illustrious pilot who helped develop flight in Alaska. Instead, its focus is primarily on eastern Alaska, where arguably some of the most important episodes in Alaska history—industrial mining, World War II buildup, commercial tourism, the Alaska National Interest Lands Conservation Act, and even Alaska Native land rights—can be explained, at least in part, through the lens of aviation.

The flyers whose stories weave throughout these pages are some of the same skyboys made famous by Beth Day in *Glacier Pilot*. In fact, few aviation tales about Alaska fail to mention the flying adventures of Charles "Harold" Gillam, Merritt D. "Kirk" Kirkpatrick, Merle "Mudhole" Smith, and Bob Reeve "the Glacier Pilot." They are the central figures in *Alaska Skyboys* as well but not necessarily for their exceptionality. These flyers represented the typical lives of pilots in Alaska, especially during the early days of territorial flight. Moreover, these men collectively embody the Alaska skyboy identity that typified their flying style and epitomize how the frontier myth can eclipse a more complicated, and arguably just as engaging, interpretation of historical reality.

Besides transforming pilots into cowboys, the "skyboy narrative" also "westernizes" the Alaska landscape (hence "the Last Frontier"), often portraying it as an uninhabited, menacing foe—a natural barrier to overcome and be conquered. Pilots in the Wrangell Mountains commonly landed on and took off from glaciers, mudflats, and even active volcanoes. Maverick behavior or adventure seeking, however, were not their motivations—it was the success or failure of their commercial enterprises that drove these early flyers to take such risks. But once airborne, there was no exaggeration: these Wrangell Mountain skyboys soared above a magnificent yet dangerous landscape. Starting from such coastal airfields as Valdez and Cordova, and following the glaciers and rivers inland to isolated airstrips and gravel bars, they navigated a skyscape that contains some of the highest and most rugged terrain in Alaska.

The eastern corner of Alaska, before it dips into the southeast Panhandle, consists of three mountain ranges: the Chugach, Saint Elias, and Wrangell. The towering Chugach Mountains brace against the Gulf of Alaska's ranging storms and surround the coastal towns of Valdez and Cordova like sharp fangs slavering waterfalls everywhere. The warm, moisture-laden oceanic air, which shrouds the Chugach range in seemingly eternal fog, collides with the frigid air of Interior Alaska, creating more snowfall in places like Thompson Pass north of Valdez—a major transportation thoroughfare—than anywhere on the planet. To the southeast lies the Saint Elias range, crowned by the 18,008-foot Mount Saint Elias, the second highest mountain in Alaska.

The jagged peaks of the Saint Elias range appear frozen in time by the world's largest nonpolar ice field, but geological forces, plunging the Oceanic plate beneath the North American plate, make these mountains exceptionally dynamic. For ten million years tectonic activity has driven this far-traveled range northward, slamming it into Alaska's continental margin, lifting the range skyward. Though most of the Saint Elias Mountains are nonvolcanic, plate tectonics produced the stratovolcano Mount Bona, located in the western end of the Saint Elias range in eastern Alaska. At 16,421 feet, this ice-covered peak is the highest volcano in the United States.[29] From the landscape over which the aviators flew most, however, rise a series of other colossal volcanoes. The Wrangell Mountain range, a massive field of volcanic and glaciated splendor, commands Alaska's eastern skyline. The unmistakable sentinels of the Wrangells include Mount Blackburn rising 16,390 feet, Mount Sanford rising 16,237 feet, Mount Drum rising 12,010 feet, and Mount Zanetti rising to 13,009 feet. Mount Wrangell, for which the range is named, is one of the largest andesite shield volcanoes in the world, rising 14,163 feet.

Snaking from the trifecta of ranges is the most extensive glacial system in North America. The stark divide between the wet-cold climate of the coast and a dry-cold of the interior, combined with the high mountain environment, creates enormous snow accumulations from which drain some of the longest temperate glaciers in the world. Originating in the high-mountain complex of the Icefield Range near the Alaska-Canada boundary, the Walsh Glacier moves westward for over sixty miles. The world's longest interior valley glacier, the Nabesna Glacier, is more than seventy-five miles long. It takes a pilot flying a small aircraft nearly one hour to cross the Malaspina Glacier, the world's longest piedmont glacier, which at its widest is forty-five miles across. Flying this country was (and still is) dangerous at best. As Walter A. Wood, a geologist who utilized aviation to conduct scientific fieldwork in the Saint Elias range noted: "These glacierized high-mountain ranges were by their very nature unsympathetic to human invasion."[30]

Yet as isolated as this region appears, the land over which the skyboys flew was never empty. Flowing life into this eternally frozen and unfeeling landscape is the great Copper River, creating a massive watershed that is home to Dall sheep, caribou, bison, moose, and bear. The river's mouth is used annually by sixteen million shorebirds, including the world's entire population of western sandpipers, the world's largest population of nesting trumpeter swans, and the only known nesting site for the dusky Canada goose. All five species of salmon return to the Copper each summer. The river's renowned red salmon constitutes the largest of the run's sizes. Today, the first fish caught of the season receives first-class treatment by Alaska Airlines, which flies it, and other coveted Copper salmon, to restaurants worldwide. The Copper River's spectacular fish runs were (and continue to be) vital to subsistence and commercial fishermen, and form the bases of the coastal economy. The river's name, however, derives not from the salmon that give it life but rather from the abundant copper deposits used for centuries by the Ahtna, the river valley's original occupant. By the early twentieth century, copper was central to the "electrification of America." Formidable "captains of industry" sought the ore so voraciously that they blazed a two-hundred-mile railroad and mining empire into a mountain wilderness in order to supply insatiable markets.

The Copper River originates at the foot of the Copper Glacier, located on the north side of Mount Wrangell. Flowing northward past the eastern flanks of Mount Sanford, the river makes a sudden turn southwestward and is joined by the Chitina River. Draining an area the size of West Virginia, the Copper River flows some 287 miles to tidewater near Cordova. Major tributaries—the Tanada, Slana, Chistochina, Sanford, Gakona, Gulkana, Tonsina, Kotsina, Chitina, Tiekel, Tasnuna, Bremner, Wernike, Allen, and Martin Rivers—swell the Copper's size as it makes its way to the Pacific Ocean. The sheer volume of water emptying into Prince William Sound produces the Copper River delta, the largest contiguous wetland along North America's Pacific Coast. Early flyers, like the river's famous copper salmon (as well as the ancient Ahtna, Russian *promyshlenniki*, American explorers, hopeful miners, and railway builders), used the Copper River to navigate the mountainous landscape. Despite the complicated rivalries and relationships these flyers exhibited, their reliable service to eastern Alaska eventually formed the primary stops along a regularly scheduled flight route in the Wrangell Mountains called the Copper Belt Line. They used the Copper River as a transportation corridor into the Interior and followed the braided course like a roadmap to find their way home.

1

Cowboys, Sourdoughs, and Alaska Bush Pilots

THE EASE IN WHICH A CENTURY OF WRITERS AND JOURNALISTS could evoke the frontier and its most iconic character, the cowboy, goes back to 1893, to the Chicago World's Fair, when history professor Frederick Jackson Turner and flamboyant showman Buffalo Bill Cody each told compelling stories about the American frontier. In the years between the purchase of Alaska in 1867 and the Chicago World's Fair in 1893, the average American considered the northern appendage an "icebox" or "Seward's Folly." But in the last decade of the nineteenth century, America's icebox image of Alaska began to thaw. The Chicago World's Fair initiated the first shift in the nation's collective thinking. There, Turner delivered his essay "The Significance of the Frontier in American History."[1]

Turner's frontier thesis positioned the westward migration of European settlers on the North American continent within the broader narrative of U.S. history by arguing the "existence of an area of free land, its continuous recession, and the advance of American settlement westward, explain American development."[2] Turner's story explained the growth of democracy, rugged individualism, and American exceptionalism. Arguing that the United States was now, according to the U.S. census, an intact nation from sea to shining sea, Turner proclaimed the American frontier closed and, in doing so, dramatically ended what he claimed was the most important chapter in the American saga: the move to the West. Because his sweeping explanation resonated with the American people, Turner's version of American history and character spread easily among academics and popular audiences alike.[3]

Meanwhile, exhibited not far from where Turner introduced his frontier thesis to the nation, Bill Cody's public extravaganza, Buffalo Bill's Wild West and Congress of Rough Riders of the World, claimed to be "a correct presentation of life on the plains." Among Cody's colorful cast of settlers, scouts, and Indians was the cowboy, the Wild West's most enduring figure. Cody took a Texas cowpuncher named William Levi Taylor and introduced him as "Buck Taylor, the King of Cowboys." Cody crafted Taylor as a wandering soul, who longed to return to the rustic life on the Great Plains. Portrayed as a plainspoken Westerner, Buck Taylor's life on the open range made him somehow more genuine than pampered Easterners. Audiences embraced Taylor's performance, and as his popularity grew, so did America's interest in the cowboy. Historian William W. Savage Jr. later remarked that thanks to Buffalo Bill's careful management, Taylor "became the first bona fide cowboy hero."[4]

Cody's invention of the American Cowboy was no small feat, for before his promotion of Buck Taylor as a featured performer in his show, the public perceived cowboys as drunken, rambunctious rustlers, who disregarded private property, law-abiding citizens, and the maintenance of the peace. The historic cowboy was likely an ex-Confederate or the son of a fallen soldier, "drifting" from town to town. Of the thirty-five thousand men who worked as "cowboys," about 25 percent were black and another 12 percent were Mexican. Instead of saving damsels and small towns from black-hat wearing wranglers, the historical cowboy was a hired hand, employed to tend cattle. His work was dirty, his hours long, and his pay pitiful. "Cowboying required no particular skills beyond the initial ability to sit on a horse and pay attention," explained Savage "The work was simply more tiring than heroic, more boring than romantic."[5] The invention of Buck Taylor, "the King of the Cowboys," idealized the cowboy. He was courageous, honorable, and chivalrous. In psychological terms, Cody's cowboy symbolized not so much what America was but what it imagined itself to be.

Moreover, "the Cowboy King," like the frontier he inhabited, was vanishing. Historian Richard White has suggested that Cody's frontier story conveyed a message of eventual decline, for his cast of characters memorialized a list of "lasts"—the last "real" Indian, the last herd of buffalo, and last "real" cowboy.[6] "Ironically," notes White, "the cowboy became an American symbol in the very era that announced the end of the West and the closing of the frontier that had created him."[7] Both storytellers—Turner and Buffalo Bill—warned that the sun was setting fast on the open frontier, but the cowboy rode on, long after the multitude of "last" Wild West encores ceased. The character of the cowboy began to appear more frequently in melodramas and popular fiction, the most influential being Owen Wister's *The Virginian* in 1902. By the turn of the century, the strenuous life typified by Theodore Roosevelt—America's first "cowboy president"—coupled with the Progressive Era's desire to toughen up America, accounted for the growth, development, and spread of the "western" as a literary form, as well as the adoption of the cowboy identity in American life.[8]

Then, just four years after the Chicago Fair, an event occurred that reopened the frontier and melted Alaska's icebox image from public perception forever. As an economic depression gripped the nation, sixty-eight Klondike miners and a million dollars in gold sailed into Seattle in 1897, sparking a rush of seekers—the sourdoughs—to the Far North.[9] The wild stories circulating about the size and extent of the Klondike discovery not only represented opportunity for ordinary Americans, but writers of the time began to link America's northern territory to the nation's frontier saga. Suddenly, as cultural studies scholar Susan Kollin has noted, "Alaska was positioned to encode the nation's future, serving to reopen the western American frontier that Turner closed in the 1890s."[10] Almost overnight Alaska's image as an icebox was replaced with an image of a land of vast natural wealth.[11] Alaska had become the Last Frontier, and personifying a new kind of American hero was the sourdough, "the invincible prospector." This image was further cemented in the public view when early-day Alaskans "took" Alaska to Seattle to promote a better understanding of the Last Frontier at the magnificent world-class Alaska-Yukon-Pacific Exposition in 1909.[12]

What drove the invincible prospectors into eastern Alaska at the turn of the twentieth century was the need for an all-Alaskan route to the Klondike. But the trail's inhospitable terrain and adverse weather convinced most miners to remain close and continue their search in the countless tributaries of the Copper and Chitina river valleys. Although Alaska miners never stopped seeking gold, the chief catalyst for mining in the Wrangells was copper, which transformed into wire and electrified the modernizing nation. Consequently, some of the most important mineral discoveries—both gold and copper—were made in the shadow of the Wrangell Mountains at places now synonymous with mining: Chisana, Nabesna, Bremner, and Kennecott.

In the final chapter of Alaska's famed gold rush era, the Chisana boom introduced the possibility of a new tool for the mining industry: the airplane. After James V. Martin made Alaska's first historic flight in Fairbanks on July 4, 1913, regional business leaders from places like Valdez and Cordova recognized the machine's value in mining enterprises almost immediately.[13] On July 29, 1913, just about a month after the first flight in Alaska, the *Chitina Leader* reported that Cordova boosters were so impressed with the possibilities of air flight that they quickly devised a plan to fly prospectors from their coastal town to the thriving Chisana gold fields located on the other side of the Wrangell Mountains.[14] Exactly why Captain Martin never began the first air carrier commuter service in the Wrangells in 1913 was never explained.[15] The lack of airfields and supporting infrastructure was a likely reason, and flight service to the Chisana gold camps, or anywhere else in the Wrangell Mountain region, would not be established for another seventeen years. The reality that faced the individual endeavors of eastern Alaska pilots and the big dreams fostered by community leaders was that mechanical flight would not take off until big business and the federal government combined forces in the early 1930s.

No doubt early pilots were pioneers, but they were hardly independent ones. They relied entirely on mining companies and federal mail contracts for their survival. In addition, it was the 1925 Alaska Territorial Legislature that authorized the federally managed Alaska Road Commission (ARC) to construct many of the early airfields that supported mineral development in the Wrangells. In 1927 the agency, supported entirely by Territorial-raised funds, scraped the region's first airfield on a bar in McCarthy Creek in order to supply the mining giant, Kennecott Copper Corporation.[16] Two years later, the ARC built a more substantial field on a bench above the creek and two additional strips north of the Wrangell Mountains: one on the Nabesna River and the other in Chisana—a decade and a half after Cordova boosters had envisioned air travel over the massif. Both strips were intended to serve the isolated mining communities, rather than attracting new settlement.[17] Similar to the incorporation of the American West, the partnership between corporatism and the federal government was crucial for the growth and expansion of Alaska's aviation frontier. But gaining the glory in the eyes of local residents as well as the media was, like the cowboy, the charismatic pilot. Helping to mold this solitary portrait was the understanding among Alaskans that the federal government supported the endeavors of outside capitalists and tended to ignore or neglect the situation of individual pilots, not to mention average Alaskans.

In the 1930s acclaimed journalist Rex Beach correctly observed that Alaska aviation lacked regulation. During these initial years when the federal government created an artificial market for gold, a free-for-all for flights ensued, depicted by many writers as a kind of Wild West. Flyer Bob Reeve admitted that to succeed in Alaska aviation business, a pilot had to do what was necessary to keep flying. "It was the rustler who survived," noted Reeve.[18] Instead of creating an environment in which healthy competition resulted in stabilized market growth, the government's lack of regulatory oversight forced rival pilots, hoping to outbid one another, to set unsustainably low prices for their services for which they rarely received full payment. To make up for those losses, rates for passengers and freight fluctuated constantly, making business arrangements with potential clients shaky at best.

Little control over the costs of their own flying businesses, combined with a fierce contest for customers, forced pilots (many of whom were still flying open-cockpit biplanes in the early 1930s) to take off in the worst Arctic conditions. Flyers who survived the night flights, frigid temperatures, and blinding storms were treated like heroes by residents of the communities they served. As the stories multiplied, the bush pilots moved into the realm of aviation legend. More times than not, however, bad weather and treacherous landscapes caused pilots to crash, in which they lost cargo, planes, and even lives. It seemed that in those first years of flight in eastern Alaska, the legendary status of pilots was equaled only by their mounting debt.

CREATING THE SKYBOY NARRATIVE

When mechanical flight came to Alaska in 1913, the territory's future position as the "compass of the world" was far from inevitable. Before World War II, the overriding perception of Alaska's aviation industry was that it involved only a small fraternity of flyers, who operated their trade in a few frozen outposts of the American frontier. Arguably Alaska's most famous flyer, Carl "Ben" Eielson spent as much time lobbying Congress as he did flying. His goal was to convince the skeptical lawmakers that they should award bush pilots the U.S. mail contracts instead of, what was presumed, the more reliable dog mushers. In fact, the inability to convince Congress to appropriate suitable and timely funds for airmail delivery and even a strong air defense in Alaska in the 1930s would have, at least in the minds of Alaskans, dire consequences.

During the advent of Alaska's "age of frontier flight," a fifteen-year period that lasted roughly from 1923, when commercial aviation began, to 1938, the year Congress passed regulatory legislation for the industry, it is true that only a handful of people piloted airplanes, even fewer flew in them, and fewer still understood how aviation worked. By the time commercial aviation service came to eastern Alaska in 1927, only forty-four rudimentary landing fields had been scraped out across the vast territory and only three Alaska-based transportation companies were in operation. Flying during those early years was dangerous and perhaps even considered exotic, but as more flyers entered the scene and air routes became established and commonplace, the air carrier business took on an air of day-in and day-out efficient dullness.

Although most of the industry's flyers strove to cultivate an image of safe, reliable service, scribes of the day ignored the routine nature of Alaska aviation. In fact, the rise of the air transport industry provided tremendous fodder for the men and women who earned their living by writing. "On the pilot," proclaimed a *New York Times* journalist, "depends much of the future of America's northern empire."[19] Likewise, another journalist writing for *Nation's Business* predicted that "airplanes will be the salvation of Alaska."[20] When flyers first took off in the mid-1920s, no simple storyline existed that fully explained to the average reader how the airplane might impact them or shape their future. Consequently, the language used to describe early flight often waxed romantic about the Last Frontier. Indeed, by using a simple, nonconfusing, and universally understood nineteenth-century narrative to explain the complexity of twentieth-century modern flight, authors and journalists were able to put into words—to describe to nonflyers—the indescribable.

Writers filled their stories with images of "huddled cabins" in which lived "grizzled prospectors," disconnected from the rest of the world. As if right out of a scene of a Jack London novel, these were men who spent their dark evenings around the fireplace of the roadhouse, playing cards and spinning tales of the north. In 1936, *New York Times* writer Calvin S. White wrote: "Lacking the facilities for other travel found in many regions, Alaska proves its claim to the title of 'America's Flying Frontier.'"[21] The *Times*'s portrayal of Arctic aviation—that "everyday travel, as well as in all emergencies," Alaskans "depend on the airplane"—reflected a largely fabled mix of metaphors depicting America's frontier past and its inevitable forward progress.[22] Airplanes were, in fact, considered a real possibility in transporting the life-saving serum to Nome's children sick with diphtheria—a headline-making story in 1925. But due to severe cold and wind, the lack of good maps, and a shortened period of winter light that limited safe flying time, Alaska's territorial governor "chose to bet against the modern age."[23]

Governor Scott Bone had weighed the risks of the new technology against the old and determined that if the plane went down, it would take with it all chances to save lives. He therefore decided upon dogs. Journalists, nevertheless, took aim at Bone, calling him somewhat ironically a "traitor to the Alaskan pioneering spirit." The governor's decision to use dog teams rather than pilots not only went against local newspaper men hoping to write gripping tales of flying machines and made-to-order heroes, but as author Gay Salisbury wrote in *The Cruelest Miles: The Heroic Story of Dogs and Men in a Race Against an Epidemic*: "The choice went against the Zeitgeist."[24] So much of the spirit of the age was predicated on America's innovation and ingenuity that anything less than modern American progress seemed to go against the public interest.

But even in their declaration of pilot-heroes bringing to Alaska a new technology, newspaper reporters from both inside and outside of the territory were misleading their readership, for few Alaskans, especially in the late 1920s and early 1930s, actually flew in airplanes. Air contracts were almost always made with mining companies and not people. Like U.S. lawmakers, average Alaskans saw the new innovation as a curiosity, even as entertainment, but irrelevant to their day-to-day life. In fact, they viewed flying as unpredictable, unsafe, and expensive. The physical act of flying fascinated crowds, but crowds were little interested in the physics of flight nor its practical application, as evident by the reportedly small turnout at a presentation on the mechanics of aviation given by Captain Martin the night before his historic 1913 flight in Fairbanks— an event that attracted a far bigger attendance.[25] Admittedly, most there that day came to watch him crash. Consequently, most people remained as skeptical in Alaska as they did in Washington, D.C. "Folks would pay to watch flyers risk their necks," explained Bob Reeve, "but nobody would think of giving you a regular job."[26] Bush pilot Oscar Winchell discovered this viewpoint the hard way. When seeking flying work in 1931, Winchell learned all too quickly that most Alaskans believed that "pilots were nuts."[27]

Several factors eventually secured a modicum of public confidence in Alaska aviation. One included a secession of around-the-world flights made by Russian ace aviators in 1937 and a year later by the globetrotting, dramatically heroic and handsome Howard Hughes, who after a brief stop in Fairbanks completed the trip in an unprecedented ninety-one hours.[28] The most important and far-reaching factor was the role of government regulation legislation passed in 1938, which through navigational aids, improved airfields, and established air routes promoted safer aviation for Alaskan passengers.

But Alaska aviation never completely dispelled its association with the unpredictable nature of the frontier. Underscoring the creation of Alaska's "skyboy narrative" was the influence that three transformative decades had on Americans' faith in their future. The disillusionment experienced by the shock of World War I not only "killed progressivism as a political and social movement," explained historian Steven Kesselman, "it destroyed the whole notion of the inevitable progress of mankind towards a better life."[29] Words that once expressed Progressive-era optimism, such as "efficiency" and "ingenuity," were used less and less. America's shaky prosperity of the 1920s revitalized faith in capitalism and free enterprise, but once the economic crisis at the end of that decade hit, a chronic fear cultivated the belief that those cornerstones of American life had reached their final conclusions. Working against the routinizing of Alaska aviation was the Depression-era's bleak outlook and America's absolute need for a heroic uplift.

Prospects for down-on-their-luck Americans were nonexistent during the 1930s. Poverty, especially in rural America, ran deep. Many claimed that technology, machines, and modernity itself had caused the nation's financial woes—that progressive science and industry had reached their practical limitations and were now the source of their problems. Moreover, most Americans, including Franklin Roosevelt himself, believed that in previous depressions, the untilled prairies of the West had afforded a haven for jobless men from the East.[30] But since it was determined that the modern age had consumed most the available free land

and abundant resources, new opportunities for ordinary men were extremely limited. "By the early 1930s, writes historian Orlando Miller, "Americans felt hemmed in."[31]

Sentiments of uncertainty caused by the Great Depression significantly shaped peoples' attitudes, which were, at best, nervous and disbelieving. Contemporary scholars argued that the nation's pessimistic state of mind stemmed from the physical closing of the western frontier. In the spirit of the era's antiurban and anti-industrial views, historian Walter Prescott Webb, whose landmark work *The Great Plains* brought him critical acclaim, argued in his largely dour *Divided We Stand: The Crisis of a Frontierless Democracy* that the frontier once worked for democracy, but its closing caused the rise of an antidemocratic force—the modern American corporation.[32] Likewise, American West scholar Robert E. Riegel wrote in 1930: "Beneath . . . a sentimental regret for the passing of the old West lies a very real and perplexing problem. What now happens to the restless, the discontented, the dissatisfied and the unsuccessful of the East who once moved West to start life anew?" Riegel's answer: outlets for restlessness on the still extant frontier of Alaska.[33]

Thus to create a storyline that lifted the spirits of pessimistic readers, Alaska boosters and newspapers in the territory and Outside began to adopt the tone and vocabulary of frontier promotion.[34] By 1934 papers espoused disenchantment with the city and industrialized civilization and in contrast idealized rural life and the nostalgia for the vanished frontier.[35] Writers ignored the technical or unknown effects of the modern aviation industry. Instead, they focused on the charismatic pilots—almost all originally from the Midwest—and the more fascinating aspects of flight: the risk and danger, selfless heroism, the freedom, not to mention the ability to explore new territory, conquer nature, and defy gravity. "The story of the development of aeronautics on and near the Arctic Circle, in a hard-bitten area which is one-fifth the size of the United States," declared the *New York Times* in 1932, "is a story of the resourcefulness of pilots."[36]

The same perceived dangers that gave Alaskans doubts of leaving the ground, writers and other pundits of the day presented as mere obstacles to be overcome by stoic, fur-clad men who had achieved the miracle of mechanical flight. In reports the day-by-day monotony was so telescoped that what was left was the picturesque incident—"the heroic episode" that, at least in the minds of nostalgic Americans, transformed the bush plane into the covered wagon of Alaska's frontier narrative.[37] For their cold-weather services such as carrying the mail, assisting miners, and saving lives, a reporter for *Alaska Life* called Alaska's aviators "angels in furs."[38] Noting the exceptionalism of aviation in the North, the *Los Angeles Times* simply proclaimed: "Flying in Alaska [is] different."[39] To the average factory worker or farmer, the stories of Alaska aviation conjured up alluring pictures of an open, mountainous, vast terrain over which flew bold and romantic flyers to whom adventure was the mundane. To someone tied to a machine or daily farms chores, Alaska appeared to be a land of freedom. This familiar narrative not only echoed the past but reinforced it.

By 1936 the *New York Times* boasted: "Alaska sourdoughs, who once took fifty-five-day musher trails over frozen tundra, relax in airplanes now and cover the distance in a few hours." The article continued to list the airplane's remarkable uses: delivering shoes for a miner's children; carrying school teachers Outside for Christmas; and transporting fur traders throughout the Territory.[40] Perhaps surprising to many who saw flying as unreliable, dangerous, and expensive, the end of the decade saw more Alaskans flying in planes. In the year 1929 planes carried only 2,171 passengers, but in less than a decade that number jumped sevenfold.[41] By 1937 the territory recorded seventy-nine planes in regular service and the number of Alaska airfields more than doubled.[42] Accounting for the boost was likely more the result of government imperatives than the success of pilots winning over the hearts and minds of average Alaskans. Indeed, just as significant as the bush pilot to the development of Alaska aviation was the federal government directing projects that built bigger and safer airfields and passing legislation that increased the gold price in 1933 and 1934.[43] Still, it is undeniable that Alaska aviators entered history just when people—as well as the fledgling industry—needed them most.

While Americans wondered whether industrial man could be as free as he was on the frontier, Alaska's heroic skyboys proved the affirmative. Besides providing escapism for the weary factory worker and farmhand, in a world that characterized the modern age as "mechanistic pessimism," the skyboy narrative showed what man and machine could accomplish together.[44] "Nowhere, I believe," marveled an observer from 1930, "does air travel mean more saving of time and effort than in Alaska."[45] Triumphant stories of the bush pilots showed the disheartened how to negotiate the world of industrialization and corporatism. These northern heroes became symbols of self-reliance, ruggedness, and, most important, captains of their own fate and dreams. By the end of the 1930s the average Alaskan could no longer afford to stay on the ground. This was the flying scene, when a young jack-of-all-trades, with absolutely no flying experience arrived at McCarthy to work for the Alaska Road Commission in 1923. His name was Harold Gillam.

2

Mines, Mail, and Mercy Flights

CHARLES "HAROLD" GILLAM IS CREDITED AS THE FIRST AVIATOR TO establish a significant commercial operation in the Wrangell Mountains.[1] Although Gillam's solitary personality and his fabled piloting skills are discussed at length in many books and articles focusing on Alaska aviation, the tightlipped pilot remains an enigmatic figure.[2] Stories of Harold Gillam permeate Alaska lore. One anonymous flyer, for example, tells how Gillam refused to hunt anything that flew because, as memory claimed, "Gillam was part bird."[3] He is remembered as being frugal with words, withdrawn, but warm to his friends.[4] "Gillam . . . never was one for . . . hanger talk," explained Alaska pilot Frank Barr. "Harold would sit slightly in the background, grin at some of the humorous remarks, and once in a while interject one of his own, but never offer information about his experiences."[5] Mostly, Harold Gillam is remembered for flying in Alaska's foulest, most extreme weather conditions. "Oldtime pilots said that there were three kinds of Alaska weather," explained writer June Allen. "Clear and unlimited, called Pan Am weather, then ordinary weather, and lastly, there was 'Gillam weather.'"[6] Consequently, like ravens riding invisible thermals skyward, stories, rumors, and hyperbole have always swirled around him. Over the years these stories have successfully transformed Harold Gillam, the man, into an aviation legend.

According to Gillam's first mechanic, Oscar Winchell, the pilot stood only five-feet-eight-inches tall, but "his muscular body made up that which he lacked in height." Winchell recalled that whenever Gillam was excited or angered, "his dark eyes would flash his impatience."[7] Many remembered Gillam as handsome and attractive to women. In her memoir *Sisters: Coming of Age and Living Dangerously in the Wild Copper River*

Valley, Samme Gallaher confessed, "I was nineteen . . . and thought I was in love with Gillam. All the ladies liked him, because he was a charming man and rather romantic."[8] Gillam was a fastidious dresser who fussed ceaselessly over the appearance of his planes. "He somehow managed to remain clean even when working on his airplane," remarked writer Jim Rearden.[9] He kept his wavy raven-black hair neatly combed, and he often wore a small knitted skier's cap on the back of his head.

Flyers and nonflyers alike considered Gillam an exceptional pilot for flying safely through extreme weather. "We use to refer to him as having a compass built into his head," recalled fellow Wrangell Mountain flyer Merle "Mudhole" Smith. "He always had a general sense of where he was."[10] "Violent winds were a daily part of the game," explained Wrangell pilot Bob Reeve, "but storms and low ceilings that blocked the mountain passes were as much of a dead end as a stone wall." With flyers facing a choice to either land and wait out the ceiling or backtrack to the first available civilization, "Gillam," Reeve marveled, "bored through." The genuinely astonished "Glacier Pilot" Reeve, a legend in his own right, acknowledged that "there was only one Gillam."[11]

THE ALASKA ROAD COMMISSION AND GILLAM'S EARLY YEARS IN THE WRANGELL MOUNTAINS

Although he is recognized as the Copper Belt's first commercial aviator, Gillam's initial association with the Wrangell Mountain region predates the start of his flying service in 1930. After four years of serving in the U.S. Navy as a deep-sea diver, Gillam joined several friends, including his father, and came to Alaska to work for the Alaska Road Commission (ARC) in 1923. In eastern Alaska, as with most of the Alaska Territory, two economic sources provided the bulk of a wage earner's income: mining and the government. "Mining was the backbone of the country," recalled Valdez resident Robert Redding, a young ARC employee, but "Uncle Sam was there [too]."[12]

The largest government payroll was the Alaska Road Commission, explained Redding, and in places where most mining jobs (except for hardrock) were seasonal, "the ARC figured prominently."[13] The Guggenheims' private railroad venture to reach the fantastically rich copper deposits deep in the Wrangell Mountains from the Pacific Coast was an unparalleled technological achievement in the annals of transportation history.[14] But it was the federal government, under the auspices of the U.S. Army-run ARC, that also played a leading and vital role in opening eastern Alaska to the public sector.

After gold was discovered in the Klondike in 1897, prospectors sought an all-American overland route to the goldfields. Because Congress felt that the Canadian discovery fell within the domain of U.S. national interests, it sent the army to explore potential routes to access the goldfields as well as the rest of Alaska's spacious, and assumedly, gold-sprinkled interior. The most logistical route moved northward, from the port of Valdez, through the Copper River valley, to Eagle, Alaska. The following year, the army blazed a trail along the 409-mile route. Because the trail connected the army's Fort Liscum in Valdez with Fort Egbert in Eagle, it was called the Trans-Alaska Military Road. Then, in 1900, Congress authorized the U.S. Army Signal Corps to begin laying a system of cables and telegraph lines in Alaska, known as the Washington-Alaska Military Cable and Telegraph System (WAMCATS). For the first time, Alaska was temporally linked to the continental United States as well as the rest of the world. In 1903 the Signal Corps began construction of a WAMCATS line along the Valdez-to-Eagle trail. This made the Valdez trail one of the most important access routes to the Alaska Interior.

Two years later a Senate committee studying Alaska's transportation needs recommended that the War Department construct a system of trails in Alaska and upgrade the Valdez-Eagle trail to a wagon road. To oversee construction and maintenance of the roads and trails, Congress created the Board of Road Commissioners for Alaska in 1905. Funding for the new agency came mostly from Alaskans. The federal government collected business license fees from residents of the territory's major towns. Alaskans who lived in rural areas had the choice of contributing two days' labor or eight dollars each year toward road building.[15] Though officially named the Board of Road Commissioners for Alaska, the agency was referred to popularly as the Alaska Road Commission, or the ARC. The War Department tasked the ARC to build roads in every region of the territory. Overall, the agency developed and maintained summer and winter trails, operated ferries, built bridges, and maintained narrow-gauge tramways—often under enormously difficult conditions.[16] By 1910 the ARC was engrossed with its premier project: construction of a spur trail from Gulkana on the Valdez-Eagle route to new mining camps near Fairbanks. That same year a ninety-mile spur road was built from Willow

Creek on the Valdez-to-Fairbanks road to Chitina on the Copper River and Northwest Railway construction route. Brigadier General Wilds P. Richardson, the board's first president and for whom the wagon road would later be named, oversaw the construction.[17]

Calling attention to the ARC early on was the promising mineral regions of the Copper and Nabesna country that lay to the east of the Valdez road. Even with the railway penetrating deep into the Nizina Mining District, prospectors still needed access to outlying districts as they ceaselessly searched for new prospects. The need for additional mining sites amplified after World War I as copper reserves quickly slumped. Kennecott mines continued to produce and ship copper ore, but miners had already removed the highest grades, and profits from the lower-grade ore declined exponentially. From the independent miner to the industrial corporation, finding the next rich "Bonanza" or "Jumbo" deposit to ensure future mining became a major priority in the region. However, a lack of transportation arteries made it almost impossible to get supplies and mining machinery into the most promising areas without prohibitive costs. Prospectors could only perform the annual assessment work to hold the ground and then wait for the federal government to build the routes. Because road building was slow and arduous, some of the most favorable mineral properties in the region remained idle.[18]

In the mid-1920s one of the most attractive mining areas within the shadow of Kennecott included the gold streams at Dan Creek and the surrounding Copper Belt of the Nizina Mining District. From Dan Creek, prospectors could search for minerals up the Chitistone River and Glacier Creek, over Skolai Pass, and into the White River and Nutzotin Mountains or down toward the May, Chititu, and Young Creeks, and into the Bremner River region. In order for prospectors to move supplies into those rich areas from the railway town of McCarthy, they needed to build a ten-mile wagon road and a sturdy bridge across the Nizina River.[19] The Nizina was a significant obstacle to prospectors. Serving once as the original path of the Kennicott Glacier, the treacherous glacial river, with its huge boulders and torrents of swirling water, had claimed many lives.[20] Efforts to build a bridge across the Nizina had occurred before, but products of those labors were always washed away by spring floods. In the early 1920s renewed speculation and corporate investment in the Nizina Mining District prompted ARC engineers to design a permanent bridge, made with steel and a concrete foundation that could withstand spring breakup as well as the Nizina River's notorious shifting channels.[21]

In the summer of 1923 the ARC hired an inexperienced twenty-year-old, Harold Gillam, as a heavy equipment operator assigned to the Nizina River bridge project. When the ARC shut down summer operations and the rivers froze in winter, Gillam went to work. His job was to move needed bridge construction materials from the railroad terminus in McCarthy to the bridge site using the ARC's Holt crawling tractor. Gillam maneuvered the Holt and its load down the Kennicott River, which ran through McCarthy, to the Nizina—a distance of about seven miles. Then he turned east down the river about another seven miles to the bridge site.[22] Gillam's winter work—replete with darkening days, cold temperature, and blinding blizzards—not only gave him experience running engine-driven machines in the unfriendly winter weather of Alaska, but "whether he was aware of it or not," suggests biographer Arnold Griese, "Gillam's work that winter prepared him for his future winter flying."[23]

EXPANDING HIS WINGS

Gillam did not remain long in McCarthy during those early years. Although he would return to the Copper Belt region a few years later with a fledgling air carrier business, Gillam decided to move to Fairbanks in 1925 to start a freight company. While working near Weeks Airfield, he fraternized with several Alaska pilots who introduced him to flying in 1927. By far, the most influential were pilot Joe Crosson, arguably Alaska's greatest bush pilot, and Joe's sister, Marvel, also a distinguished pilot in her own right. At the Crosson siblings' encouragement, Gillam left Alaska in January 1928 to stay with their family in San Diego, fittingly called the "air capital of the West," and learned to fly.[24]

San Diego's rich aviation history duly matched its immodest slogan, for the city's ideal weather and protected bay provided supreme aviation opportunities. Within a decade of the Wright brothers' first flight at Kitty Hawk, air pioneer Glenn Curtiss had opened a flying school at San Diego's North Island. The first seaplane took flight from there soon after. With the advent of aviation in World War I, the military commissioned North Island as a Naval Air Station in 1917. A decade later, at San Diego's Dutch Flats Airfield, inventor T. Claude Ryan developed a modified monoplane, the *Spirit of Saint Louis*, which Charles Lindbergh would fly during his transatlantic flight. The first leg of that historic flight originated from Rockwell Field on North Island. Eight months later, Gillam was in San Diego learning to fly from the nation's best. According to Griese, "Gillam's ability to listen when talk turned to aviation, especially when new ideas were being considered, leaves no doubt that he spent every extra waking moment looking and listening to everything going on in this frontier of flying."[25] During Gillam's four-month stay in California, Claude Ryan started the Ryan Aeronautical Company and, following in the footsteps of the successful Glenn Curtiss, the aviation innovator established the city's latest flying school. Perhaps inspired by Ryan, Gillam returned to Fairbanks in May 1928 with a Curtiss JN-4D "Jenny" to start his own flight school—the first in Alaska.

While in San Diego, Gillam met Marcel Leroy "Danny" Danforth, a former navy pilot. The two navy men made a business pact that on return to Alaska, Gillam would provide the plane and Danforth would move to Fairbanks to become the instructor for Gillam's flight school.[26] What began as a promising plan, however, ended in tragedy. After only two weeks of the school's operation, Gillam's Jenny stalled after takeoff at Weeks Field. "The plane went into a spin," reported the *Farthest-North Collegian*, "falling less than a thousand feet to crash into some burned-over ground a mile or two west of Fairbanks."[27] The headline for the *News-Miner* read: "Spinning Biplane Falls to the Ground Here—Gillam and Danforth Are Hurt."[28] Danforth was fatally wounded in the accident. Gillam, who was flying the plane, survived the first fatal aviation accident in Alaska.[29] Despite the deadly crash, and shortly after he left the hospital, Gillam purchased another plane, a Swallow biplane called the *Arctic Prospector*. Seven months after the mishap, he received a limited commercial pilot's certification for single engine aircraft in Fairbanks on April 11, 1929.[30]

One of the swirling stories of Gillam's life in Fairbanks left unsubstantiated by historical fact was his relationship with Marvel Crosson, Alaska's first female pilot and Gillam's best friend's sister. Gillam got to know Marvel while both eagerly partook in the interior town's growing aviation scene. Marvel was undoubtedly hard to ignore. She was beautiful, engaging, and lively. "Young people who shared a love of airplanes and flight were a tightknit crew," explained writer Dirk Tordoff. "Marvel's cabin became a social gathering place for pilots and aviation aficionados who spent hours 'hangar flying.'"[31]

We know that Marvel and Gillam shared a common passion for aviation and reportedly liked and respected each other tremendously. Some accounts say they remained only excellent friends.[32] Others speculate that the two pilots were "dating."[33] One account states the two were engaged and had decided to start an air service company together in McCarthy.[34] Engaged or not, Marvel left Alaska in 1929 and returned to California. There she set an altitude record over San Diego for female pilots, and that summer she entered the National Women's Air Derby.[35] One story stated that Marvel and Gillam intended to use the prize money to stake their McCarthy flying business.[36] The race featured some of the best female pilots of the day, including Amelia Earhart. But on August 19, on the third leg of the derby, Marvel Crosson became violently ill and disoriented, likely from carbon monoxide poisoning. Although she tried to jump, the plane crashed, killing the aviatrix. Her broken body was found crumbled, entwined in her parachute cord. In a letter to her mother just weeks before, Marvel had written, "Don't worry; every flyer would rather go with her plane instead of a more lingering way. Just think of the thrill of making immediate contact with the spiritual while doing the thing one loves to do most."[37] Discovered in the wreckage was a love letter to Marvel. "Sweetheart: Goodbye and good luck. . . . Will be with you every minute and waiting for you at Cleveland."[38] The letter was signed not by Gillam but rather by Emory Bronte, a fairly well-known aviator who had made the first civilian flight between California and Hawaii in 1927 and to whom Marvel had become close after she returned to San Diego.

Whether Gillam was in love with Marvel or the "Star of the Clouds" was just a friend, her death would have filled Gillam, someone who had spent a great deal of time with the Crosson family, with terrible grief. Nevertheless, the fledgling pilot apparently decided to move on with his life and forward with his flying ventures. In autumn of 1929 he established a partnership with Chitina and McCarthy businessmen, most likely investors with interests in the mining sectors of Nabesna and Bremner. That November a headline for the *Fairbanks News-Miner* announced, "Gillam Will Fly for New Company." The new flying firm had apparently secured for its head pilot a passenger-friendly New Standard biplane, which would be shipped to Cordova in the spring. The purpose of the new stock company, according to the article, was to provide transportation over the Wrangells' rugged terrain to the region's isolated mining districts, and to fly hunting parties to the White River area, described by the *News-*

Miner as one of the best hunting regions in Alaska. Gillam's Swallow biplane, the paper explained, was also purchased by the company and would be used for student instruction and short commercial flights.[39]

Yet again, plans for Gillam never materialized. That same month world-famous pilot Carl Ben Eielson and his mechanic, Earl Borland, went missing in Siberia. Gillam, flying an open-cockpit Stearman C2B biplane NC 5415, participated in the highly publicized search with his good friend Joe Crosson. The search for Eielson, combined with Marvel's death, postponed Gillam's plan to return to the Wrangell Mountains and likely derailed local investors' efforts to start an aviation business there. For more than two months Gillam and other Alaska flyers fought ranging storms and bitter cold in an environment that Crosson described as akin to "flying inside a milk bottle." The *New York Times* called the search the "greatest rescue armada ever assembled in the Arctic."[40]

The fact that Gillam and Crosson were the pilots who located the bodies of their missing mates brought them immediate fame. Gillam's flying in those months also earned him the respect of the flying fraternity. With a growing reputation as a solid pilot and penchant for flying in treacherous weather, the twenty-eight-year-old Gillam was finally able to attract enough financiers to back his dream of starting an air service company in the Wrangell Mountain region. On March 18, 1930, within just ten days of returning to Fairbanks for Eielson's funeral, Gillam took off in the *Arctic Prospector* to embark upon his delayed venture. Without the fierce competition that had formed around Weeks Field in Fairbanks, Gillam, on returning to the Copper Belt, established Gillam Airways, Inc.,—the first air service company in the Wrangell Mountain region—and quickly began to round up business.

COMMERCIAL AVIATION'S EARLY SUPPORTERS

The month following Gillam's return to McCarthy, he traveled to snowbound Valdez to pick up a second Swallow biplane.[41] After assembling the plane in Owen Meals's garage, residents gathered at the airfield on that April day to watch Gillam prepare for takeoff for McCarthy. There, Gillam made his first landing as captain of his own company on an aviation strip atop a flat and narrow terrace overlooking the town cleared by the Alaska Road Commission the previous summer.[42] As Gillam glided in for a landing, the Root and Kennicott Glaciers glistened, while the copper mill at

Kennicott, situated along the glacial moraine at the base of the Wrangell Mountains, stood in the distance. A few months later, Gillam passed his airman's examination, receiving his air transport pilot license.[43] The future seemed so promising for the pilot that he planned to purchase an amphibian aircraft in the spring.[44]

Gillam's flying business was indeed a first for the region. But had it not been for the federal government's support for the mining industry and supplying the initial, albeit modest, aviation infrastructure to the region, Gillam would not have been any better prepared to serve the Copper Belt than Captain James Martin and the Cordova boosters were seventeen years earlier. But after the successful establishment of commercial aviation in the Far North by the likes of Ben Eielson, Joe Crosson, and Noel Wien, territorial officials recognized that for economic productivity, settlement, and growth, aviation fields were crucial to Alaska.[45] In 1929 the *Fairbanks Daily News-Miner* promised readers that the government was moving forward, for in eastern Alaska the paper declared: "The Alaska Road Commission is doing everything possible to push forward the lines of transportation."[46]

The bureaucratic advancement for an aviation infrastructure began in 1925, when the Territorial Legislature authorized the expenditure of five thousand dollars for "aeroplane landing fields." It directed the territorial Board of Road Commissioners to select appropriate sites for such construction and handed the responsibility of constructing the airfields over to the federally managed ARC under the terms of a 1919 cooperative agreement.[47] Congressional funding was usually never enough, so the board also asked citizens from various communities to form local aviation committees to select the sites and raise local contributions. Moreover, expenditures only covered construction costs and ignored the flyers' need for radio, lights, accommodations, depots, and hangers.[48] ARC engineers adopted a standard size for aviation fields—fourteen hundred by six hundred feet—extending in the general direction of the prevailing winds to permit planes to take off and land against the wind. Ideally, fields were supposed to be smooth and firm, and this required a location with good drainage.[49] Rarely was this the case, however.

Besides government involvement, individual supporters from the mining sector also played a significant factor in bringing aviation to the Wrangells. Four men who factor prominently in Gillam's early commercial activities were New York politician William Sulzer, longtime prospector Carl Whitham, and brothers Lee and Peyton "Pete" Ramer.[50] Their interest in aviation was directly associated with developing their mining claims in the Wrangells—specifically at the isolated districts of Chisana and Nabesna, tucked between the Wrangell, Nutzotin, and Saint Elias Mountains, and Bremner, situated deep in the Chugach Mountains. These men, through political influence, tenacious prospecting, and a strong desire for empire building, pushed the ARC to bring aviation fields to the high country of eastern Alaska.[51]

After the discovery of gold in Chisana in 1913, William Sulzer acquired copper claims in the White and Snag River areas and, soon thereafter, started Chisana Mines Incorporated.[52] The Chisana strike initiated the last of Alaska's famed "gold rushes" and drained the populations of local towns such as Blackburn, Chitina, and McCarthy.[53] Once word reached the Outside, woefully unprepared prospectors approached the goldfields from every possible direction—from Fairbanks via the Tanana, from White-horse via the Donjeck. Others came from Cordova, arriving at McCarthy on the northbound train, then hauling their supplies for over a hundred miles along the Chitistone River to Skolai Pass, traversing raging streams, glaciers, and a trail so treacherous that one miner called it nothing more than a "goat trail."[54] In 1927, Sulzer lobbied for the construction of landing fields near McCarthy and the White River Mining District, specifically "near the Chisana Post Office."[55] Sulzer explained that airfields would be good for growth: "If the White River Country had a landing field it would help materially, and I would come in that way from Fairbanks or Eagle, and it would only take a few hours."[56] Sulzer even suggested that people living in the White River country build the landing strip themselves and that the territory of Alaska pay for half of it.[57]

A fellow veteran of the Chisana stampede, Carl Whitham had also invested in the White Mountain area in the 1920s and was anxious to get his gold claims at Nabesna developed and producing. But without direct access to the Nabesna site, this was a fruitless endeavor. Whitham first had to ship all the necessary milling and mining equipment from Seattle via the Alaska Steamship Company to Cordova, and then freight the equipment on the Copper River & Northwest Railway to Chitina. From there, he and six or seven men hauled loads up to the Richardson High-way to the Gakona Roadhouse. Next, a team of horses and a tractor pulled bobsleds over the Eagle Trail to Slana and then down the Nabesna Trail for nearly one hundred miles.[58]

Meanwhile, prospector Lee Ramer had worked the placer claims on Golconda Creek in the Bremner Mining District back in 1910. The remote region in the Chugach Mountains once supported several early placer mining operations, which eventually faded as World War I drained the region of labor. Located approximately thirty miles southwest of McCarthy on a mountain pass spanning eleven miles between the North Fork of the Bremner River and Monahan Creek, the district, like Chisana and Nabesna, was difficult to reach. Bremner's prospectors and miners could only move mining equipment during the winter months to a point near the mouth of the frozen Nizina River, from where they hauled their outfits by sled up the Chitina and Chakina Rivers to Monahan Creek and over the divide to the gold placers of the Golconda. Geologist Fred Moffitt noted that the cost of such freighting was expensive, calling it "the greatest" in the region.[59] Despite dogged efforts, Ramer made little progress on the Golconda and eventually returned to Nevada, but he never shook the belief that the lode gold deposits, feeding the placer gravels, were there to be found.[60] In 1928, Ramer returned to the Bremner District, during which time he and fellow miner Charles Nelson located the "Grand Prize" vein. Encouraged, Lee and his brother, Peyton "Pete" Ramer, spent the following year pursuing investors for their new gold mining company.

Not surprisingly, the Ramer brothers, like Sulzer and Whitham, having had difficulty reaching mining claims, saw the potential of aviation to their respective enterprises. Each miner felt strongly that air service would be vital for development and accordingly convinced the Board of Road Commissioners to act. In 1929 the ARC hired Gus Johnson to build a strip at Chisana in an abandoned channel of Chathenda Creek. The Chisana airstrip was a thousand feet long by one-hundred-fifty feet wide and possessed a grade of about 2 percent.[61] That same year Johnson also constructed an airfield at Nabesna. The Nabesna facility was slightly shorter and wider, measuring about nine hundred feet by two hundred feet.[62] With government subsidization that exponentially lowered transportation costs, Whitham and five other members of the Board of Directors from Chitina formed the Nabesna Mining Corporation in 1929 and began to process ore that same year.[63]

The gold quartz strikes at both Nabesna and Bremner prompted the first, albeit failed, attempt to organize an airplane company, which, according to Gillam himself, expected "to develop a considerable business in carrying miners and supplies to the scene of the stampedes."[64] Despite setbacks caused by Eielson's fatal crash, Gillam returned to the region in 1930, and the Ramer brothers hired the pilot to make a reconnaissance flight to Bremner to locate a landing field they could use to introduce potential investors to the area. Gillam found a fine river bar, probably near the confluence of the Golconda and Standard Creeks, suitable for landings and takeoffs with full loads. Soon thereafter, the Ramers cleared the landing spot and by autumn Gillam was making a number of flights with engineers and company officials to the promising mining site.[65]

Newspapers across the territory reported that the Ramer brothers were making demonstrable progress at Bremner, but access continued to be a problem. The conditions at the Standard Creek airstrip were so poor that a Gillam Airways plane mired in breakup muck forced pilot Adolph Dieterle to abandon his aircraft and mush out on foot. This, combined with the mine's potential, convinced the ARC to strip and level a far more substantial airstrip at a better location, about two miles upstream from the Standard Creek strip and closer to the lode claims.[66] Local businessmen were so pleased with the government's efforts that McCarthy merchant and mining investor Charles T. O'Neill sent territorial highway engineer William Hesse a letter expressing "the appreciation and sincere thanks of the prospectors and residents . . . for the splendid co-operation you have shown by making this landing field available. There is no question," continued the commissioner, "but with this field available this spring there will be even more prospecting and development work in the Bremner section than was possible last year."[67]

Besides Sulzer, Whitham, and the Ramer brothers, one other individual played an important, though more subtle, role in supporting the establishment of commercial aviation in the Wrangells. His name was Thomas M. Donohoe, a Cordova attorney, a strong advocate for Gillam Airways, and a professional with the means to facilitate the business side of things.[68] Tom Donohoe came from a prominent Prince William Sound family. His father, Thomas J. Donohoe, was continuously in the legal limelight. He had served as the Democratic committee chairman from 1916 to 1930 and was known as "one of the keenest barristers in Alaska." The senior Donohoe started practicing law in Valdez in 1903 in partnership with John Y. Ostrander, and then with Anthony J. Dimond, a previous Wrangell miner and present territorial delegate to Congress. Donohoe first came to Cordova as one of the town's founders, when he and several other Valdez men surveyed the land that became known as "Donohoe's

Homestead." Within three years the Copper River & Northwestern Railway would pierce the richest copper country in the world from that homestead. Early in 1920, the partnership of Donohoe & Dimond established a branch office in Cordova, which quickly became the foremost law firm in the Third Judicial District.[69]

In the early 1930s Donohoe relinquished his place in the firm in favor of his son, Tom, the youngest man to date to graduate from Stanford Law School. Beyond developing a friendly relationship, Tom Donohoe served as a direct link between regional mining companies and Harold Gillam. Donohoe was the aviator's attorney and financial adviser, but he was also the public notary who signed the Nabesna Mining Corporation's incorporation papers in 1929 and, by 1937, served on the company's Board of Directors. In addition, Donohoe, along with Peyton Ramer and Lee Ramer, both of McCarthy, formed the Bremner Gold Mining Company on October 2, 1931.[70] Collectively, these "Chitina and McCarthy businessmen" were some of the original backers of Gillam's air transport company. Moreover, regional mining companies like the Nabesna Mining Corporation and Bremner Gold Mining Company were looking to mimic the industrial giant Kennecott Copper Corporation by controlling not only the mining but regional transportation too.

Through the combination of public and private efforts, quality airfields had been established at McCarthy, Chisana, Nabesna, and Bremner by 1931. It was clear to all participants—the government, the mining companies, and the aviators—that a successful relationship had been established.[71] In addition, the ARC built several other regional airstrips designed to almost exclusively serve the Wrangell Mountain mining industry. Throughout the summer of 1929 aviation fields were surveyed, scraped, and leveled at Copper Center, Cordova, and Valdez.[72] The *Fairbanks Daily News-Miner* reported that "airplane landings at Chitina are made on a bar in summer and on a lake in the winter."[73] In 1930, ARC engineers cleared, stripped, and leveled the irregular-shaped aviation field at Chistochina and provided a detailed survey and map for the proposed Chitina aviation field near the townsite.[74] Miner Martin Harrais cleared a strip near his claims on a flat near the headwaters of the Chitina River. Far from roads or railways and surrounded by mountain ranges and raging glacial rivers, the Harrais site showed promise, so the ARC decided to improve the landing field by leveling it, expanding its dimensions, and placing landing markers by summer's end. Within a year of

Gillam's return to the Wrangell Mountain region, the pilot had seven newly built airfields on which to land.

Gillam had originally founded Gillam Airways out of Chitina—centrally located due to the railroad station—but preferred to base his two Swallows and a recently acquired Stearman and a Zenith biplane Z6-B at the airfield in Copper Center.[75] The location, north of Valdez via the Richardson Highway, also allowed him to supply the developing mining enterprises with their new airstrips, scattered northeast and southwest of the Wrangell Mountains. He left his Ireland Neptune amphibian at Chitina, where he could take off and land from Town Lake.

Treasurer of Gillam Airways was the enterprising O. A. Nelson, the town's postmaster and onetime magistrate, who owned the grocery store, the drugstore, and a clothing store. Nelson was not exactly the "little tramp" for whom locals believed he resembled. He was a civil and surveying engineer and held several PhDs. He served as U.S. commissioner of the Chitina Precinct and maintained interests in the Nabesna Mining Corporation. He was also the primary backer of Gillam Airways. His sons ran the local paper, *The Chitina Herald*. On January 17, 1931, Adrian Nelson announced "Harold Gillam Landed Yesterday," noting that, with a larger number of residents at the landing field to meet him, "it is the first time in history that an airplane has landed in the town itself."[76]

For his coastal base Harold Gillam favored Cordova over Valdez. The seaport and the railroad provided more economic incentive for the pilot whose majority of flying was along the Copper River corridor and the rail belt. On June 24, 1930, flight logs report that Gillam landed his second Swallow NC430N on a newly scraped field near Cordova on the flats at Mile 17, coming from Copper Center in just "one hour and thirty minutes of flying." He ran into fog shortly before reaching the field and circled for a few minutes before landing. The pilot carefully loaded 200 feet of cable and some marlin pins for the Nabesna Mining Corporation and was away again, using only 350 feet of the strip on the takeoff.[77]

Ore was hauled by pack horse six miles down to the landing field near the Nabesna River. From the airfield Gillam flew the ore 120 miles to Copper Center so that it could be trucked down to Valdez and shipped

Outside.[78] With the successful establishment of a mining-aviation relationship, miners throughout the Wrangell region began contracting Gillam to fly equipment, gasoline, labor, and ore to and from their isolated mining operations. After flying with Gillam Airways from one mine to the next, mining inspector B. D. Stewart recognized how important the new air service was to the developing industry. "The establishment of airplane service in the Chitina precinct by the Gillam Airways," wrote Stewart, "which base of operations is at Copper Center, has been an important factor in facilitating and encouraging mining development in the Nabesna region as well as elsewhere throughout the Copper River Basin." The mining expert continued: "There is thus rendered a very large area of favorable territory that heretofore has remained unexplored, owning to its remoteness from transportation routes." Stewart, like so many mining entrepreneurs, saw aviation as key to accessing hard-to-reach prospects. "The marked success that has attended the recent development of the gold mine of the Nabesna Mining Cooperation . . . should bring out extensive exploration and prospecting throughout this region."[79]

The motto for Gillam Airways was "fly anywhere, anytime, in any weather for a dollar."[80] According to territorial mining inspector Earl Pilgrim, however, the cost of chartering a plane into the northern Wrangells was a bit more pricy: from Copper Center to Nabesna it was $125; to Chisana it was $150; and to Snag River it was $160. The added cost of freight ranged from thirty-five to forty cents a pound.[81] Although these prices were prohibitive to most, Gillam, besides flying exclusively for local mining companies, transported a handful of intrepid passengers around the region. Passengers who recalled these early flights were amazed by the time flying saved. "In a little over an hour after takeoff," gushed a Valdez passenger, "Gillam landed the craft at the little Copper Center airstrip, a journey that in the gold rush days took weeks of hard work to accomplish."[82] Gillam flew law officers to Valdez—"the court city"—for work at the Alaska's Third Judicial District headquarters. He met passengers disembarking steamships in Cordova, flying them to scattered locations throughout the Interior. Independent prospectors also chartered Gillam to transport them and their supplies to previously hard-to-reach sites.[83]

Local miner Martin Harrais contracted Gillam to transport his wife, Margaret, from McCarthy to the couple's mining claims on the Chitina River in 1931. This was Mrs. Harrais's first airplane flight and one she recounted in her journal. The flight took only forty minutes, and as they sailed above the braided Chitina River, Mrs. Harrais tried to follow the route that ordinarily took her five grueling days to travel. "I'll admit a feeling of apprehension from the beginning as to how we were going to land," noted Mrs. Harrais. "The feeling of apprehension deepened as we circled the field several times." Although she was surprised by the smoothness of the landing, Mrs. Harrais reported that Gillam looked grim. She asked whether it was not a successful landing. He replied that any landing that you can walk away from is a successful landing. "Good enough!" wrote Mrs. Harrais. "I was there safe and he would go away and boost for a government-made field."[84]

Gillam's constant need for additional work led him to embark upon another important Wrangell Mountain aviation service: delivering the U.S. mail. Between 1922 and 1938 no regular airmail service existed in Alaska. During that time the federal government shipped the mail to Alaska and then authorized, what Congress termed the Star Route contractors, to carry first-class mail at regular first-class rates to destinations throughout the territory. It was never stipulated that the Star Route carriers had to fly planes, but "it was natural that the Post Office Department should often find contractors equipped with planes as offering the best faculties for the quickest and most economical transportation of the mail," reasoned an editor of the American Air Mail Catalogue.[85] But even though Alaska's vast and vertical terrain inevitably made aviation the preferred means of mail delivery, it was hardly Washington's first choice.

Prior to air-carrier service, dog teams delivered the mail for the federal government. Routes radiated from population hubs across Alaska, connecting the most isolated individuals with the rest of the world. Sprouting up around the dog team mail carriers was an elaborate business system, from sled makers to sellers of dried salmon to feed for the dogs.[86] Along the trails, roadhouses catered to the teams, supplying overnight lodging, food, and dog care. This entrenched system was first challenged in winter 1924, when Carl Ben Eielson made the first U.S. Airmail test flight from Fairbanks to McGrath. The postmaster general was so impressed with the young pilot's feat that he read Eielson's trip report at a Cabinet meeting. President Calvin Coolidge, captivated by the tale, wrote a personal letter to the airmail pilot congratulating him upon the successful completion of the flight.[87] Despite the president's positive interest, Eielson's desire to bring airmail to Alaska was met with bureaucratic red tape. With the assistance of Alaska delegate Dan Sutherland in

Washington, D.C., Eielson and his Farthest-North Airplane Company eventually received Alaska's first U.S. Airmail contract. Leary postal officials, however, paid the pilot less than half of the rate that a contractor received for delivering the mail by dog team.[88]

"Alaska mail-team drivers and their sled dogs were in a category of their own," Sutherland reportedly warned the eager pilot. "They would be difficult to replace."[89] Within a few years of Eielson's first mail flight, Sutherland's prediction that Alaska's dog team mail-delivery system would slide into frontier mythology proved to be true. The arrival of the airplane began to push many of the enterprises involved with dog teams out of business, but as on writer put it, "not without a struggle." A typical late 1920s response representing the view of the dog sled carriers was a sign posted on a roadhouse door reading, "Drunks, Indians, and Airplane Pilots not Welcome Here."[90]

Nevertheless, Alaska's immense territory and hostile climate made the dog team mail service irregular at best. Rural Alaskans almost immediately began to reap the advantages of air mail delivery. For those who were either afraid to fly or could not afford to pay exceedingly high passenger and freight rates, they could still benefit from aviation. Though slow and imperfect, the U.S. airmail first-class postal rates represented one of the few tangible economic subsidies that rural Alaskans received from being part of a national system.[91] With mail delivery, aviation extended its practical use beyond the mining industry to the broader residential community.

However, the rate of change in Washington, D.C., seemed to Alaskans to move at glacial speed. After a decade Alaska's latest nonvoting representative in Congress, delegate Tony Dimond, was still pressing for regular airmail in Alaska: "I do not suppose I can make you realize what air mail service means to the people in the remote regions of Alaska," remarked the delegate before the U.S. House Appropriation Committee. "I remember back in 1905, or thereabouts, the great thrill of pleasure we all had in the camp when the first mail came in. . . . Why it was better than almost anything else that could have been offered us. . . . So I can testify from my own experience the great advantage and benefit that is given to the people in these remote regions by having their mail, and having it delivered speedily." Dimond pointed out that the costs for Star Route contracts had actually decreased over the years with the employment of bush pilots. He then put his colleagues on the spot: "The question is whether we wish to go backward or forward." Responding to his own rhetorical query, Dimond assured the committee: "Air transportation, and particularly the transportation of mail by air, is here to stay."[92]

Another feature worthy of congressional consideration, according to Dimond, was the link between modern mail delivery and the increasingly worrisome issue of national defense. Dimond argued that air service would connect Alaskans to the rest of the nation. Minimal air service, on the contrary, left America's Far North vulnerable and opened the door to foreign attack.[93] The *Anchorage Times* touted Dimond's ambitious mail-delivery plan as "one of the biggest federal enterprises ever contemplated for Alaska."[94]

Through the efforts of Alaska leadership, the federal government finally supported a territorial airmail system, transforming it from a public curiosity to a practical and dependable service. Not surprisingly, Harold Gillam was the first pilot in the Wrangell region to fly in the mail. In January 1931, with the help of Nabesna Mine owner Carl Whitham, the U.S. Postal Service awarded Gillam Airways a Star Route mail contract for eastern Alaska. This included mail and the right to carry passengers from Cordova to Chitina, to McCarthy/Kennicott to Copper Center, and return to Cordova.[95] By April, Gillam obtained a contract to deliver mail twice monthly to the mining communities of Nabesna and Bremner.[96] In 1934, Kennecott Copper Corporation contracted him to fly in the mail after the Chitina Bridge went out during spring, preventing mail delivery by rail.[97]

By 1935, Gillam Airways had successfully expanded its Copper Belt contract to carry mail to Katalla once each month and to Yakataga Beach once each three months.[98] With the assistance of his financial adviser, Tom Donohoe, Gillam managed to purchase a potbellied Pilgrim, a large enclosed plane suited for heavy cargo, long distance, and passenger comfort, after visiting Tulsa, Oklahoma, where the plane was made. On July 5, 1935, the aviator and his new ten-seat plane—equipped with plenty of cabin room, leg-space, and a lavatory—made front-page headlines in Cordova.[99] "Gillam," the paper trumpeted, "brings large plane" to town.

CREATING THE LEGEND

Flying the mail route also helped cultivate Gillam's legendary skyboy reputation as a confident flyer in treacherous weather conditions and deteriorating light.[100] An often-repeated story about Gillam places a handful of grounded bush pilots waiting out a snowstorm in McGrath. Then, in the darkness, they hear Gillam's Pilgrim roar overhead. "Gillam, in furs, and looking like an arctic explorer, climbed out of the plane, unloaded mail sacks and packed them into the roadhouse."[101]

As with Gillam's future Kuskokwim mail route in southwest Alaska, the triangulated route between Cordova, McCarthy, and Copper Center was equally hazardous. Storms originating in the Pacific Ocean constantly move into the area, bringing fog, clouds, and mountain air turbulence. It could be whiteout conditions in Nabesna, sunny in Kennecott, and raining sheets in Cordova. Nevertheless, residents say it was common to hear Gillam's plane roar off into a storm. Witnesses recall Gillam landing his ski-equipped Waco 10 biplane on bare ground in Cordova after a flight from the snowbound interior. Even skilled pilots admired Gillam's ability to negotiate such a landing on metal-bottomed skis, without crashing nose-over on the dry ground.[102] Such piloting talent inspired newcomer Bob Reeve, who around the same time devised his own unique ski-landing techniques. "Harold Gillam had developed into the finest bad-weather pilot in the Territory," asserted Reeve. "[He] flew contact through incredible hazards that left the other pilots opened mouthed with awe."[103]

Gillam's courageous flying also made his name synonymous with humanitarian missions. The Kennecott mill town had the only fully equipped hospital in the Copper River basin. When Owen Meals's Eagle-rock crashed near Gakona in 1928, victims were transported to the hospital at Kennecott, which maintained the best health facility in the territory beyond Fairbanks.[104] Regional mines had made arrangements with Kennecott Copper Corporation so that they too could send injured or sick miners there for treatment.[105] McCarthy and its airstrip became an immediate destination for wounded miners or others seeking medical care. On October 3, 1929, when Gillam was on the verge of establishing his business in the Wrangells, he accompanied Fairbanks pilot A. A. Bennett on the medical flight in which they transported Chisana miner Jack Carroll, who had been severely crushed in a mining accident, to Kennicott where he was hospitalized.[106]

One of Gillam's most repeated mercy mission stories involved Copper Center trader John McCrary, who became bedridden with a perforated ulcer. Gillam not only flew McCrary to Kennicott for medical treatment, but he flew through a snowstorm to Cordova to retrieve McCrary's son, in case his father died. McCrary lived and the legend grew. Another medevac story included a Copper Center resident who fell down a cellar and put a nail through his stomach. Again in foul weather, Gillam loaded him into his plane at dusk and flew him on a wintery night to Kennicott's hospital. Sometimes the most severe injuries required the attention of doctors in Fairbanks, at Alaska's largest hospital. One particular story involved Gillam's friend and benefactor, Carl Whitham, who almost died after falling down a mine shaft at Nabesna. Gillam left Cordova in the middle of a snowstorm, reached Nabesna after dark, picked up Whitham, and flew him to St. Joseph Hospital in Fairbanks, 250 miles away.[107] The feat was considered so impossible that some papers reported that Whitham had died from his injuries, only to report a week later that he miraculously survived.[108] Bob Reeve, who called Gillam's mercy flight "the most sensationally brave job of rescue work," recounted that night's mission from Fairbanks. "It was pitch dark and ceiling zero." When he heard the roar of Gillam's Zenith, Bob noted, "that could be only one man in this world—Gillam."[109]

Gillam's astonishing flying feats earned him the nickname "Thrill'em, spill'em, no kill'em" Gillam.[110] Mechanic Oscar Winchell did his best to keep Gillam's planes in flying condition. Winchell recalled that the pilot "flew as though the devil was on his tail, continually hopping from one plane to another."[111] Indeed, by 1931, Gillam had amassed a fleet of five planes—but by the middle of 1932, Thrill'em Gillam had wrecked six planes (one plane twice) and his investors lost more than thirty thousand dollars.[112]

The high number of wrecks came on the tail of one of Gillam Airway's most lucrative contracts. In January 1932 a series of snow slides forced the Copper River & Northwestern Railway to halt its run to the copper mines at Kennicott. Consequently, the Kennecott Copper Corporation subcontracted Gillam to haul passengers and freight from Cordova to Chitina and Kennicott. Apparently the contract came with "a substantial sum of money," but the pressure to please his new patrons caused Gillam to push his flying into the realm of sheer recklessness. Gillam's first few trips with the amphibian were successful, recalled his mechanic Oscar Winchell, "but one day he was in too much of a hurry and rammed the landing gear through the ice, making the plane immobile for the rest of winter."[113] Flying as though he had not a moment to lose also put pressure on Gillam's overworked mechanics, Winchell and Earl Woods. Despite the numerous accidents, Winchell noted, "[Gillam's] planes were expertly pieced together, to keep him going on his runs."[114]

By the end of spring breakup, the railroad was repaired and cleared of snow, but the Great Depression hit the copper mining industry hard, as the price of copper plummeted to five cents per pound. The combination of a depressed economic market and dwindling copper ore reserves forced the Kennecott Mine to temporarily close operations in 1932.[115] Cancellation of the Kennecott contract only added to Gillam's financial problems. To efficiently transport heavy equipment and ore, Carl Whitham had recently been expressing publicly his desire for better access routes to the industry's more isolated mines. "Airplanes could be as thick as gulls," Whitham told the *New York Times*, "but Alaska needed roads."[116] Within a year Whitham had received his wish. The ARC constructed the Nabesna Road, linking the mine to the Richardson Highway and Valdez. Transportation costs decreased so much that Whitham could eventually afford to ship in first-grade fir lumber from Seattle rather than paying crews to cut and haul lower-quality native logs to the mine.[117] Road access represented a major obstacle to Gillam's business operation that likely pushed him to fly even harder. Consequently, by the end of 1932 the pilot, with his six wrecked planes, found his flying business in the red. "Gillam had been notified by his stockholder that he was not going to get any more money and that he was on his own," recalled Winchell. "[I] knew that time had come for [me] to leave."[118]

Finally, what drove Gillam's determined, and what some might call reckless, flying was competition from other pilots. Although copper prices had declined during the Great Depression, gold prices skyrocketed in 1933 and 1934, which created a demand for more air transportation from gold miners. Nabesna Mine, with its new spur road, was fully operational by the early 1930s. The Ramer brothers, in the isolated Bremner District, were also moving their mine toward full production. In addition, prospectors on Dan and Chitutu Creeks near McCarthy had resurrected small placer mining outfits on those rivers. Common to each new mining enterprise was their increasing use of aviation.

With so many requests for air service, Gillam Airways struggled to keep up with growing demand. Gillam increased his business with additional planes, pilots, and mechanics. Besides Winchell and Woods, over the years he had hired pilots Adolph Dieterle, Johnny Moore, A. J. Valley, and Chestochina flyer Morgan Davies.[119] Gillam's well-known mechanics included Tom Appleton and Bud Seltenreich, whom Gillam befriended in McCarthy when Bud was ten-year-old. Gillam took the interested grade-schooler under his wing, giving Bud lessons in mechanics at the Anderson Garage in McCarthy, which the ARC had leased for the season. In later years Gillam taught Bud and his two brothers, Ted and Fred, to fly a Swal-low airplane, which at the time was one of the first airplanes based in McCarthy.[120]

But not all of Gillam's employees had such a relationship with the moody pilot. His flying style and detached personality were equally demanding, and rarely did an employee stay long at Gillam Airways. Though some sought work for air carriers beyond the Wrangells, others decided to stay and compete for the Copper River's growing clientele. Within just a few years of bringing commercial aviation to the Wrangell Mountains, Gillam was no longer the region's sole air service operator. It appeared that Gillam's most significant competition would come from his most promising former employee, Merritt D. "Kirk" Kirkpatrick. Local investors, who had once courted Gillam, had established a new regional carrier business in 1934 called Cordova Air Service and made Kirkpatrick president, manager, and chief pilot.[121] Concentrating chiefly on airmail delivery, Gillam replaced the outgoing Kirkpatrick with Bud Seltenreich and gradually moved his operation from Copper Center to the more modern facilities at Cordova.[122] Meanwhile, everyone looked to McCarthy as the staging area for Wrangell aviation. By 1934 the airstrip on the bank above town buzzed with activity, as Wacos Swallows and Stearmen served the gold mines, delivered the mail, and conducted mercy flights. Seltenreich, with support from the Bremner Gold Mining Company, built the hanger at the McCarthy airfield to keep Gillam's assortment of biplanes airborne.

By the mid-1930s Kirkpatrick and Gillam had worked out a coopera-tive flight schedule that complemented their respective operations. Upstart Bob Reeve, however, caused the biggest ruckus among Wrangell Mountain flyers, when he appeared on the Valdez aviation scene in 1932 with his proverbial guns blazing, inserting himself as *everyone's* primary rival. Reeve admitted that the more established Alaska flyers like Gillam and Kirk were "a little stiff-necked about a competitor." Still, when Gillam slipped off his icy wing in the spring of 1934, spraining his wrist and ankle, he called the self-proclaimed maverick for help. Though busy flying a freight-run that day, Reeve dropped everything to aid the injured aviator, flying him to the nearest hospital for treatment. He even completed Gillam's flying job.[123] But as the Great Depression became more pronounced and pilots still had to convince skeptical Alaskans to fly, Reeve unapologetically saw aviation in Darwinian terms: "It was get some business or starve."[124]

By the mid-1930s the emerging aviation infrastructure from Cordova to Nabesna began to attract more and more flying businesses to eastern Alaska. As new flyers arrived, they gathered in hangers to trade their best stories of the day. As tales of pilots pushing the region's natural boundaries grew more and more daring, none forgot that it was Thrill'em Gillam who blazed their early air routes. Despite his reputation for being too reckless, Gillam was nevertheless intent on bringing safe, reliable, and regular service to the region.[125] The pilot would later pioneer communication and instrument flying by hiring locals at the roadhouses to tend his stations. He installed a direction finder, a directional gyro, sensitive altimeter, and an artificial horizon—at a time when most pilots were content with compasses.[126] So even while flying in dense fog and blinding whiteout conditions, Gillam managed to get in. "Those flights," according to flying newcomer Merle Smith, "constitute the greatest flying ever done."[127] "Gillam didn't think he was taking chances when he flew through bad weather," explained Frank Barr, "he was simply trying to achieve perfection in flight."[128] "Pilot Harold Gillam," wrote Pat Wachel, "is a part of the early Alaskan aviation legend. He flew, fought, and loved with the same kind of fervor as that of his contemporaries."[129] Most pilots agree that Harold Gillam was legendary. But the pioneering aviator's unique methods of overcoming the elements were talents—or *cajones,* some of the hangar-talkers would say—that other pilots simply lacked.[130] Alaska's frontier flyers, as well as those flying today, place Gillam in a category all by himself. To bush pilots like Bob Reeve and the rest of the Wrangell Mountain skyboys, "There was only one Gillam."

3

Mudflat Takeoffs
and Glacier Landings

IN 1932, DURING THE DARKEST DAYS OF THE GREAT DEPRESSION, A stranger drifted into Valdez with no money, no job, and no plane. Valdez residents who witnessed his arrival recalled that he was tall, gaunt, and sporting a thin and rather shady Errol Flynn–style mustache. He dressed in knee-high laced boots, dirty hiking pants, and a long leather jacket that hung almost to his boot tops. A tight-billed cap hid his salt-and-pepper hair, casting a shadow across his squinting, steel blue–gray eyes. "He looked," according to observers, "like a tramp."[1]

But the stranger wasn't a bum—he was a flyer. Everyone in Valdez knew that the high boots he wore were a hallmark of bush pilots of that period. Rumor had it that the stranger had recently come from South America, where he had acquired high-altitude flying skills transporting the mail for Pan-American-Grace Airways above the spine of the Andes Mountains.[2] He supposedly lost his savings in the stock market. Broke, he stowed away in a steamship's chain locker, seeking in Alaska a fresh start.[3] This stranger, through innovation and sheer resourcefulness, would apply lessons learned flying the high coastal range of the Southern Hemisphere and adapt his aircrafts and unconventional takeoff and landing style to the extreme, multifaceted environments of eastern Alaska. By carrying clients—from miners to mountaineers—to new, unexplored destinations, he became one of the territory's most famous flyers. People from Valdez to Virginia would know him as the "Glacier Pilot." His name was Bob Reeve.

Robert "Bob" Campbell Reeve liked to joke that during the year he was born, "the weather was so bad that not one plane got off the ground!" The year happened to be 1902, twenty months before the Wright brothers made the first successful air flight at Kitty Hawk.[4] Even though heavier-than-air mechanical flight had yet to be achieved, Bob Reeve was born to fly. He was raised in the American heartland, where daredevil stuntmen embraced the new technology, soaring over the undulating terrain made low and spacious by ice age glaciers thousands of years ago. At the start of World War I, he joined the U.S. Army at age fifteen, eventually reaching the rank of captain. Soon thereafter he paid five dollars for his first airplane ride. "It was a thrill few people are privileged to know," Reeve later remarked, "in the airplanes of the modern age."[5]

Reeve's passion for planes halted his plans for higher education. He was kicked out of the University of Wisconsin in Madison because he spent more time at the airfield than in class. Following in the footsteps of other Midwestern pilots, he became a barnstormer, an exclusive occupation taught to him by two Texas flyers with the oddly appropriate names of Maverick and Hazard.[6] America, at the time, had yet to take aviation seriously. "They'd pay to see you get killed," commented a fellow barnstormer, "but you couldn't get 'em to take a ride—even for free!"[7] Reeve, conversely, took flying very seriously, making aviation his profession. With the passage of the Air Commerce Act in 1926, he attained one of the first engine and aircraft mechanic's licenses, along with his commercial pilot's license. In 1929 he pursued adventure and work in South America, where he delivered the mail in a Ford Trimotor and a Fairchild 51. One of Reeve's colleagues in the Andes was famous pilot Antoine de Saint-Exupery, whose classic *Night Flight* memorialized the exploits of the South American flyers. Reeve flew between Lima, Peru, and Santiago, Chile, the longest aviation route in the world at the time, and one in which he sailed in record time.[8]

Like so many other Americans, the pilot faced economic hardship with the deepening Depression. So, on his first day in Valdez, Reeve wasted no time. He immediately found Ford dealer Owen Meals and offered to fix his cracked up Eaglerock biplane. In return, Meals paid Reeve one dollar an hour to work on the aircraft, and once it was fixed, Reeve leased it back for ten dollars an hour. Putting to rest any doubt that he was just another "fast-talking Cheechako," Reeve took off in the open cockpit of the Eaglerock from Valdez's small airstrip, which was lined with spectators eager to see a spectacular crash. Surely some in the growing crowd compared the brash pilot to "Thrill'em" Gillam, who despite being the region's best pilot, still managed to crash six planes in as many months. Owen Meals later described Reeve's safe and unspectacular flight, saying, "Bob handled that little Eaglerock just like he would big powerful planes—nice and easy." Unlike the spectators, Meals knew Reeve was an experienced pilot. "I wasn't worried," he later recalled, "I'd seen his logbook."[9]

A STUDENT OF THE WRANGELL MOUNTAIN ENVIRONMENT

Once airborne, Reeve felt at home above the towering peaks of the Chugach Range that surrounded Valdez. While circling summits and studying the tongues of ice that flowed forth from the barren, steep slopes, the pilot, with a prospector's instinct, remembered thinking, "It was hard to realize that in such an inhospitable, nearly impassable land lay the riches of the earth." Prompting his interest in the high mountain peaks was the fact that the so-called "easy-to-gather" ore had long since disappeared from Alaska and the Yukon. By 1932, "Valdez," as Reeve described it, "was a dead town."[10] Geologists and prospectors alike claimed that rich quartz lodes still lay in the inaccessible mountains, but those prospects were "scarcely touched because of the expense and physical labor of reaching them."[11] Besides the famous Chugach mines that once made Valdez a mining hub before the Great Depression—the Big Four Mine, the Ramsay Rutherford, and the Mayfield—Reeve guessed that the ranges stretching eastward, with little or no distinguishable break on the horizon, held the type of riches that to the pilot meant more flying and a promising future.

To serve this region of perpetual mountains and ice efficiently, Reeve figured he needed to know it from the ground up. But preventing him from the arduous work that lay ahead was a bad leg weakened by a childhood bout of polio. "The vast stretches of unpopulated country," explained Reeve, "convinced me that flying Alaska would require maximum physical fitness."[12] So after a few experience-gathering charters that summer, Reeve joined a couple of Valdez prospectors on a gold-seeking trip to Mount Sanford—a magnificent, glaciated shield volcano—mostly for the exercise. From Valdez the exploration party drove over Thompson Pass and one hundred miles to Copper Center, which offered Reeve the best vantage point (at least from ground level) to soak in the startling beauty of the Wrangell Mountains. Being the closest peak, the free-standing 16,237-foot Mount Sanford dwarfed the surrounding landscape. With the promise of gold beckoning, the party crossed the Copper River and traveled on foot for seventy miles over boggy rough tundra to Sanford's base. There they spent ten days scouring its foothills for the lost mine. The searchers never found gold, but Reeve, besides developing an interest in mining, regained full use of his leg. He also soon discovered that gaining a commanding knowledge of the Wrangells' natural landscape would not only earn him the moniker "Glacier Pilot," but it would also save his life.

WINTER FLYING IN THE WRANGELLS

It did not take long for Reeve to encounter extreme weather conditions, which provided him a strong awareness of the natural surroundings that, among other things, was crucial for success in Alaska's aviation business. Adapting particularly to eastern Alaska's constantly changing weather was mandatory for pilots flying in the uncharted territory, for at any given moment a situation could quickly turn dangerous. And indeed, nature was never predictable. Sharp winds from the coast swept inland, tumbling across mountains and creating downdrafts as rough as waterfalls on aircraft. Shifting fog from the sea could enshroud a plane in a blanket of mist. Frost on the wings prevented airplanes from taking off. Temperature inversions made it colder at ground level, wreaking havoc on planes landing. Whiteouts, blizzards, and brilliant, blinding light were commonplace hazards. Wrangell Mountain pilots flew in an environment where temperature variations ranged from eighty degrees above to eighty below zero, where light conditions varied from continuous daylight in summer to continuous darkness in midwinter. Flyers understood the region as a land of contrast and change. "The way of the pilot is hard in that country and the perils which lie over and beneath the white blanket of snow are many," warned the New York Times in 1932. "In the Alaskan winter-time this means . . . a fight for life."[13] "It is no wonder," remarked writer Harmon Helmericks, "that the old pilots were all weather-wise."[14]

To Reeve, being "weather-wise" was simply part of the job, a skillset he most certainly perfected during his first contract work in the Wrangells. The job consisted of flying supplies into the isolated Chisana region. At the time the only way into or out of the struggling, year-round mining camp was hauling supplies over the mountains by horse and sled, or if one could afford it, charter a flight with Gillam Airways. Reeve was hired to fly supplies to Chisana at twenty cents a pound—an affordable price. To keep costs low, Reeve found the most efficient way to fly in goods was to truck fuel and freight up the Richardson Highway from Valdez to Chistochina, where he based his rented Eaglerock at the Chistochina roadhouse. From there he flew supplies over the Wrangells to Chisana.

By 1932 roadhouses were well equipped to serve Alaska's flyers. Their original purpose—positioned in incremental locations, dictated by the distance a dog sled driver could travel in a day—was slipping toward nostalgia. Roadhouses had not only accepted the transition from sled dogs to air service by this time, they embraced it. Instead of kennels, many roadhouses now provided airstrips, encouraging weary pilots to stay overnight. However, not all the roadhouse airstrips were safe. Bob Reeve once described the privately run Chistochina airfield, apparently managed by oblivious nonflyers, as equipped with a tall pole at one end with a high radio antenna and a tall timber at the opposite end, book-ending the runway with obstacles. "An Alaskan pilot," retorted Reeve, "is apparently supposed to be half bird."[15]

According to Reeve, roadhouses along the Richardson Highway maintained "a club-like atmosphere," where "at night, twenty or thirty flyers, truckers, trappers, and miners" gathered. Besides room and board, roadhouses also served as a place for locals to gather, hosting from time to time parties, dances, and holiday celebrations.[16] Such events presented the typically solitary pilots a chance to socialize with other usually isolated residents.[17] The Copper Center roadhouse, run by Florence "Ma" Barnes, was a preferred base for flyers from Cordova, Juneau, McCarthy, and Seward. Because it offered a telephone line, pilots could call in for weather reports.[18] Roadhouses also offered pilots a place to conduct, as one journalist described, "creative mechanics" so that their aircraft were prepared to fly in temperatures that could reach sixty below.[19]

By mid-November in the Copper River basin, temperatures drop as quickly as the daylight disappears. No matter the duration of the flight or how tired they were, pilots in the age before the invention of antifreeze immediately drained the oil from their plane upon landing. If a pilot neglected this critical procedure, the oil would freeze like water, irreparably damaging the engine. Reeve recalled that during these first winters, he had to beg the roadhouse proprietor to allow him to warm the oil overnight near the stove. Through cooperation and good manners, Reeve found that the cooks became "as plane-wise as the flyers," for they routinely set the oilcan next to the stove before they started to grill the hot cakes.[20] "Alaska roadhouses all smelled the same," recalled Reeve, "a mixture of warm oil and boiling coffee."[21]

Before taking off the following morning, pilots had to warm the motor with a fire pot, which had to be covered with a tarpaulin to keep wind from extinguishing the flame. A fire extinguisher was also handy, in case the flame made contact with highly flammable grease or gas and ignited the tarpaulin. Unfortunately, far too many inattentive eyes watched their entire investment go up in smoke. It took a pilot at least a couple of hours to thaw a motor in frigid weather. On the coldest of days, Reeve warmed the engine, then took off empty, flew around the field for a few minutes, then landed, allowing the heat generated from the brief flight to spread and diffuse while he loaded the plane.[22] Perhaps no yarn about Reeve's cold weather "creative mechanics" is more outlandish than that told by Pat O'Conner in a 1934 article appearing in *The Alaska Weekly* that described how Reeve, replacing the carburetor with a meat grinder, kept his engine hot by running through it South American chile peppers.[23]

Equally important for surviving winter flying in open-cockpit planes was a pilot's attire and gear. Reeve quickly learned that protection from the deadly elements required a typical Alaska bush pilot uniform, starting with traditional Alaskan long johns, heavy wool clothes, and a fur parka that covered from head to toe. Mittens and warm boots were also necessary. Finally, all pilots wore goggles. In open air at forty below, unprotected eyes promptly froze.[24] Trumping freight for cargo space was a pilot's spare gear, usually consisting of emergency rations, camping outfits, stoves, tools, and other equipment.[25] Many pilots even flew with extra parts, like propellers. If trouble during a flight occurred, it meant that a pilot and mechanic were forced to conduct emergency repairs in the remote backcountry or walk out to the nearest community, usually miles away.

Once Reeve reached the Chisana airfield, the pilot realized that although he was paid by the mine owners, in reality his true customers were the miners, whose consistent supply of mail, fresh food, and tobacco in the dead of winter kept them connected and happy and, in turn, productive workers. Although new, Reeve was not naïve: "A bush pilot was expected to serve as mailman, message-carrier, and purchasing agent for the men who stayed the year-round at the mine sites." Like the roadhouse staff that accommodated pilots, to the isolated miners who appreciated items brought to them from distant markets, pilots recognized their role in a new elaborate system linking Alaskans to the modern world. Still, Reeve maintained that instead of transporting modern American life—along with its commodities, technologies, and business—into the most remote places of the North, his air services carried on a spirit of frontier Alaska. "It was much more than a packet of needles or a can of snuff. It was their assurance that they were still a part of the outside world," explained Reeve, "and it was a tradition of Alaskan fellowship."[26] But in spite of Reeve's extolling of frontier camaraderie, the bold pilot's success with the Chisana route compelled him to start competing with Harold Gillam for Nabesna's business, making separate arrangements with mine owner Carl Whitham to fly out to Valdez a cargo of bullion and gold concentrates as well as supplies and other equipment back to the mine.[27]

Several times Alaska's winter environment tested Reeve's resourcefulness. In February 1933, while flying a couple with their four-year-old son and four-month-old baby to Nome, ice fog forced him to land and wait out the weather. Temperatures that night reached fifty-five below zero, but Reeve kept the family alive while ceaselessly hauling logs to keep their bonfire going for twenty-five hours straight.[28] Then, a month later, he experienced a pilot's worst nightmare. Reeve had finished ferrying supplies to Chisana for the day, and while returning to Valdez with passenger Charlie Hawkins, high over the Wrangell Mountains, his engine stalled. The only airfield in the vicinity was the Nabesna landing field. Realizing that he was not going to make it to Nabesna, Reeve managed to glide his crippled plane into the steep-walled canyon of Jacksina Creek, about fifteen miles below the mine, and land safely. Though seasonal daylight had returned to the Wrangells, the harsh winds reminded the stranded pair that it was still winter. After tying down the plane, Reeve and Hawkins strapped on snowshoes and "mushed out" into the deep spring snow.[29] Thanks in part to his leg-strengthening expedition to Mount Sanford, Reeve safely reached Nabesna at one in the morning, announcing his arrival by pounding on Carl Whitham's cabin door. The next morning, Whitham sent a four-horse team to pull Reeve's abandoned plane up the frozen Jacksina to the confluence of the Nabesna, and finally to the Nabesna airfield situated near the river. Whitham then found a local dog team to carry Reeve and Hawkins from Nabesna to Salana, and then on to Chistochina. From there Reeve hitched a ride home with a fellow Valdez flyer. The next day he enlisted Gillam's new mechanic, "Kirk" Kirkpatrick, to help him ferry his disabled plane back home.

Episodes like this made it difficult for the Wrangell Mountain flyers to keep up with the cost of doing business in such an unforgiving environment. Flyers amassed some of their greatest expenses while grounded at a roadhouse waiting for the weather to clear. "The first time I paid my bill at a roadhouse, I was shocked," admitted Reeve. "I was use [sic] to paying thirty-five cents instead of a dollar for my ham and eggs."[30] Likewise, after working as Gillam's mechanic and second pilot during the 1931–32 winter season, Oscar Winchell still had no money to pay his eight hundred dollar Copper Center roadhouse bill. Recalling later he had promised to repay every penny, Mrs. Barnes simply nodded at his assurances and "smiled a warm comforting smile." This was not the first time a pilot promised to repay Ma Barnes a room and board bill he could not afford.[31]

Besides bad weather and emergencies, just paying for gas was the bush pilot's biggest worry.[32] Refueling stops alone consumed most the profits made during a trip. Despite Reeve's contention that aiding isolated miners was the Alaska way, during the worst years of the Depression, the gesture nevertheless lacked good business sense. As Reeve himself pointed out, it was always difficult to receive actual payment from them. For carrying passengers or delivering supplies in 1932, Reeve received for his payment dozens of post-dated checks, government bonds, and gold dust. Sometimes pilots received meat, furs, and mining interests in exchange for chartered flights. "All of those guys meant well," explained Reeve. "It didn't occur to them to pay bills more than once a year, during cleanup season." But, as the pilot acknowledged, his plane did not fly on pay dirt, "pilots had to pay for their gas year-round."[33] So instead of concentrating on well-intended, cash-strapped passengers, Reeve specialized in the transport of freight. His competition in the Wrangell Mountain area seemingly preferred to fly people, because passengers could, as Harold Gillam put it, "use their two legs" to walk off his plane. The pragmatic Reeve had a different view. His response to Gillam: "It [freight] didn't ask questions."[34] But more important, the mining companies that chartered flights with Reeve generally paid their bills.

Even though the cost of doing business in Alaska was extraordinarily high during the winter of 1932–13, Reeve described that first year as "the greatest winter of my life . . . I was doing what I wanted to do—fly. And I was building my profession."[35] Scrimping every cent, he managed to save two thousand dollars on the Chisana route, earning enough money to buy his first plane, a Fairchild 51.[36] Though used, the aircraft had certain advantages over Meals's Eaglerock. It was familiar, for Reeve had flown a Fairchild while working in South America. It was spacious, good for hauling heavy mining freight. Finally, its cockpit was enclosed, making the Fairchild a far more practical plane to fly in arctic weather. Reeve built a modest shop next to the Valdez airstrip and lived in a tiny cabin close to his plane. By the beginning of 1933, his new Fairchild aircraft became emblematic of his new business: Reeve Airways. The advertisement in the *Valdez Miner* announced to potential clients, and rivals too, that Reeve was in the aviation business to stay: "Not the cheapest," the ad admitted, "but I attempt to give the best in service."[37]

A GOLDEN BOOST FOR AVIATION

It turned out that Reeve started his airfreight business at the perfect time. Even though the mining giant Kennecott Copper Corporation had temporarily closed its mines, and the lack of any new ore discoveries added to the decline of the region's copper production, the impact of the Depression cut costs for equipment and other supplies, which effectively reduced overhead costs for gold lode mining operations in eastern Alaska exponentially. In addition, Congress passed legislation in 1932 relieving owners of the obligation of having to conduct annual assessment work, except those who were required to pay federal income taxes. Most significantly, however, prosperity in the gold mining industry came from new federal policies directed at replenishing the nation's precious metal reserves.[38]

Across the nation desperate people were pulling their life savings from local banks, forcing them to close. Without capital available for new investment, the economy stagnated, coming nearly to a complete halt in 1932, the year Reeve arrived in Valdez. Soon after his inauguration in 1933, President Franklin Roosevelt signed a series of executive orders designed to prevent the run on and ultimately failure of the banks, which culminated in the Gold Reserve Act of 1934. This piece of New Deal legislation made the Federal Reserve Bank the only financial institution that could legally buy gold. In fact, the law criminalized the holding or acquiring of gold by any U.S. citizen. The law also required that all newly mined gold in the country had to be purchased by the U.S. Treasury. Most significant, the Gold Reserve Act increased the nominal price of gold from $20.67 per ounce to $35. The nearly doubling in value inflated the federal government's gold-holding $2.82 billion overnight. The surge in gold prices made it remarkably profitable to mine gold.

In Alaska, where stories of gold rushes and independent sourdoughs continued to resonate with citizens, the Gold Reserve Act gave a tremendous boost to the depressed mining industry. As Governor John Troy reported: "Never before have the material prospects for this Territory been brighter than now."[39] Writer Rex Beach referred to such federal support as "a bit of intelligent government aid."[40] Thanks almost entirely to an artificial, federally controlled market, mines that had not been working for years suddenly reopened. The independent-minded citizens of the Last Frontier were too busy to be concerned that gold mining had become a noncompetitive industry. Valdez, like other dormant gold rush towns, retuned to life, as miners streamed into town with "cleanups" of gold bricks.[41] Territorial journalists proclaimed the Prince William Sound port as "the Key to the Golden Heart of Alaska."[42] Most significant for flyers, mining investors could now afford to charter flights to remote prospects and develop new lode claims. While the country's economy would remain stalled for several more years, Alaska's revitalized mining industry took off with the help of the federal government and a new mining tool—the airplane.[43] In early 1934, Reeve placed an announcement in the *Valdez Miner*: "Prospectors, Attention!," it publicized. "Gold is where you find it; but you can't beat the Chisana, Nabesna, Slate Creek, Chistochina and Bremner gold bearing districts as some of the best bets in Interior Alaska in which to make that pile." When a miner had his outfit ready to go, the ad insisted, "Always use REEVE AIRWAYS!"[44]

Without the federal law significantly increasing the price of gold, it is likely that Reeve Airways never would have left the ground. But the reopening of the high-altitude lode mines, combined with increasing investment in exploration, kept Reeve in the air almost around the clock.[45] For the summer months Reeve made a deal with the mine owners that when they needed fresh supplies, they would send a man on foot down to the town with the order. Bob would then fly the order out to the mine and deliver it by airdrop.[46] Clarence William Poy, mining engineer and manager of a local lode mine, told the *Valdez Miner* that "parachuting a 1,000-pound diesel engine from an airplane above an Alaskan mine is one of the latest achievements of aviation in assisting the prospector in the pioneer country, to say nothing of dropping dynamite, carbide, canned goods, lumber, drill steel, meat, oil and, in short, everything but eggs into the heart of the frozen North."[47] One of Reeve's mechanics who also helped him conduct the airdrops in those days was Valdez resident and fledging airman Bill Egan, Alaska's future governor.[48] Besides the booming mines in the vicinity of Valdez, Reeve Airways—thanks in part to strategic advertising—also picked up increased business from mines in Chisana, Nabesna, and the new gold mine at Bremner.

The rising demand for business after 1934 allowed the pilot the opportunity to develop such a distinctive operation that it would quickly manifest into a brilliant reputation and moniker for which he would forever be known. Following trends set by European aviators landing in the Alps, Reeve began flying supplies into mines throughout the Chugach and Wrangell Mountains, landing on makeshift strips near the diggings. Existing in close proximity to most high mountain lode mines were alpine glaciers, where even in summer, winter ruled. Reeve found that for the most part the snow on glaciers froze as hard as concrete. He replaced the Fairchild's wheels with wooden skis, instantly making each glacial field a possible landing strip that provided access to the protruding quartz lode deposits.[49]

After a series of trial-and-error attempts landing on the constantly changing and potentially deadly rivers of ice, Reeve perfected his new niche by paying close attention to the relatively unknown glacial environment. He learned to land in flat light on a featureless glacier by making a preliminary pass while throwing out dark objects, such as gunnysacks dyed black, or willow boughs, anything that gave him depth perception.[50] He also set up flags and sprinkled lampblack to mark the landing area. Reeve learned to identify the location of the mostly hidden crevasse by looking for a slight undulation on the surface, where snow was not quite as blue as the surrounding field. Reeve's rule of thumb: the lighter and drier the snow, the more dangerous on which it was to land. The wet and heavy snow characteristic of the coastal mountains tended to be more solid and thus better to land on; the powdery snow of the Wrangells could sink a plane to its belly.[51] Finally, he learned to turn his plane to a ninety-degree angle on the slope before cutting the engine so as not to slide backward. The main problem facing Reeve's innovative glacier flying was that by May, snow on the Valdez airstrip had melted, making it impossible to reach the alpine mines with skis during the warm months of late summer.

While crossing the glistening mountains during those summertime charters, it did not take long for the pilot to catch his own case of "gold fever." Reeve used his prospector eye to look for unclaimed lode sites. He would notice several quartz strata running through the mountainsides, but his wheels prevented him from landing and getting a closer inspection. By winter, when he could finally replace his wheels with skis, the lodes had disappeared with the quickly accumulating snowfall. Reeve, something of a mechanical virtuoso, solved this problem by fixing his Fairchild with stainless-steel homemade skis and taking off from the mudflats that fronted Valdez at low tide. But unlike snow the sticky mud created suction on his skis, making it extremely difficult to get airborne. Once in motion, Reeve had to physically rock the plane in order to tear the skis loose.[52] The hassle proved prosperous, however, for this inventive mudflat takeoff technique allowed him to serve mines year-round. "While other pilots were operating by clock and calendar," recalled Reeve, "I began using a tide book for a manual of operation."[53]

Tourists arriving via steamship often gawked curiously at Reeve's "airport," dubbed "Mudville" by his rivals. Within a year and a half of his arrival, Reeve had developed a reputation as being "intensely competitive" and "fiercely proud of his skill in the air." Valdez residents remember that he wore an oiled, floppy fisherman's rain hat while puttering around town, whether it was raining or not. One account describes the pilot as "a chain-smoking aerial entrepreneur whose locutions were sprinkled with many a vivid profanity."[54] Reeve's manner was both confident and curious. Over the door of the wooden shack that served as his office he had painted a skull and crossbones, and the words: "Opportunity makes damned rascals out of all of us. But opportunity is not knocking here: HANDS OFF OUR TOOLS." "Always use Reeve Airways," ordered a sign painted on the side of his Valdez hangar. Next to the advertisement were the words: "Slow Unreliable Unfair and Crooked. Scared and Unlicensed and Nuts. Reeve Airways—the Best." He didn't write them, but apparently Reeve was proud of the anonymous graffiti. Adding a final personal touch, Reeve hand-painted on the side of an old Model T Ford used to drive passengers to and from the mudflats the words "Airways Officials."

Because work kept him up to his knees in a mired mess that smelled of rotting salmon and decaying seaweed, Reeve was known as a fairly filthy flyer. While in the air, "Reeve had worked out a way that he could pee past the stick and out a hole in the floor," recalled one of his passengers years later. "The whole damn plane smelled of dried piss."[55] Perhaps coincidently (or not), the spirited pilot was dirty in other ways. He would pay for a "Fly Reeve Airways" advertisement in the *Valdez Miner* that was often strategically placed near the headlines of a reported aviation mishap associated with one of his rival pilots. By 1934 not everyone was impressed with Reeve's dirty flying. As the meticulously clean, neatly groomed Harold Gillam put it (also Reeve's frequent advertising target), "Reeve can have it!"[56]

THE FLYING FRONTIERSMAN IN THE NATIONAL SPOTLIGHT

At a time when people around the country struggled to make ends meet, Reeve's glacier and mudflat flying skills sparked the imagination of a depressed populace whose collective lives had little opportunity or reason for excitement. In the 1930s celebrated writer and onetime Alaska gold prospector Rex Beach wrote several articles promoting Alaska mining that centered on Reeve. Beach wrote passionately on his contention that the federal government should invest even more money to create a modern infrastructure for aviation in Alaska. For its efforts, argued Beach, the territory would attract a fleet of "sky prospectors," who, in Beach's mind, were "the quickest way to unlock Alaska's golden treasure chest and provide thousands of immediate jobs for young, out of work Americans."[57] Illustrative of these so-called sky prospectors was Valdez pilot Bob Reeve: "One pilot with a battered, nine-year-old ship," crowed Beach, who "has [single-handedly] started a boom which promises to put that town back on the map." [58] Perhaps because he perfectly adapted his flying to the seasons, Beach called the pilot a "Flying Ptarmigan." He even patterned his lead character upon Reeve in his 1939 novel *Valley of Thunder*:

> "Anyhow he's a winter bird and he's doing the wildest flying I ever saw. He's carrying mine supplies up into the sawteeth—grub, gasoline, machinery, dynamite. When he can't find a landing place he drops it." "I heard about him," Red admitted. "He dropped a Diesel engine by parachute. The guy is cuckoo."[59]

In the "Flying Frontiersmen," an article appearing in the 1936 issue of *American Magazine*, Beach credits Reeve for solely igniting Valdez's economic upturn. As Beach explained, it was Reeve who gave discouraged miners wings to access onetime impossible to reach sites. "The hazards, the hardships and the expense of moving mining supplies through such a country can be imagined," wrote Beach. "Valdez was a prosperous, live town until the struggle against nature's odds became too exhausting. The operations were abandoned, promising lodes were deserted. Discouraged owners swore they'd never go back until they grew wings."[60] Beach, and similar writers of the Depression-era generation, understood that the only real foundation supporting Alaska's modern economy was the extraction of natural resources. Such endeavors, particularly industrial mining, however, required an enormous amount of capital rarely secured in the North. In addition, the development of the mining industry in places like eastern Alaska benefited from federal support ranging from geographic exploration, construction of overland trails, roads, and airfields, and a host of federal laws that artificially kept mineral prices high.

Beach argued that federal influence—particularly federal interest— did not go far enough: "Isn't it high time we lent a hand to those intrepid Alaskan fliers who haul its freight and passengers, who gamble with its glaciers, and risk their lives on blind mercy fights?" asked an indignant Beach. "This state of affairs," cried the writer, "is the result of that habitual indifference which has always characterized the government's attitude towards Alaska."[61] But whether absentee investors or government subsidization answered Beach's call to support bush pilots, and consequently boost Alaska's mining industry, the combination made the territory dependent upon outside entities. Such dependency, however, blatantly contradicted Alaska's independent pioneering spirit embodied by the central figures of the Last Frontier—the miner and his trusty flyer: "Prospecting is not a lost art in the Northland," wrote Fairbanks mine owner Ernest N. Patty, "and the prospector finds that his days in the hills can be greatly lengthened by using the airplane to land him and his outfit in the center of a likely area."[62]

Even though it was an economic necessity and, quite frankly, a historical reality when it came to the West or the North, dependency was neither an American nor an Alaskan trait. To resolve the contradictions and counter accusations of Roosevelt's "overreaching," if not "socialistic," New Deal approaches, writers like Beach simply linked rugged individualism to capitalist individualism.[63] Accordingly, pioneers seeking in the North the freedom to make unlimited profits first had to conquer Alaska's formidable wilderness. To succeed in this quest, these pioneers would need to be courageous, resourceful, and self-reliant—characteristics necessary to confront the cold and brutal natural environment, and ultimately conquer it. Success came only when the rugged pioneer stood independent, not so much from corporate giants or big government but from nature, or in the pilot's case, from gravity itself.

According to Beach, Bob Reeve and other Alaska bush pilots maintained the necessary qualities, as well as the tools, to overcome Alaska's inaccessible natural barriers. Thus instead of recognizing Reeve's winter flying and glacier landings as remarkable examples of knowing one's environment, his piloting methods were portrayed as potent weapons in the dramatic war against nature. Like the western cowboy, bush pilots became symbols of independence and freedom, evoking what might be considered the last chapter in the frontier saga: "How the North was won." Ignoring Alaska's dependency on the federal government and corporate America, ignoring bush pilots' constant debt or their command of *modern* flight, Beach solely credits Reeve as winning the "struggle against nature's odds" by defying gravity and literally giving the lowly miner wings. "We're not getting rich," a modest Reeve told Beach of his fraternity of frontier flyers. "But the country is progressing and it's our job to push it along."[64]

FLYING MOUNTAINEERS TO NEW HEIGHTS

Rex Beach's popular articles attracted the attention of another arctic adventurer needing the Glacier Pilot's talents. Twenty-six-year-old Harvard instructor, explorer, and photographer Bradford Washburn sought a pilot to fly his climbing party and gear to the Walsh Glacier at the base of 17,150-foot Mount Lucania, the highest unclimbed mountain in North America at the time. The duke of the Abruzzi, who first scaled Mount Saint Elias in 1897, had named the nearby peak for the Cunard steamship on which he sailed to America—the luxury ocean liner *Luciana*.[65] Nearly forty years since the duke's ascent of the higher Saint Elias, mountaineers still considered Lucania too remote to climb. Even the most skilled declared the peak to be "virtually impregnable."[66]

Washburn's climbers traveled to their icebound destination in far less luxurious conditions than Abruzzi. The climbing party, comprised chiefly of members from the Harvard Mountaineering Club, was without question America's most ambitious collection of mountaineering scholars. The club specialized in remote, unclimbed peaks of the Far North, and its members were most certainly inspired by Britain's Oxford scholars—men such as George Mallory and Sandy Irvine—who just thirteen years earlier had achieved international acclaim and redemption for their country in their epic effort to reach the top of the world, the treacherous Mount Everest. Washburn's generation, primarily through their Alaskan and Canadian expeditions, "changed the face of American mountaineering." "They belonged," wrote David Roberts, a fellow Harvard Mountaineering Club climber, "to a different subspecies of human beings."[67] Thus with Mount Lucania standing in the midst of the vast, desolate Saint Elias ice cap, the largest glacier system in the world, it presented the Harvard climbers an opportunity to make history.[68]

Washburn had read about Reeve's innovative mudflat takeoffs, which allowed for a summertime ascent of Lucania. In addition, by flying to just south of the sprawling mountain, the climber reasoned that it would preclude a demanding, if not impossible, overland approach. In January 1937, Washburn wrote the Valdez pilot, outlining details of his proposed trip to Lucania. In closing, Washburn wrote: "We believe that you are plenty experienced to handle this work—and that if we succeed on Lucania, you are certain to get a lot of favorable publicity, both for you as well as of the town of Valdez. We hope that you'll agree to be our pilot."[69] Reeve replied to Washburn's request in typical Reeve fashion. He sent the Harvard mountaineer a one-sentence telegram vowing: "Anywhere you'll ride, I'll fly."

In March, climbing-party member and Washburn protégé Russell Dow arrived in Valdez to help Reeve establish a base camp on Walsh Glacier. A deep blanket of snow still covered the Wrangell Mountain lowlands, allowing for ski landings at nearby airstrips. In cloudless weather the men left Valdez on May 2 then refueled at McCarthy, staying only long enough to eat lunch. Witnesses report that Reeve took off for a flight over what McCarthy prospectors called Alaska's "big blind spot" and landed a load of food supplies near the nine-thousand-foot level of Mount Lucania.[70] On his first attempt at landing, Reeve faced violent winds, but on a second try the Glacier Pilot landed his Fairchild competently onto the condensed snow. At 8,750 feet above sea level, this seemingly routine landing broke the world's record at the time for the highest ski-equipped landing, and Reeve had done it with a fully loaded plane.[71] "This shows what planes can do," trumpeted John Barrett from McCarthy. "Two days of freighting by air—which took three months by dog team a few years ago."[72] Over the course of a week due to a batch of rough weather, Reeve and Dow managed to ferry two thousand pounds of gear and food in three trips from the McCarthy strip to their base camp on Walsh Glacier.[73]

Washburn and the rest of the climbers arrived in June, during a period of unseasonably warm temperatures. While waiting for the weather to clear, Reeve considered the situation. The snow had long since melted off the McCarthy airstrip, and because they could not refuel at the mining town, Reeve would need to carry enough five-gallon gas cans for the return flight. Just before noon on June 18, the sun broke through heavy clouds, prompting the first leg of the charter: transporting the climbers in a single trip from Valdez, more than two hundred miles over remote wilderness, toward the Saint Elias Range. After taking off from the mudflats fronting the Prince William Sound town, the Fairchild's route crossed over Thompson Pass and quickly descended into the Copper River basin. They passed over McCarthy, "the last outpost of civilization," headed up the gorge of the heavily braided Chitina River, and toward the frozen confluence of the Chitina, Logan, and Walsh Glaciers. Washburn described in his journal the feeling he had experienced when looking out the cockpit window down onto the Chitina Glacier: "Till my dying day I shall never forget that nauseating desolation of dying masses of ice . . . the valley walls on both sides were vertical rock and scree, bare, snowless, and bleak. Potholes full of horrid muddy water filled every depression in the hellish sea of stagnant ice."[74] The plan was to drop off Robert Bates and Washburn at the Walsh base camp, then return for fellow climbers Russ Dow and Norman Bright. A month later, Reeve would retrieve the party and fly them out by pairs.[75]

As Reeve's Fairchild reached the lower reaches of the Walsh Glacier, the reliable plane hit a strong headwind. Long past the point of no return, the chain-smoking pilot spotted the cache despite the brutally flat light. Washburn later wrote that the Walsh was "a chaos of filthy, rotten ice and twisted moraines, gutted and crisscrossed with crevasses."[76] Telling his passengers, "We're going to land, boys. Hold on!" Reeve landed the plane in an astonishingly short distance. The men disembarked from the plane and immediately sank thigh-deep into an ocean of slush. The strange warm weather caused the glacial snow to deteriorate. After numerous failed takeoff attempts, Reeve realized that he was marooned.

Bad weather had stranded the pilot before, but this was his first extended grounding since meeting Janice Morisette in 1935. Indeed, Washburn was not the only person interested in Reeve after reading the

Rex Beach articles. Morisette had also read about the aviator's exploits and decided to write him a letter, asking if he needed an assistant. The Alaska-Wisconsin correspondence lasted for four months until Morisette decided to move to Valdez. Terrified, the confirmed bachelor fled on a prospecting trip, rather than greet Morisette's arriving ship. Undeterred, the black-haired Morisette got a job for the Alaska Road Commission, and while "punching that ole typewriter," she reminded Reeve of "Tillie the Toiler," the hardworking flapper-turned-stenographer comic book character. Love eventually caught up with the fast moving Reeve. The pilot and "Tillie" were married in 1936.[77]

Now, with the sun blazing down through broken clouds and Lucania towering above, Reeve began to grasp his predicament. Tillie had given birth to the couple's first child, Richard, in January. Without any way to communicate with the outside world, his wife would fear the worst. With thoughts now only of his family, the pilot was, Bates later wrote, "wild to get home."[78] On Reeve's fifth day it had become clear to the party that Dow and Bright would be excluded from the Lucania expedition, for a return trip to the glacier was too risky. Furthermore, if Reeve was even able to get his Fairchild, currently encased in slush, airborne, he'd be forced to abandon Washburn and Bates at Walsh Glacier.

After five days of rain and several more disastrous takeoff attempts, Reeve decided to try again. The temperature had finally dropped to below freezing. Desperately determined and hoping to lighten his load, the pilot threw out of the cabin all excess gear, including tools, an emergency sleeping bag, first-aid equipment, survival food, and even the crank for the engine.[79] Without so much as a wave goodbye, Reeve left camp, moving down the glacier to his plane. According to Bates, the plane "went bouncing down the runway."[80] At about one hundred feet on takeoff, Reeve hit a crevasse, which knocked his plane off course and into the path of another large crevasse, "big enough to hold a boxcar." Reeve made a sharp turn and then shot his plane into a swan dive off a 250-foot icefall. While witnessing Reeve's plane disappear over the side of the glacier, Bates and Washburn breathlessly waited for the sickening sound of a crash. "All of a sudden," a rejoicing Washburn described, "[Reeve's plane] was going like fury, but this time she was sturdy, her right wing lower than her left."[81] While in descent, Reeve had achieved enough forward speed to become airborne, "just ten feet from the bottom."[82]

Upon his safe return, the *Valdez Miner*'s headline declared, "Most Hazardous Trip in Career; Says Pilot Reeve."[83] Although plans to retrieve the rest of the climbing party (and gear) were canceled, Washburn and Bates still managed to scale Mount Lucania. In order to flee the Saint Elias wilderness, they also had to traverse the summit of 16,650-foot Mount Steele, descend its 9,000-foot east ridge toward the Wolf Creek Glacier, then hike a grueling thirty miles to the Donjek River, almost fatally fording it, and finally crossing tundra and brush to Burwash Landing on the shores of Kluane Lake in Canada.[84] "From that day on," Brad Washburn later recalled, "through the rest of his life, Bob Reeve always called me 'Burwash.'"[85]

Life magazine, highlighting Reeve's mudflat takeoff technique, heralded the expedition a national success.[86] David Roberts, Harvard climber and author of *Escape from Lucania: An Epic Story of Survival*, described the expedition as "one of the great American adventures of the century."[87] "In the light of the history of mountaineering," explained Roberts, "it was certainly not technical difficulty that made the first ascent of Lucania such a benchmark. . . . On Lucania, it was the collision of the risky new gambit of using a ski-equipped plane to approach a remote mountain with some of the weirdest weather either Brad [Washburn] or Bob Reeve would ever see in the North that led to the men's dramatic dilemma."[88] After returning safely to the East Coast, Washburn credited the Glacier Pilot with the climbers' historic achievement. "It is impossible to praise pilot Bob Reeve highly enough for his flying skill and resourcefulness which have got at least two of us safely into the highest glacier camp ever established by airplane," wrote Washburn in a letter that later appeared in the *Valdez Miner*. "Any success which our expedition may have during the work we are about to do will be entirely due to his four magnificent flights which have landed us and our supplies at so great an altitude and so near our objective."[89]

About a month after the Lucania expedition, Robert Bates received a letter from Reeve. The pilot began the letter with rare praise for the climbers and then ended it with a brief story that underscored the miraculous nature of their stint on Walsh Glacier:

> By the way, three weeks ago I was flying the Fairchild 51 (the ship we used) down the Columbia Glacier on skis with a load of timber when the motor quit cold . . . , and I had to make a forced landing in the ocean. I had to swim to shore. We got the ship out at low tide, repaired the motor, and flying reg-

ular again, none the worse for the dunking. Trouble was a broken timing gear. Don't say we hadn't luck on Lucania. I've only flown the ship four or five hours since we returned from that flight. . . . I don't mind forced landings but I sure would have hated to walk out from there. . . . Bob.[90]

Over the years Reeve would claim even more national fame. For his flying feats (and apparently his good looks), he was called the "Adonis of Alaskan Aviation" by the soon-to be-famous war correspondent Ernie Pyle.[91] During his time as the Chugach and Wrangell Mountains' sky prospector, Reeve made more than two thousand glacier landings and dropped more than a million pounds of freight to area mines.[92] In 1938, Reeve made his last glacier flight when he flew Washburn and his latest Harvard climbing party to Mount Marcus Baker. The pilot later described the importance of his final glacial landing in typical feigned fashion: "This was the last time I landed anyone on some damn unknown hunk of ice."[93]

The Copper Belt Line

ALTHOUGH THE CHISANA GOLD RUSH IN 1913 SPARKED THE DREAM of supporting flights over the Wrangell Mountains from Cordova, a practical vision for an air carrier service based from the railroad town emerged twenty years later, in 1933, when local business leaders successfully convinced the Territorial legislature to pass an appropriation bill that would fund construction of an airport there. Cordova had been a transportation hub into the Interior since the completion of the Copper River & Northwestern Railway in 1911, but signs were evident that the Kennecott copper mine and mill, the impetus for the railway and engine for the local economy, was in decline.

Between 1932 and 1934 copper prices remained so low that the Kennecott Copper Corporation suspended operation on Bonanza Ridge, and in 1934 Copper River floods destroyed the bridge near Chitina, temporarily taking the railway out of operation. By 1935 the Kennecott Corporation reopened the mines, but dwindling ore reserves, combined with the depressed market, darkened the region's once bright copper-producing future. Signaling a worsening economy, Kennecott ceased railway operation between December and April, forcing the U.S. Post Office to contract pilots to fly passengers and mail between Cordova and McCarthy.[1] Although the sun was fading on the region's titanic copper-mining industry, the region's other mineral, gold, had regained much of its nineteenth-century luster. Thus Cordova's business leadership, particularly those with financial ties to the prospering Bremner District, as well as other merchants desiring to transport their products into the Kennecott mine area during the winter months, focused their fortunes on a new mode of transportation for the Copper River basin: aviation.

Pilot and mechanic M. D. "Kirk" Kirkpatrick, along with G. Earl Means of the Alaska Transfer Company of Cordova and O. A. Torgerson, the new vice president of the Bremner Gold Mining Company, founded Cordova Air Service on September 13, 1934, with the purpose, among other things, "to transport passengers, machinery, goods, wares and merchandise by airplane . . . within the Territory of Alaska, from the Territory of Alaska to any state in the United States, to Canada, Siberia, or to and from any state, Canada, Siberia, or any other country."[2]

Connected to the Swallow Aircraft Company in Wichita, Kansas, Kirkpatrick originally came to Alaska to work for Gillam Airways in 1931.[3] Joining Kirk on his journey to Copper Center was his wife, LeahDean, whom he affectionately called "Dean." After a year in Copper Center, where Dean's only companions consisted of Florence "Ma" Barnes and a huskie named Oscar, Gillam suggested that the Kirkpatricks move to Cordova for the winter. There, Gillam worked with Kirk to establish an air service for passengers and mail arriving on stateside steamships. This was such an important service for the local community that it made headlines: "The S.S. *Alaska* got into Cordova last night at midnight," reported the *Chitina Weekly Herald* in 1932, "and Gillam and Kirk were waiting with their planes to bring the mail up today." Even when the pilots couldn't fly, headlines were made: "It was snowing all day and they [Gillam and Kirk] could not fly. They will bring it [the mail] up tomorrow if the weather is right."[4]

Besides timely airmail delivery, the pilots promised passengers a quicker route into the Interior. Cordova to Fairbanks air service routes devised by Gillam and Kirk competed with the traditional steamship route that disembarked in Seward and then transported passengers northward on the federally built Alaska Railroad. Gillam and Kirk boasted a savings of four to seven days for Interior-bound travelers.[5] The frozen Lake Eyak, located just out of town, made a perfect platform on which to land ski-equipped planes.[6] The arrival of spring, however, melted the town's ice-covered landing strip, bringing an end to Cordova's popular, yet experimental, air service operation. The Kirkpatricks, with mixed emotions, returned to Wichita in 1933, just before hearing word that Cordova had received funds to build an airfield. Back in the Midwest, the couple quickly realized that the Depression had exhausted most aviation jobs, and after two months of looking, Kirk and Dean decided to return to Alaska.

By January 1934, Kirk was back in Cordova, but this time he flew for Noel Wien, owner of Northern Air Transport (NAT). The short-lived NAT company maintained bases in Nome and Fairbanks as well as an additional coastal base in Cordova. Four planes flew out of the Cordova operation.[7] Now flying for another company, Kirk, it appeared, was poised to become Gillam's biggest competition. But because of the stimulated growth of the gold-mining industry sparked by the passage of the Gold Reserve Act, there was more than enough work to go around. Consequently, Kirk and Gillam worked out a "gentlemen's agreement," splitting flying responsibilities to better serve the Copper River region. Gillam concentrated on what he did best, flying the scheduled mail routes, while Kirk took over the irregular flights to the mines.[8]

One district, however, kept Kirk particularly busy. On January 27, 1934, the *Cordova Daily Times* reported: "Pilot M.D. Kirkpatrick returned early yesterday afternoon after a trip to McCarthy with L.C. Ramer and others for the Bremner mine."[9] This was the first indication of the Ramer brothers' interests in the Kansas pilot. Over the course of the next several months, Kirk would make numerous trips to Bremner. In April, Kirk increased his flying time to the mine: "Pilot M.D. Kirkpatrick has been extremely busy here lately freighting in a quantity of provisions to the Bremner Mining Company," wrote the Cordova paper. "He completed two trips to the mine with foodstuffs Saturday and expects to make two more trips to the same place today."[10]

Fueling regional mine development was the recent gold boom, sparked by the passage of the 1934 Gold Reserve Act, which incidentally created a stable, and profitable, market for gold-mining enterprises in eastern Alaska.[11] Experts predicted that the Bremner District bared "all the earmarks of being one of the foremost potential producers in this part of the Territory."[12] The federal gold laws, coupled with government airfield construction projects, quickly encouraged mining in the Bremner District. By the end of January newspapers were reporting on the Ramers' plans to ship a mill to Bremner for processing ore. The mill would be partitioned into pieces small enough for airplane transportation.[13] To facilitate the transportation of construction material and personnel from the Copper River & Northwestern Railway terminus to the Bremner mine, the Ramers made a swift and bold real estate purchase on January 5, 1934, of the property encompassing most of the McCarthy airstrip.[14] To keep pilots content and their critical planes in service, the company also apparently supported the construction of an airplane hangar at McCarthy, built by Gillam's mechanic, Bud Seltenreich.[15] Just as the previous generation looked to McCarthy as the staging area for mining in the Wrangell Mountains, twenty years later the Ramer brothers had helped transform the railroad town into a staging area for regional aviation. By July 1934 the Ramer brothers had secured funds for the mill at Bremner.[16]

Meanwhile, Kirkpatrick had decided to leave NAT and strike out on his own, reportedly making a purchase of a Kinner Bird two-seater.[17] He had recently met with the Cordova Chamber of Commerce, and although the meeting proved promising, his wife, Dean, was leery. She worried about the risk of putting their entire life savings into an aviation business. "I could think of a lot of other games to play than that of going in debt forever," she later confessed.[18] As an independent flyer, Kirk continued to be the Ramers' pilot of choice. In August he flew O. A. Torgerson, Cordova banker and by then vice president of the Bremner Gold Mining Company, to the mine to investigate the site firsthand.[19] The press called Torgerson an important local investor, contrasting him to the big eastern bankers who financed the region's copper industry. "The Ramer gold mine is essentially an Alaska mine," boasted the local paper. And thanks to Torgerson, Bremner was "more particularly a Cordova mine."[20] Admittedly, Torgerson knew little about mining. And despite the local media's characterization, he did, in fact, pay close attention to the business strategy applied by the region's industrial easterners, J. P. Morgan and the Guggenheims. The Alaska banker was a pragmatic businessman and understood the importance of controlling costs, particularly transportation. When it came to advancing that strategy, Torgerson reportedly put his money where his mouth was: "The present operation and prospects for the immediate future looked very promising," boasted the banker to the *Cordova Daily Times*. His only disappointment, quoted the paper, was the mine's "meager aviation facilities." As Torgerson stressed, a new airfield built closer to the gold claims was the mine's "most crying need."[21]

A new airfield at Bremner was not Torgerson's only priority concerning transportation. Like the McCarthy airstrip, Torgerson saw the Eyak airstrip as another crucial link in Bremner Gold Mining Company's transportation plans. Construction of the Cordova Airport at Eyak Lake had taken a little under two years and was completed during the summer of

1934. "With government help," wrote Dean, "huge bulldozers were brought in from Seattle and the townspeople were all agog watching the side of Eyak Mountain blasted into Lake Eyak."[22] The two-thousand-foot runway was dedicated on June 21, 1934. Cordova's mayor, William Chase, dedicated the Cordova Airport "to the memory of those gallant men who pioneered the airlines for this great territory—to Governor Troy, who assisted so greatly in procuring the necessary funds to construct this magnificent field, and to the future prosperity of Cordova."[23] Fittingly, Harold Gillam, in his large Stearman, was the first pilot to land on the Eyak airstrip.[24]

Missing from the dedication ceremony because of bad weather was another major advocate for the Cordova Airport, Captain Austin E. "Cap" Lathrop. Alaska's homegrown millionaire promised an additional twenty thousand dollars to construct a hangar at the new Eyak Lake airfield, if the city raised five thousand dollars.[25] According to Dean, it was Lathrop who originally encouraged Cordova's aviation venture and even promised to build the hangar to Kirk's specifications.[26] With the town's approval, Lathrop also arranged a fifty-year lease on the adjoining land to the hangar to erect a large machine shop. When construction was finished, Cordova had one of the most modern airfields in Alaska.[27] "There is no other place in Alaska," boasted Lathrop, "and perhaps no place anywhere in the states with such adequate and conveniently arranged facilities for both wheel and pontoon-equipped planes."[28]

Before the first golden-birch leaf of autumn began to fall, the Bremner Gold Mining Company had launched an aviation company. "The Cordova Air Service, whose incorporation papers are now on file in Juneau," announced the *Cordova Daily Times*, "is strictly a local concern. It is financed by residents of Cordova and the Copper River valley and its chief pilot and manger is M. D. Kirkpatrick, well-known Alaska flyer and airplane mechanic."[29] What these local businessmen failed to accomplish with Gillam in 1929, they achieved with Kirkpatrick five years later. The Eyak facility became the home base for the newly incorporated Cordova Air Service, and by the time winter's snowflakes began to fall, the buzz around the new Cordova airfield even lured Gillam from Copper Center.

To more practically serve the vastly different environments of the coast and the Interior, Kirk invented a ski-wheel combination for one of his planes.[30] Kirk's landing apparatus solved the major difficulty that most airmen faced each spring flying between the soggy coast and the still frigid Interior. But the Department of Aeronautics sanctioned Kirk's landing combination, unlike Bob Reeve, whose innovative ski designs lacked regulatory approval. Moreover, Kirk's repair shop at Eyak Lake was one of only two or three in the territory that was government accredited. Thus a main reason pilots flew into Cordova in those early days was plane repair, and Kirk's mechanical skills put the Eyak airfield on the map.[31]

Lathrop, who funded the shop, had five shares of Cordova Air Service (CAS) stock.[32] Not surprisingly, the savvy businessman demonstrated remarkable foresight when it came to the future of air carrier service in Cordova.[33] With its new Bellanca Pacemaker, CAS expanded its services beyond big mining companies to individual miners, hoping to locate new areas to develop. They offered flights over promising districts, allowing prospectors to investigate leads spotted from the air. In addition, the company offered to "grubstake" a prospector on the chance that a paying piece of property would be discovered. "Every ten days or so, or oftener if regular business takes the pilot into the vicinity," wrote the *Cordova Daily Times*, "the prospector is contracted, more supplies are taken in, and a check-up is made on the work. Benefits are derived by both parties and there is always a chance that 'paydirt' will be struck."[34] Lathrop recognized, however, that during the Great Depression, mining alone could not sustain the aviation industry. Knowing that Cordova was primarily a fishing community, he promoted Cordova Air Service to the fishing sector, explaining that planes could fly out over the Pacific to locate schooled fish and alert the fleet. Indeed, during the worst years of the Depression, supporting Alaska's commercial fishery helped to keep Cordova Air Service afloat.

Other key contracts came from Sears-Roebuck and Montgomery-Ward, which asked the air service to haul their catalogs into the Interior for the first time. "These were heavy and going by the pound," explained Dean, who served as the company's first office manager, "plus orders coming back really paid off."[35] Taking off for almost any request, whether it held the promise of a paid charter or not, Kirkpatrick once flew down to the isolated and glacier-bound Yakataga Beach in response to a distress call sent by way of the U.S. Signal Corps. Kirk was more than surprised to find the president of the Standard Oil Company of California, who was there scouting for oil with his geologists, waiting patiently for a plane.[36]

Soon thereafter, Kirk expanded his business eastward, toward the remote coastal areas, where storms originating from the Gulf of Alaska consistently brutalized the landscape. Gillam, by that time, had expanded his operations westward, into the Interior and the Kuskokwim area, to takeover southwest Alaska's mail run. Consequently, Gillam subcontracted most of his coastal flying to Kirkpatrick, including his mail route to Cape Yakataga, Yakutat, and Juneau. Indeed, unlike Gillam who focused on reliable mail service, and Reeve who focused on freight, CAS's niche was pretty much anything goes. As Dean put it, their combined "resources paid off and we [the Kirkpatricks] were out of debt in one year!"[37] This willingness for diversification probably accounts for Cordova Air's ability to scrape by and go on to dominate air service in eastern Alaska for the next thirty years.

CORDOVA AIR: A TRUE REGIONAL CARRIER

Although establishing regional relevancy meant necessitated services for mail delivery, responding to distress calls, and scouting for the commercial fishery, the main concern for Cordova Air's stockholders continued to be serving regional mines.[38] "Many of the directors of Cordova Air Service were heavy investors in the Bremner [Gold] Mining Company," explained Merle Smith, "and they were keen that the mine should be well serviced during the summer months when the cleanup was coming in."[39] Indeed, the company's lenders, B. W. Sargent and W. H. Field of Wilson-Fairbanks & Co., told residents of the Copper Belt to dream big: "It takes such courage and confidence to make dreams become reality. Our close observation and firsthand information regarding Bremner needs but visualization of only a few years ahead to see a busy, profitable real mining operation."[40]

In 1935, Kirkpatrick convinced the Cordova Chamber of Commerce's aviation committee to back an emergency landing field in the Chistochina District, which according to Kirk would also have the added benefit of "opening some promising mining property."[41] Bremner Gold Mining Company investors hoping to secure funds for improving its airstrip likewise appealed to the Cordova Chamber of Commerce, citing that in 1934 pilots flew into the district with an excess of twenty thousand pounds of freight and transported in and out of the mine ninety-one passengers. By the spring of 1935 planes had already transported nineteen thousand pounds to the mine, while the mining company predicted that passenger numbers would likely double that year.[42]

Moreover, the Bremner Gold Mining Company, with backing from the

Seattle brokerage firm Wilson-Fairbanks Company, planned to transport a mill, machinery, and other supplies into the mine over the winter of 1934–35. With so much of the success of their investment depending upon aviation, the Ramer brothers decided to move ahead with their plans for a runway, themselves clearing ground for the district's third strip. The runway was located even farther up the valley at the saddle of the pass and provided direct access to their claims and permanent camp. The construction of the Upper Airstrip marked the completion of their transportation trifecta—the McCarthy Airfield (which they owned), Cordova Air Service at Eyak Lake (in which they were significant investors), and now the airstrip fronting their Bremner claims. With a new milling facility matched by improved economic conditions stemming from the passage of the Gold Reserve Act, a confident Bremner Gold Mining Company petitioned the Cordova Chamber of Commerce in 1935 to finance necessary improvements on its partially completed field, reasoning that "the Bremner district [is] one of the most highly mineralized sections of Alaska. . . . A safe landing field here is absolutely necessary in the furthering of this district."[43]

Transportation success, however, failed to parlay into business success. While the Ramers waited for news on the pending airfield improvements, several financial setbacks confronted their organization. Suffering from high construction costs and nonproducing veins, the Bremner Gold Mining Company (originally capitalized at $250,000, comprising one million twenty-five-cent shares) found itself short on cash. Seeking to entice new stockholders, the company reduced its stock to ten cents a share.[44] Bob Reeve even lobbied on behalf of his friend and business associate Clarence William Poy, Bremner's general manager, while meeting with a group of potential Anchorage investors in early 1935. Reeve pitched that the price of gold promised to bring many properties into production, and airplanes, not to mention the added cost of building airfields, would be vital in their success.[45] But by the end of the year, Bremner's brief aviation monopoly began to collapse. In February 1936 the company was forced to sell its parcel of land surrounding the McCarthy airstrip to the Alaska Road Commission (ARC).[46]

Bremner's officials, including president Peyton Ramer, vice president O. A. Torgerson, and board director V. G. Vance, assured potential investors in a full-page advertisement that the Bremner Gold Mining Company's mine was "well equipped with mining machinery ready for immediate operation on a large scale."[47] The ad highlighted the new mill's capacity of processing "fifty tons of rock a day," which could "easily be increased in size with very little expenditure of money." To qualm doubts regarding transportation difficulties, the advertisement trumpeted the recent acquisition of two thousand dollars to enlarge and develop the upper airfield, boasting that "supplies are landed right at the mine."[48]

But Kirkpatrick knew, like Cal Lathrop, that for his aviation business to survive, even if Bremner's third airstrip did increase investment and flights, he nevertheless needed to look beyond the mines to increase business. In what can only be described as the region's first professional marketing effort promoting the practical application of the aviation industry to the larger public (at least one that was not hand-painted on the side of a tool shed), Kirkpatrick painted each of his aircraft orange, then launched an advertising campaign highlighting the numerous uses of Cordova Air Service's Orange Fleet. "Time flies," announced an ad for the company, and "so should you" in "comfortable, fast planes, equipped for year-round service."[49] Kirkpatrick provided a professional and timely alternative for passengers wanting to fly around eastern Alaska and beyond. The Orange Fleet offered service into Prince William Sound, the Copper River valley, the Chisana District, and the Tanana River valley.[50] Even though both Gillam and Reeve flew into those areas, Kirk set Cordova Air Service apart simply by its name; Gillam Airways and Reeve Airways implied that those businesses were essentially "one man shows," whereas Kirkpatrick's company reflected the interests of the larger geographical region, indicating that Kirk's goal as a bush pilot was building clientele rather than cultivating a legendary self-image.

Despite Kirk's invisible individualism, Cordovans still treated their aviator as a hometown hero. A *Cordova Daily Times* account of Kirkpatrick's interstate flight from Washington state to Cordova, on which he carried influenza serum bound for Barrow, emphasized the region's optimism for the promising new air carrier: "Appearing suddenly out of the gray mist which hung low on the horizon for the past few days, a plane piloted by M.D. Kirkpatrick . . . landed on Lake Eyak."[51] Carried with him were also two passengers, Peyton Ramer, president of Bremner Gold Mining Company, and J. L. Galen, president of the Alaska Transfer Company and co-owner of Cordova Air Service: two men Cordovans hoped would be capable of manufacturing golden dreams.

Even though the gold mines made Bremner an important air stop, especially in the minds of Cordova Air Service investors, the copper mining communities of McCarthy and Kennecott, along with the outlying camps of the Nizina and Chitina Rivers, still remained the region's largest population center and the best place for the air carrier to expand. Hoping to attract new clients with regular mail and fresh groceries, Cordova Air Service started a subsidiary, Airways Inc., based at McCarthy, intended to serve what Kirkpatrick called the Copper Belt Line. The company didn't hesitate to remind potential customers living and working off the road system that the "government's attitude toward road building in the territory and its penchant for putting tolls on what road is built" made flying the ideal choice for travel in the Wrangells.[52] The planes that served the Copper Belt Line featured a large green belt painted around the fuselage, acknowledging the region's affinity for the mineral copper. When demand grew beyond what Kirkpatrick could fly himself, he hired a new pilot, a fellow Kansan and Midwestern barnstormer named Merle K. Smith.

Merle "Smitty" Smith arrived in Cordova in 1937. On his first day of work Smith's boss wasted no time easing his inexperienced pilot into the job. Kirk instructed Smith to fly to McCarthy, about 150 miles north on the Copper River, in the Stearman C2B biplane. "You can't miss McCarthy," encouraged Kirkpatrick. "Just follow the railroad tracks." On the way back to Cordova, Smith hit fog rolling up the valley from the sea and had to make an emergency landing in an area surrounded by a swamp. On a fluke Smith landed in the only dry spot that could have held his plane's weight without sinking. Hearing the story of the young pilot's sheer beginner's luck, Harold Gillam dubbed the emergency landing site "Smith Field."[53]

The Stearman C2B biplane Smith flew that day became as legendary as the pilots who flew it. Aviation pioneer Noel Wien first brought the aircraft to Alaska in 1928. A year later it served as part of Carl Ben Eielson's Alaskan Airways fleet. When Eielson and Borland went missing in the winter of 1929–1930, Harold Gillam flew it on the search. Joe Crosson flew the Stearman on several mercy missions. Jerry Jones made the first glacier landing on Mount McKinley in the Stearman in 1932. In 1934 it was sold to Pacific Alaska Airways, a subsidiary of Pan American Airways. Three years later Kirkpatrick purchased the Stearman C2B to serve the

Copper Belt Line from the Cordova Air Service base at the McCarthy airstrip, where the legend of the biplane continued to grow.[54]

In May 1937, Kirk transferred the young Smith to McCarthy permanently, from where he flew and managed the Copper Belt Line twelve months a year for $175 a month. Cordova Air Service maintained a cabin near the McCarthy airstrip for its pilots. The cabin had a good stove for both warmth and cooking. In the corner was a barrel buried in the permafrost, where butter and meat could be stored. When Smith's new wife, Bertha, arrived in McCarthy, the couple rented a small furnished house from Kate Kennedy. The little house had a wood stove, on which Bertha learned to cook. One of Smith's first runs on the Copper Belt Line was to Horsefeld, where Cordova Air Service had recently hired a local resident to build an airstrip. Smith made several trips to Gillam's old stomping grounds in the Nutzotin Mountains, delivering large orders of mining equipment to William Sultzer. Once on the other side of the Wrangells, Smith flew on to Nabesna. On one trip in particular, Smith was sent to retrieve two prostitutes. The flight earned him some grief from his wife but, most important, it resulted in the acquisition of his trademark beaver hat.[55]

From Nabesna the Copper Belt route always included stops at the Bremner gold mine before going on to Cordova. It was on a flight into Bremner in the usually stormy month of August that Smith received his infamous nickname "Mudhole." Flying the Stearman biplane, Smith landed at the Bremner Gold Mining Company's upper airstrip, in the saddle of the pass. The headwaters of the Golconda River made this area extremely wet and soggy. What Smith landed on was a long strip built on the sponge-like tundra, which the company had scraped and leveled a few years before. For arriving planes to land on hard and, if possible, dry ground, Bremner employees dug drainage ditches on each side of the soggy strip and laid large flat shale-type rocks close together across it.[56] While taking off in a heavy rain squall, Smith's Stearman sunk in a mud hole made by an uprooted rock in the middle of the field. The plane skidded off the rocky strip, ending up on its nose. Smith spent a miserable night at Bremner scraping mud off his plane. The next day, Harold Gillam flew in a propeller for him. Keenly embarrassed about the crash, Merle Smith would later become immortalized because of it.[57]

The story of Smith's misfortune spread along the Copper Belt Line. Weeks later, when Smith ran into an almost gleeful Bob Reeve in Valdez, the older pilot, who had apparently heard the story from Pete Ramer, christened the greenhorn "Mudhole" Smith.[58] The nickname stuck. The story, repeated many times in aviation lore, depicts the dangers encountered by bush pilots even on everyday flights. Moreover, the story's seemingly innocent humor, provided gregariously by Bob Reeve (who decried regularly that the young Smith had "stolen" the Bremner run) underscores a far more serious contest brewing among regional flyers by the end of the decade.[59] No longer were pilots flying under "gentlemen agreements." Cordova Air Service butted heads with Reeve Airways on numerous occasions, especially in the advertised contest for customers. "If you need seaplanes or aerial ambulance service," announced an advertisement placed by Kirkpatrick, "wire the Cordova Air Service—the Copper Belt Line." The Cordova ad, situated just above Reeve's "old reliable" ad in the *Valdez Miner*, seemed to really tick off the Glacier Pilot: "Afterthought," stated a Reeve's ad published not long after CAS ran its ad. "Why don't you wise up and also locate in a good Town (Valdez as opposed to Cordova) and Gold Belt (as opposed to the other, dwindling industry in the region)."[60]

Despite the ribbing by Reeve that christened his "Mudhole" moniker, not to mention the heated rivalry growing among air carriers, Smith continued to build a positive reputation as a competent Copper River area pilot. Bad weather, zero visibility, and tight canyon flying were daily hazards. "I must have made a thousand trips up and down that Copper River," recalled Smith. "I got to know it real well. . . . I knew every bush and tree."[61] Because of its reliable service, Cordova Air Service was able to renew its contract with Sears-Roebuck to fly packages and freight from Cordova to Chitina and McCarthy. The large retailer would ship one large package on the Alaska Steamship Company to Cordova. Then Cordova Air Service would open it and load the individual packages into the airplane for Smith to deliver. The packages were mostly shoebox size, already addressed, and easy to handle. With six hundred people at the Kennecott mines and McCarthy, and probably another two hundred at Chitina, as Smith explained, "this was a very good account."[62]

THE END OF THE LINE

Even though the late 1930s were the most profitable years of Alaska's gold-mining industry, the year 1938 meant the end of the line for most residents of the Copper Belt, and almost for Cordova Air Service as well.[63] Unlike the booming gold-mining operations, copper miners fared poorly during the Great Depression as the price of copper plummeted to five cents per pound.[64] Moreover, no other large deposits had been discovered in the Wrangells, despite extensive attempts by Kennecott to prospect the region. The region's economic engine had exhausted its richer ore reserves. The Kennecott Copper Corporation therefore decided it was time to close the Bonanza Ridge mines, which collectively produced upwards of two hundred million dollars in high-grade copper over the years, and move its attention to more lucrative properties in Utah and Chile.

Earlier that spring, Kennecott's president, E. T. Stannard, announced the October closing of the Kennecott Copper Mines, which also meant the stoppage of Kennecott's primary means of transportation, the Copper River & Northwestern Railway. At the time, Smith believed that this would be a boost for the air industry. The naïve flyer recalled thinking: "Those people had only two ways in or out: walk or fly."[65] Instead, they did neither. Most Copper Belt residents left with the last train on November 11. The towns of Chitina, Kennecott, and McCarthy were practically deserted. Cordova Air Service, as Lathrop had earlier predicted, was forced to look beyond the Copper Belt to keep business from sinking.

Cordova Air Service's first business after the closure of the railway was to Chisana. That winter and spring Smith transported all the mining community's freight from Cordova. Although mining was in decline and camp populations had dwindled, this route became a mainstay of Cordova Air Service over the next few years. Besides flying freight, Smith also flew several passenger charters that winter. One was for a young game warden, Clarence Rhode, on the hunt for fur smugglers near the Canadian border. Rhodes later became well-known for his work at the U.S. Fish & Wildlife Service.[66]

Summer of 1938 also brought back explorer Bradford Washburn, who had returned to study eastern Alaska's mountains and glaciers by air.[67] Sponsored by the National Geographic Society, Harvard University, and the New England Museum of Natural History, Washburn chartered Gillam, Reeve, Kirkpatrick, and Smith to fly him over "the most interesting and spectacular glacier systems on earth." The purpose of the aerial expedition was twofold: the first was to obtain material for mapping unexplored regions of Alaska, and the second was to secure as complete as possible a series of aerial photographs illustrating the fundamental principle of glaciation.[68] Because of the fickle nature of Alaska's weather, Washburn considered hiring a pilot for the season but quickly decided that it would be fiscally impossible. Researchers therefore remained at local airstrips waiting for the weather to clear. On the rarest of occasions when the clouds cleared enough to photograph the targeted geological formations, the party chartered with the local air carrier. "Our whole project was broken down into a series of minor sub-projects at the beginning of the season," Washburn wrote, "and we rarely knew until just before we took off exactly what job the weather was going to let us tackle."[69]

In August, Bob Reeve and Harold Gillam flew Washburn, along with his party consisting of geologists G. Dallas Hanna and Garrett Eddy, across the coastal barrier range toward Mount Saint Elias. Washburn mounted his mapping camera out the cabin door of Reeve's Fairchild 71. To make the cabin as comfortable as possible while in flight, they built a special door inside the cabin that left an opening for the camera.[70] As the pilots circled the peak, Dr. Hanna and Washburn made a significant geological discovery. Located "in the very face of the great cliffs of St. Elias" was the previously undiscovered contact between the massive core rock of the Saint Elias Range and the coastal sediments lying to the south. "From the great folds of rock clearly visible in these cliffs, reported Washburn, "it is clear the highest peaks of this range have been bodily thrust southward over the top of younger coastal rocks and this gained their position as one of the greatest coastal ranges in the world."[71]

By fall, Washburn had chartered a flight with Kirkpatrick, who completed a circuit of the Prince William Sound shoreline, then flew up to McCarthy. From McCarthy, Smith flew Washburn out past the north side of Mount Logan, between the peak and Mount Walsh, and around Mount Lucania—a landscape in which Washburn was quite acquainted. The team returned to McCarthy by way of the Donjek, Klutlan, and White Rivers and Sokolai Pass. Washburn left Cordova in October 1938, remarking that he had never worked in any area where he had received more wholehearted and sincere cooperation. He especially noted "the efficient and splendid service of the Cordova Air Service and pilots Kirkpatrick and Smith."[72]

In part because of Washburn's geological work, people outside of Alaska were beginning to pay attention to this remote, and increasingly deserted, part of Alaska. Boosting Alaska tourism with the goal of enhancing the local economy was indeed on the mind of future territorial governor Ernest Gruening when he also chartered a flight with Merle Smith that summer. At the time, Gruening was director of the U.S. Department of Interior's Division of Territories and Island Possessions and was interested in developing Alaska's recreational potential. One issue concerning Gruening was public access to these places—or more specifically, the lack thereof. Smith flew Gruening and his entourage on an aerial tour of the Chitina Valley, on which Gruening determined the area to be, as Smith recalled, "national park caliber."[73] The ensuing pullout of the Kennecott Copper Corporation and the Copper River & Northwestern Railway distressed the director, who correctly believed would cause the region's economy to collapse. "The most superlative of all scenic trips in Alaska," lamented Gruening, "would soon be unavailable to the public."[74]

That September, Gruening recommended that the Chitina valley be incorporated into the National Park Service system and designated the Kennicott National Monument. The threat of war, combined with the argument that wilderness preservation was unnecessary in a region already dominated by wilderness, caused President Roosevelt to reject the proposal in 1939.[75] Although the federal government tabled the plan for the time being, a relationship between aviation and tourism in eastern Alaska had been established.

In the fall of 1938, Cordova Air Service returned service to the near ghost towns of Chitina and McCarthy, while increasing frequency to Alaska's main urban center, Anchorage. Wrangell, Juneau, and Petersburg of the southeast Panhandle were also among its destinations. The air carrier commenced a flight route for tourists, sightseers, and recreationalists, promoting local fishing trips to places such as Tebay Lakes, located near the Bremner Mining District. But as Gruening predicted, the region's economy crashed with the closing of the copper mine and railway, and Kirk was forced to transfer Smith from McCarthy to Copper Center for his base of operations. There, business continued to include taking freight to mines.

That same year, Asa Baldwin, a highly valued surveyor for both the Kennecott Copper Corporation and Nabesna Mining Corporation, took over the struggling Bremner Gold Mining Company and consolidated all lode-mining claims in the Golconda Creek area, forming Yellow Band Gold Mines, Inc.[76] Although new gold strikes were few and far between, the value of gold production rose to record levels between 1938 and 1941, hence the continued interest and investment in gold-mining ventures at places like Bremner and Nabesna.[77] Smith, like Reeve had done five years before, began trucking freight up to Copper Center and then flying it across the Wrangells to Nabesna. Still, by early that year the charter business throughout the Copper Belt continued to plummet, and Smith also felt that the end of the line had finally come. He began to look elsewhere for work. That spring, Noel Wien offered him a far more profitable job flying out of Nome, where dredge mining looked to make millionaires out of ragged miners.[78] Kirk offered to pay him more, but as Smith later admitted, he planned to accept Wien's offer.

Talk of work that day had to wait. It was April 10, 1939, and Kirkpatrick had a load of miners waiting for their charted flight to McCarthy and Dan Creek. Kirk left McCarthy with passenger Con Miller on his return flight to Cordova. Soon after takeoff, a spring snowstorm, unleashed from the Gulf of Alaska, smothered the Chugach Mountains in a blanket of white and engulfed the Copper River basin in an impenetrable wall of weather. Smith waited out the blizzard in the warmth of the Cordova Air Service cabin in McCarthy, eagerly listening to the radio for a report from Kirk. None came. After five days, the bodies of M. D. Kirkpatrick and his passenger Con Miller were found inside the Bellanca aircraft in Orca Bay, not far from the landing field at Cordova. Kirk's plane reportedly clipped a tree and crashed into the cold water.[79] The death of Kirkpatrick inspired scores of newspaper articles, each expressing residents' heartfelt sadness for the loss of Cordova's unlikely skyboy.[80]

Merle Smith, in light of the tragedy, turned down Noel Wien's job offer. The Cordova Air Service board elected Merle K. "Mudhole" Smith into the position of president and general manager. Not only was his friend and mentor dead, but Smith had to take over the flying business at an economically impossible time. Moreover, the death of one of Alaska's most competent pilots and his well-known passenger only cemented aviation's biggest obstacle: the public's fear of flying. Change, however, was on the horizon for the Wrangell Mountain flyers. That summer the newly created Civil Aeronautics Board (CAB) arrived in Anchorage to hold hearings and make recommendations that would profoundly impact Alaska's the aviation industry.

Asked to write a poem about his favorite person, a third grader from Cordova captured perfectly public sentiment for pilot Harold Gillam: "He thrilled 'em/ Chill 'em/ Spilled 'em/ But no kill 'em/ Gillam." Courtesy of the Cordova Historical Museum, 95-46-11.

A self-proclaimed maverick of the Wrangell's aviation scene, Reeve embraced an Old Frontier style. He felt that in the dog-eat-dog competition for Alaska aviation business, "only the toughest— and the shrewdest—survive." Bob Reeve in front of his Valdez machine shop, wearing his trademark rain hat, around 1937. Russ Dow Papers, Archives and Special Collections, Consortium Library, University of Alaska–Anchorage, uaa-hmc-0396-14a-30.

A lone Cordova Air Service plane flies over a boundless sea of mountains and ice. Walter A. Wood, a geologist who used aviation to conduct scientific fieldwork in the Saint Elias range once noted: "These glacierized high-mountain ranges were by their very nature unsympathetic to human invasion." Merle Smith Collection, Alaska Airlines, Seattle, Washington.

Cordova Air Service pilot Merle Smith spent several years flying scheduled flights to mining camps around the Copper Belt. On one such flight he crashed his Stearman C2B biplane after attempting a takeoff from Bremner Mine's muddy strip. Word spread of the rookie's misfortune and when he ran into Bob Reeve days later, the senior pilot bestowed upon the Copper Belt's newest competitor the nickname "Mudhole." Merle Smith in front of his Stearman C2B biplane in McCarthy in 1937, his first year flying the Copper Belt route. Courtesy of the Cordova Historical Museum, 95-46-45.

To bush pilots like Bob Reeve and the rest of the Wrangell Mountain skyboys, "there was only one Gillam." Gillam preparing to take off in his Pilgrim, around 1935. Courtesy of the Cordova Historical Museum, 95-46-95.

Harold Gillam conducted some of the first reconnaissance flights into the Bremner Mining District in 1930 for the Ramer brothers, owners of the Bremner Gold Mining Company. Lee Ramer and his dog team, and possibly Gillam's Swallow biplane, high in the saddle of Bremner pass in the early 1930s. Bertha Ramer Collection, McCarthy-Kennicott Historical Museum, McCarthy, Alaska.

Harold Gillam pioneered commercial air service in the Wrangell Mountain region. He was famous for his pet polar bears, his cat-like vision, and his uncanny ability to fly in weather that kept most flyers grounded. Gillam Airways Corporation Capital Stock Certificate, January 23, 1930. Courtesy of the author.

In her memoir *Sisters: Coming of Age and Living Dangerously in the Wild Copper River Valley*, Samme Gallaher confessed: "I was nineteen . . . and thought I was in love with Gillam." Gillam frequented the family's homestead along the Copper River in the early 1930s. Although most Wrangell Mountain residents lived far apart, the airplane supplied speedy travel that allowed isolated people to come together as a community. Samme Gallaher Darnall Collection, Thousand Oaks, California. Courtesy of Geoffrey Bleakley, Maui, Hawaii.

Well into the 1930s, Alaskans received mail via dog teams. Through persistent lobbying efforts of Alaska's leadership, Washington, D.C. finally granted a territorial airmail system, which transformed Alaska aviation from a public curiosity to a practical public service. Harold Gillam obtained a contract to deliver mail twice monthly to the mining communities of Nabesna and Bremner in 1931. In 1934, Kennecott Copper Cooperation contracted him to fly in the mail after the Chitina Bridge went out during spring breakup of ice on the river, which prevented mail delivery by rail. By 1935, Gillam Airways had successfully expanded its Copper Belt contract to carry mail to Katalla once each month and to Yakataga Beach once each three months. Harold Gillam refueling his Pilgrim at Yakataga Beach during low tide on August 20, 1938. Courtesy of the Cordova Historical Museum, 99-2-20.

Pilot Bob Reeve "drifted" into the coastal town of Valdez in spring 1932. Called by his clients a "scout of the sky," Reeve used his modified Fairchild 51 to prospect for undeveloped mineral deposits throughout the Chugach and Wrangell Mountains. Courtesy of the Alaska Heritage Aviation Museum, Anchorage, Alaska.

Because work kept him mired in a muddy mess that smelled of rotting salmon and decaying seaweed, Reeve was known as a fairly filthy flyer. Not everyone was impressed with his dirty flying, however. His major rival, the meticulously clean Harold Gillam, once remarked, "Reeve can have it!" Russ Dow Papers, Archives and Special Collections, Consortium Library, University of Alaska–Anchorage, uaa-hmc-0396-14a-50.

In 1937, Bradford Washburn sought a pilot to fly his climbing party and gear to the Walsh Glacier at the base of Mount Lucania in the Saint Elias range, at the time the highest unclimbed peak in North America. Reeve replied to Washburn's request in typical Reeve fashion: "Anywhere you'll ride, I'll fly." On landing at Walsh Glacier, Reeve broke the world's record for the highest landing at 8,500 feet on skis. Bob Reeve's Fairchild 51 in several feet of slush on the Walsh Glacier in 1937. Russ Dow Papers, Archives and Special Collections, Consortium Library, University of Alaska–Anchorage, uaa-hmc-0396-14a-75.

Kirkpatrick started a subsidiary (Airways, Inc.) to serve the Wrangell Mountain mines from McCarthy. The planes that flew the Copper Belt line featured a large green belt painted around the fuselage, acknowledging the region's affinity for the mineral copper. He hired a young Merle Smith to manage the route in 1937. Smith and Kirk relax at the CAS McCarthy Station in 1938. Merle Smith Collection, Alaska Airlines, Seattle Washington.

Merritt M. D. "Kirk" Kirkpatrick, along with several Cordova business leaders with connections to the Bremner Gold Mining Company, started Cordova Air Service in 1934. As manager and pilot, Kirk set the company apart simply by building clientele rather than cultivating a legendary self-image. He expanded business to fly contracts for the retailer Sears-Roebuck and Cordova's commercial fishing industry. He provided a professional and timely alternative for passengers wanting to fly around eastern Alaska and beyond. With the distinctive Orange Fleet providing a reliable public service, Cordova Air Service had become a truly regional carrier. A Cordova Air Service plane loads passengers and their luggage from the beach, a common place to land and take off. Courtesy of the Cordova Historical Museum, 95-46-1.

Merle "Mudhole" Smith became famous for his beaver hat, but the warm garb added more than just local character to the pilot's persona. When flying at forty below in open cockpits, furs were a necessary part of the flyer's wardrobe. Merle Smith Collection, Alaska Airlines, Seattle, Washington.

Kirk prepares to fly renowned scientist, mountaineer, and photographer Bradford Washburn over the Saint Elias range in 1938 to conduct geological aerial studies. Within a year Kirkpatrick would die a in a plane crash ferrying passengers from McCarthy to Cordova in a spring blizzard. Courtesy of the Cordova Historical Museum, 99-2-8.

"Harold Gillam had developed into the finest bad-weather pilot in the Territory," asserted Bob Reeve. "[He] flew contact through incredible hazards that left the other pilots opened mouthed with awe." Although the men respected each other as pilots, their views on government regulation of Alaska aviation diverged. Gillam believed regulation would make flying safer and more economical, while Reeve believed it would bring more government interference to flying. Reeve and Gillam share a rare face-to-face moment in Anchorage before attending the Civil Aeronautics Board hearings in 1939. Jack Peck File, Alaska Aviation Heritage Museum, Anchorage.

The road from a waning regional air carrier that depended on a practically defunct mining industry, to an interstate airline that flew hundreds of passengers and tourists on scheduled regular routes between Anchorage, Juneau, and Bristol Bay started near the war's end, when Cordova Air Service stockholders asked Merle Smith to return to the failing company. In July 1944, Smith returned with a plan. First he bought out all stockholders. Then he expanded his fleet. In 1945 he acquired a Lockheed L-10E Electra from the Morrison-Knudsen Company (M-K) for twenty-five thousand dollars. It was the first all-weather, twin-engine airplane to fly between Anchorage and Cordova. The Electra was kept for a year then replaced with an even more passenger-friendly DC-3. The *St. Elias*, Merle Smith's Lockheed Electra, in 1945. Merle Smith Collection, Alaska Airlines, Seattle, Washington.

The federal government granted the Morrison-Knudsen Company (M-K) the contract to construct the Northway airport in the spring 1941, just a few months before Germany invaded the Soviet Union and Japan bombed Pearl Harbor. Before construction could begin at Northway, engineers had to improve and enlarge the Nabesna "bush" strip. With Bob Reeve's guidance, M-K built a six-thousand-foot main runway and two two-thousand-foot cross-runways near the Nabesna River. By summer the Nabesna Landing Field had become one of the biggest in Alaska, shorter only than Elmendorf and Ladd army airfields. After Reeve left to assist the military in the Aleutians, Gillam replaced him as head pilot for M-K, while bush pilots from across Alaska flew the "Nabesna-Northway airlift" in 1942. Pictured are (left to right) Smith (Smitty), Rudy Billberg, John Walatka, Frank Barr (sitting), Don Emmons, Jack Scavenius, Frank Kammer, and Herman Lerdahl. Courtesy of Johanna Bouker, Dillingham, Alaska.

5

Taming the "Wild North"

FOR MOST OF THE AMERICAN POPULATION, ALASKA IN THE 1930S
remained one of the few remaining places still considered a land of opportunity. Alaska, like the continental United States a century before, was a
large land mass endowed by endless resources, waiting to be exploited by
an enterprising, entrepreneurial spirit. By the middle of the decade, the
airplane had become the tool that Alaskans—from the Ramer brothers
to the industrial mining giant the Kennecott Copper Corporation—
used to develop commercial prospects in the untapped regions of the Far
North. But as historian Nick A. Komons points out in his seminal study
Bonfires to Beacons, "the airplane's potential would not—in fact, could
not—be realized by a community of businessmen acting alone."[1]

By 1938 federal intervention into the nation's aviation industry would
overcome the daunting barriers that had prevented the industry from
reaching success from its inception. Economic instability had limited
Alaska pilots from making a viable living, forcing them to fly in extreme
and dangerous conditions to pay the bills. This economic reality caused
perhaps the most intimidating obstacle to practical, everyday air service:
the public's fear of flying.[2] Nationally the federal government, according
to Komons, would stand at the side of business, "becoming, in effect, civil
aviation's indispensable partner."[3] In Alaska, where the air charter business was considered aviation's "wild north," federal oversight also effectively put an end to bush pilots' "anything goes" approach to flying. But for
many Alaska pilots the federal process of moving away from the "reckless
barnstormer image" toward "the realm of the professional" stripped them
of their "frontier" identity. At times, the transformation was painful, con-
fusing, and divisive among Alaska's flying fraternity. Some aviators saw

the federal government as facilitators of commercial growth while others saw federal authority as a threat to their freedom and independence. And some, like Bob Reeve, simply would not go down without a fight.

"LAISSEZ FAIRE IN THE AIR"

After several aviation accidents in 1924, the Buffalo *Courier* called upon the government "to bring some order out of the chaos of laissez faire in the air, where constantly increasing numbers of . . . flyers . . . disport without let or hindrance."[4] Although many on the voices demanding regulation included "hardheaded businessmen," unbridled business activity was considered an economic virtue upheld by the champion of free enterprise, President Calvin Coolidge.[5] Because of such strong advocacy for "laissez faire" legislation by the White House, Congress passed the Air Commerce Act in 1926 "to encourage, foster and promote civil aeronautics" rather than to regulate the industry's economic growth or address safety concerns. Powers granted in the Air Commerce Act would be exercised by the head of the Department of Commerce, which, according to the framers of the original bill, "is now and always should be under the direction of a successful and able business executive."[6] In 1926 the successful businessman serving as secretary of commerce was Herbert Hoover.

Hoover, who was elected president in 1928, was also a staunch believer in self-reliance. He stood at the national helm when the stock market crashed in 1929, and his belief in self-help shaped the federal government's response to the tremendous financial shockwave that immediately followed. To issue direct aid to the thousands of homeless "Okies" fleeing dust storms on the Plains, or the homeless living in cardboard shacks of "Hoovervilles," went against Hoover's deep conservative grain. He believed that volunteerism and nongovernment-relief programs should supply charity to the poor. Americans needed to work harder to pull themselves up from misfortune. That was the American way; he considered anything more socialism.

While running against Hoover in 1932, the Great Depression's worst year, Franklin Roosevelt promised to use the power of the federal government to turn the economy around by assisting the "forgotten man at the bottom of the economic pyramid," rather than continuing his predecessor's policies of laissez-faire, "trickle-down" economics that tended to benefit big business and the ultrarich. Admittedly, economic transition would take time. The Roosevelt administration recognized that the economic reality of dormant factories and rotting crops affected the national psyche. Americans had lost confidence in their ability to move forward. The county was steeped in pessimism; a crisis of morale. Roosevelt therefore promised to tackle what he saw as America's immediate threat: fear itself. This proved to be an equally challenging task when it came to aviation.

In terms of shaping the financial stability of Alaska's aviation industry, a modicum of economic confidence became manifest with the passage of the Gold Standard Act, an expression of federal government's New Deal approach to dealing with economic decline. The Gold Standard Act facilitated a strong relationship between aviation and the mining industry throughout the 1930s, but it failed to increase passenger service in the territory. Indeed, before aviation could become a viable business, the public had to be convinced that is was safe to fly.

Weighing on the industry's ability to grow from the beginning was Alaskans' unapologetic, commonsensical fear of flying. Like a majority of Americans, the idea of leaving the ground simply terrified them. "It's one of history's great ironies," wrote historian Robert Serling, "that the nation where heavier-than-air flight was first achieved was the last major industrialized country to realize the commercial potential of the airplane."[7] Even delivering the mail—aviation's first practical benefit to the American people—gained a notorious reputation. Of the two-hundred-plus pilots hired by the federal government between 1918 and 1926, thirty-five died flying the mail. The nation's aviators ominously referred to the service as a "suicide club."[8] When Carl Ben Eielson established commercial air service in Alaska in 1923, promoters knew "they had a big job ahead selling the airplane to the general public."[9]

Despite the media attention that glorified northern aviators, aviation itself was indeed a tough sell in Alaska. Unlike in the Lower 48, where a pilot flying in the 1920s and 1930s was reasonably sure of finding a place to land if he or she should develop motor trouble, a pilot on a prolonged flight in Alaska had a far less chance of safely landing if confronted with trouble. In a 1929 article titled "Problems of Alaska Aviation," Joseph Dunn painted a dire scenario that likely caused most potential passengers to think twice before taking off with a local pilot: "If the Alaskan aviator makes a forced landing," wrote Dunn, "he has a very small chance of being near civilization and must depend upon his own ability to make repairs. . . . If he is unable to do this he must make his way overland to some town or village, secure the necessary parts and then complete his repairs."[10] If the scenario of being stuck on a glacier while their pilot hikes out for help didn't deter people from flying, then Dunn gave readers a litany of reasons why aviation should be considered dangerous in Alaska: bad weather; the inability to forecast favorable conditions; no markers or beacons for night flying; confining flight time to the daylight hours, which in the middle of winter, numbered about six or seven.[11]

Confirming the dangers and undoubtedly fueling Alaskans' fear of flying were several highly publicized airplane crashes that occurred just as the industry in Alaska struggled to move from its barnstormer image to one of a professional air carrier. In November 1929, Ben Eielson and his mechanic Earl Borland died in Siberia while attempting to evacuate furs and personnel from the *Nanuk*, a cargo vessel trapped in arctic ice. The winter search for the missing plane, according to Alaska writer Jim Rearden, "became the climactic Alaskan aviation event of the 1920s that was followed in news accounts by millions around the world."[12] But the most sensational and shocking air-related accident to occur in Alaska was the "crash felt around the world" that killed humorist Will Rogers and celebrated pilot Wiley Post near Barrow in 1935.[13]

At the time of the accident, Rogers was at the peak of his popularity, rising from a vaudeville lasso-twirling comedian to syndicated columnist, best-selling author, cowboy philosopher, world-renowned Broadway performer, and Hollywood movie star. He befriended everyone from the "home folk" to the president, proving his quotable saying true: that he never met a man he didn't like. His pilot, Wiley Post, was also famous. Post had become a national figure in 1931 when he obliterated the record for flying around the world in eight days. Two years later, Post beat his own record by a day, flying around the globe in an unpressurized monoplane at extremely high altitudes. At thirty thousand to forty thousand feet the air is thin and hard to breathe. Post solved this problem by developing an early version of the pressurized suit that NASA astronauts would later wear in space.

Both Rogers and Post were part Cherokee Indian and from the West. Together these self-proclaimed Oklahoma cowboys decided on a trip to the Last Frontier. Besides the adventures the two friends had planned to share, Rogers sought fresh material for his newspaper column, while Post sought a new air route to Europe. On August 15, Post's customized Lockheed aircraft crashed while trying to take off from a tidal flat near Point Barrow. The crash made international headlines, for death had taken one of the world's most innovated aviators and the most influential voice of the Depression-era's "common man."[14] The news rocked the nation from California to New York. Los Angelino Charles Harris remembered: "About mid-afternoon two newspaper boys came down the middle of the residential street . . . 'Extra, Extra, Will Rogers and Wiley Post killed at Point Barrow."[15] The *New York Times* headline read: "Will Rogers, Wiley Post Die in Airplane Crash in Alaska; Nation Shocked By Tragedy."[16] The outpouring of national grief was said to have rivaled that felt for Lincoln. Eddie Cantor, Mary Pickford, and Clark Gable were among those who mourned at Rogers's funeral. President Roosevelt expressed deep sadness for the loss of his "old friend." Alaskans were especially stunned by the accident. Attempting to put their heartfelt sorrow into words, writer Rex Beach feebly wrote: "This tragedy is still too incredible for belief."[17] Perhaps the words of child star Shirley Temple were the most prophetic. When told of Rogers's death she bitterly cried, "I hate airplanes!"[18]

REGULATING THE "WILD NORTH"

Making matters worse, by the mid-1930s, with the exception of the Gold Standard Act that affected aviation in Alaska, most of the New Deal programs dealing with aviation nationwide were viewed as ineffectual. The recent handling of airmail contracts that led to scandal and political embarrassment, the seemingly unrestricted power of the temporarily created and bureaucratically minded Bureau of Air Commerce (BAC), and the administration's apparent disregard of the report of the Federal Aviation Commission, which experts hailed as a policy breakthrough, combined to create a crisis of confidence in the Roosevelt administration among the aviation community, Congress, and the public at large. One area, however, where the administration effectively responded was to the issue of aviation safety, which in the mid-1930s was considered abysmal.

The Bureau of Air Commerce, under pressure by Congress, the press, and the aviation industry, renewed its focus, revitalized its leadership, and began to work toward real reform. The result was the Civil Aeronautics Act, signed into law on June 23, 1938. When the act became operative that August, the Civil Aeronautics Authority (CAA) subsumed the Bureau of Air Commerce functions. As a government agency, the BAC existence became no more. The act provided air carriers with a national economic charter, which the industry had pushed for since 1934 and, perhaps most important, created an independent safety board.[19] The Civil Aeronautics Act was created to curb the fear the average American felt toward flying and instill faith in the aviation industry. The landmark legislation called for the establishment of a safe and reliable air transportation system throughout the country, including Alaska. The motivation for the 1938 law was expressed mainly in terms of public safety, a fair and balanced expansion of services between the private and public sectors, and providing a rational institutional framework for the industry. This meant to Alaskans that the federal government planned to employ navigational aides, build more airports, set safety standards, and stabilize fares. It also included for the first time a distribution of mail contracts in the Far North. Most important (and worrisome) to aviators, however, the CAA would establish Alaska's first scheduled commercial air routes.

The objective in Alaska for the Civil Aeronautics Board (CAB), which was created by Congress to oversee implementation of the 1938 law, was to integrate Alaska's small, independent, charter-driven air carrier industry into the larger and more stable nationwide network of scheduled services.[20] This was no small task. The cutthroat practices of rival arctic aviators had become legendary throughout Alaska by 1938. What was also "legendary" was the widely held belief that such practices forced pilots to fly in dangerous conditions that often resulted in unnecessary crashes or even death. Thus putting an end to Alaska's version of "laissez faire in the air" by increasing the safety of both passengers and pilots justified the federal government's need to regulate the so-called destructive competition and bring order out of the chaos that apparently existed in Alaska's aviation industry.

The CAB's main challenge in achieving this goal was to overcome the individual carriers' penchant to constantly adjust passenger and freight rates, even offer flights on credit, in order to entice paying customers away from a competitor and in the process undercut the cost of doing business for all of the industry's participants. Raymond W. Stough, director of the Civil Aeronautics Board's economic bureau, stressed that the existing business practices in Alaska warranted urgent regulation, warning that unless significant reforms were made, "Alaskan aviation may soon become unsound."[21] Thus, CAB saw the concerns for public safety and economic stability as one in the same.

Director Stough regarded such cutthroat competition as a boost for private interest but harmful to the public—not to mention, bad for the individual air carriers. Stough reasoned that continuously altering rates on the more lucrative routes eroded profits that should be used to supplement lower revenues accrued in the thinner markets.[22] This meant that the public residing in small communities and villages received less air service than mining companies, and they were charged a higher rate. In the end, this caused the erosion not just of profits but of the public's confidence in Alaska's aviation industry as a whole. "The result of Alaska's intense and unrestrained competitive struggle," lamented Stough, "is a demoralizing situation, which may well become chaotic if permitted to continue."[23] Moreover, Stough noted pointedly that the Alaskan aviation industry was largely responsible for its own problems, citing that "rate-cutting, the race for traffic, unwillingness to coordinate or pool business, the insistence upon maintaining independent rather than consolidated operations, the desire to carry traffic anywhere in the Territory, and other like practices have brought about conditions from which most of the carriers now claim to desire relief."[24]

To provide that relief to struggling carriers, as well as to meet the needs of small communities and villages, encourage public confidence, and promote the development of the air service network, the federal government therefore gave the CAB direct financial operating subsidies and oversight of the country's aviation industry. Federal regulation came in the form of Certificates of Convenience and Necessity, which through CAB recommendations to Congress granted individual air carriers the authorization to fly people and property as well as the mail for those carriers holding Star Route contracts on scheduled routes. Certification also meant that carriers would serve a general territory rather than a specific route.[25] Policy makers assured Alaskans that the CAB aimed to boost the economy but at the same time promised to protect the public interest in the new transport service.[26]

Although the new law and its ability to subsidize commercial routes meant salvation to many of Alaska's air carriers, including Cordova Air Service, not everyone was happy about the new rules. Most pilots, like most Alaskans who emphatically identified with the Wild North's culture of independence, distrusted the federal government. They saw the new law and federal regulation as intrusive—a disruption to "business as usual." As Smith explained: "It took a lot of guts to turn down a guy that came along and said I only got twenty dollars and I'd sure like to go along (on a trip that was set at thirty dollars)."[27] The consequence of failing to follow government guidelines, however, were severe. The CAA might fine a company or pull federal funds all together. However, pilots like Harold Gillam tended to favor the federal regulations because the laws under the CAA, according to biographer Arnold Griese, "supported [Gillam's] own goal of providing air transportation in Alaska where it was most needed."[28] But for pilot Bob Reeve, the king of the cutthroat competitors, the new legislation meant the end of his flying career in Valdez. To put it bluntly, Reeve was "spitting mad."

CAB HEARINGS IN ANCHORAGE

To determine Alaska's air routes and decide how to allocate those routes to the various pilots, the CAB sought testimonials during hearings held throughout the territory in 1939, the first of which took place in Anchorage. That August a large group of apprehensive flyers converged in town, including Gillam, Reeve, and Smith. Anthony Dimond had sent notice to all the territorial pilots, requesting their attendance. For all the years of competing with each other, most pilots maintained fairly isolated routes and rarely met other pilots face-to-face. "It was," recalled Bethel pilot Ray Petersen, "just like a bunch of lions and panthers tossed in one cage!"[29] According to Merle Smith, the flyers assembled in the hotel room of Don Goodman of Star Airlines the night before the hearings to discuss the intent of the CAB and the new federal law. "With the terrifying prospect before them," explained Reeve, Alaska's cutthroat pilots chose to "band together."[30]

For the first time in all their scrapping, competitive years, the Alaska pilots turned to each other. "They had a common enemy," wrote Beth Day: "government interference." But more than government oversight, Day reasoned that Alaska pilots "were not particularly good representatives of national law and order."[31] Of course, the CAB's real intent was to simply explain the new Civil Aeronautics Act to all the Alaska operators. Besides explanation of safety standards and the subsidy system, the CAB shared the government's concept of exclusive areas for small airlines. Exclusivity meant that a company or pilot would be confined to a certain geographical zone, which would restrict the carrier's radius of operation and curb vicious and unfair competition, from which neither the passenger nor the pilot benefited. Eventually air carriers would have the freedom to serve clients within that general area by pairing the scheduled routes with a continued charter service. For Cordova Air Service that meant a lot of bush flying to canneries and mining camps. Still, at the time, Smith recalled that most of the pilots assembled at the Anchorage hearing were fairly naïve about this plan. When Smith himself testified for the board, he admitted that he lost the lucrative Juneau route because when asked if he still wanted it, all he could recall was how miserable flights were to southeast and replied: "No." Smith later recalled, "I spent much money to get the very route I could have had that day for simply saying yes."[32]

Meeting participants recall that Harold Gillam remained "serious, unruffled, and thoughtful" about the new regulations. He was the only pilot who fully realized the "real purpose of the conclave." Gillam had studied the forthcoming legislation and, unlike the rest of the pilots, "actually understood what it meant." He saw regulation of Alaska's aviation as inevitable. Unlike his laissez-faire associates, Gillam knew the future for instrument flying was unavoidable and in his mind the only way to accurately deliver scheduled and efficient service. Several of the pilots interviewed by Day later recalled that Gillam cautioned them that "the modern air age was inexorably upon them and they must all prepare for it." They admitted Gillam had no love for government, but rather "he bowed to the future." "The only thing to do," he urged them, "was to make a clear statement of their facilities, their standing as pilots." Gillam advised pilots to figure out what they needed for a successful business and ask for it. "There was no point," he warned, "in trying to fight anything as powerful as the law."[33] Bob Reeve apparently took only part of Gillam's advice. At the August hearings, Reeve stated in unequivocal terms what he wanted, and what he emphatically believed he had a right to. However, in typical Reeve fashion, the pilot prepared to fight the government. He and his attorney, Tom Donahoe (who also represented Gillam and Smith), had come to request an appeal of the CAB's ruling on the Reeve Airways application that essentially kicked out the Glacier Pilot from his base of operations—the place that made him famous: Valdez. The year 1938 was especially bad for Reeve. After his nationally recognized glacier flying achievements in 1937, a combination of landing accidents, a windstorm, and a hangar fire left him without a plane for six months. This allowed Cordova Air Service to monopolize service to

Chisana, Nabesna, and McCarthy, and the upstart Lyle Airways to take over the Valdez run to places like Bremner. More significant, the CAB determined outcomes and ultimately granted certificates to a flyer based on the "Grandfather Clause." The clause stated that any pilot or air service that provided regular flights over a given area between May 14 and August 22, 1938, would retain exclusive rights to serve that area from that time on. At the time, Reeve had no planes to conduct business, and therefore the competitive pilot was ironically squeezed out of Valdez and most of eastern Alaska by an unlucky fluke in the federal law.[34]

Reeve, however, had no intention of giving up his Valdez business. He planned to take on the federal government. A straight shooter when it came to voicing his opinion, Reeve did not mince words at the hearing. He called the new CAA law the "folklore of Alaska Air Transportation," a government fabrication, that to Reeve was based on nothing but "planes on paper." Reeve appeared before the CAB and began his prepared statement: "I, R. C. Reeve, emphatically protest and take exception to that part of examiner's recommendation which denies Reeve Airways that right to engage in territorial charter flying, and aver that said recommendation is contrary to the long record of Reeve Airways as a common carrier charter operator over the entire territory and western Canada, and that, in order to arrive at a conclusion which will limit Reeve Airways to the benefit of other operating companies."[35] Reeve, in his seven-page testimony, continued to question federal intentions, adding his own unscripted verbiage when necessary, in a statement that many of the pilots likely supported: "I question [the] Examiner's right to legally abrogate my Alaskan operating rights by invoking the 'Grandfather Clause' or any other such ill-fitting act that was tailored to remedy an airline situation in the U.S.A. proper, but which is just about as relevant to the Alaskan set up as a sack of peanut shucks."

Reeve continued to defend his position, arguing that the federal government and the newly enacted Civil Aeronautics Act of 1938 hindered individualism and free enterprise:

The old time Alaskan operator, who made this country what it is, was a man who made business where there had never been business before; he was a man who in most instances was forced to hustle and rustle or starve. It was the rustler who survived. Listen, I have deliberately gone prospecting with my airplane, and discovered, staked, and sold gold mining property at far below its actual value for the sole purpose of building up airplane transportation business to that district. On one property alone over $90,000 has been spent for transportation, wages, machinery, etc. Gentlemen, suppose I had waited until that district or any of those other districts required service by virtue of public convenience and necessity? It would still be a wilderness, and I would have been in the hands of the receivers or PWA [Pan American World Airways] some years ago. By the same token and by such enterprise I have succeeded in giving my tenth year of unbroken service as an Alaskan pilot and airplane operator. My business has been run on such an economically sound principle that it has enabled me to remain solvent and support a family of four.

Reeve went on to criticize the federal government and attacked Examiner Stough personally for being oblivious to the more independent and capable manner of frontier flight:

All this, however, is an angle of an Alaskan airman's creed which is no doubt beyond comprehension to Mr. Stough. With due respects to him, he is nevertheless a sedentary salaried employee of the government, ensconced in a safe, secure government position. However, the very elements in his makeup which led him to seek such security in preference to facing the grim reality of existence in the rough and tough competition of public endeavor, do, in my mind, render this examiner incapable of passing fair judgment on Reeve Airways' application, and be able to recognize and take cognizance of the fact that to Reeve Airways, the art of making a living is not a cut and dried proposition, but an art depending on enterprise, nerve, hardships and, above all, the ability to be a producer, and hit the ball.

The CAB denied Reeve's appeal, and a disgusted Reeve soon moved his operation and family to Fairbanks.[36]

For Reeve the decision meant more than just business—it was personal, for the pilot was intimately connected to the surrounding mining operations. Not only had he made a nationally recognized name for himself taking off from the Valdez mudflats to support mining year-round, but Reeve owned 846 shares of Yellow Band stock at Bremner and had even named his youngest son Whitham for his friend Carl Whitham, owner of Nabesna mine.[37] While looking to start an aerial photography business in the Interior, Reeve didn't realize that his luck—and his relationship with the federal government—was about to change dramatically. In part, that change came to all the pilots assembled at the Anchorage hearings. It was September 1, 1939, and for a brief moment in time all were united—bitter flying rivals, territorial representatives, even federal bureaucrats—as word quickly spread among meeting attendees that Germany had invaded Poland. As Merle Smith put it: "It was evident to everybody that we were going to have another world war."[38]

6

World War II, Reeve's Field, and the Northern Air Route

LIKE SO MANY AMERICANS IN 1941, BOB REEVE EXPERIENCED THE New Year with a great deal of uncertainty. After starting over in Fairbanks, the discouraged pilot had to borrow money to pay his fuel bills as temperatures dipped to sixty degrees below zero that January.[1] He later confided to his biographer, Beth Day, "I was forty years old, with a growing family, one beat-up plane and no future." But in that infamous year, Reeve, like the rest of the country, went to work instead of giving up.

It's true that in years past the charismatic flyer brought world attention to eastern Alaska, but this time Reeve would make his most significant contribution to Alaska—and the world. He helped the United States military transform the Alaska Territory into an air bridge, which greatly aided the victorious Allied campaign in Europe and left behind an expanding web of aviation infrastructure that would underpin modern Alaska.[2] But in January 1941, when Reeve was struggling in Fairbanks, no one knew what the future held, including President Roosevelt himself. After the failed Munich agreement with Adolph Hitler in November 1938 that led to the Poland invasion in 1939, and the attack on China by the empire of Japan the previous year, the United States faced the very real possibility of a two-front war in Europe and the Pacific. By December 1941 aviation would shrink the protective span of the oceans and play a crucial role defending America around the globe. In Alaska the heavy burden of swift transportation between points would fall on the airplane.

Ever since the United States purchased the northern appendage from Russia in 1867, America's political and military leaders perceived Alaska's Aleutian chain of nearly three hundred islands as a strategic route across the North Pacific.[3] In a speech to the U.S. Senate on the Alaska purchase, Secretary of State Charles Sumner referred to the islands as "stepping stones to Asia." Some of the most important military strategists of the nineteenth century, including Admiral Alfred Thayer Mahan, suggested that because of its proximity to Asia, the United States should make the island of Kiska a naval reservation. When the Russo-Japanese war broke out in 1904, the Army-Navy Joint Board ruled that Kiska's retention would be vital in a major war with Japan.[4]

After World War I, however, intense public support for isolationism influenced American military policy, even though Japan had been showing signs of aggressive expansion since Theodore Roosevelt's administration. Responding to antiarmament sentiments stirred by the promise of the Great War, "the war to end all wars," the United States, Britain, Japan, France, and Italy negotiated the Washington Naval Treaty in 1922, which among other naval restrictions, banned new bases and forbade the improvement of existing Pacific facilities controlled by the signatories. New bases in Australia, New Zealand, Singapore, and Hawaii, however, were exempted from the treaty—mainland Alaska and the Aleutians were not. In keeping with the general cutbacks, the military closed its Alaska forts, including Forts Egbert and Liscum, which two decades earlier had played vital roles in the building of the Valdez-Eagle Road and the laying of the Washington-Alaska Military Cable and Telegraph System (WAMCATS).[5] To Alaskans, it seemed as though the U.S. mainland had once again marginalized the territory. Whether this was a fair assessment or not, any realistic plan to place the Pacific Fleet in Alaska became moot, while Pearl Harbor became the center of operations for the U.S. Navy in the Pacific theater.

Meanwhile, the treaty terms negotiated at Versailles in 1919 had come to be characterized as the "peace to end all peace," as totalitarian regimes unleashed by the Great War's bitter end began to march across Europe and Asia. By the close of the 1920s a few voices cried from the Far North, concerned with Alaska's lack of defense. In 1931, Governor George Parks, in his report to the secretary of the interior, argued that the U.S. Army Air Corps should station planes in the territory to train their pilots in flying under extreme conditions. In addition, these planes could transport government doctors and nurses to their stations. The governor noted that large sections of the territory were not unsurveyed and aerial photography could be used in the preparation of topographic maps. But mostly, Governor Parks stressed that Alaska occupied an important strategic position because the northern territory existed "on the only feasible air route to Asia."[6]

Considering Americans' concerns for the worsening economy, combined with their continued isolationist tendencies, it is not surprising this recommendation fell on deaf ears. Within three years, however, worldwide hostilities would heighten military interest once again in the North Pacific. In 1934, Japan notified the United States that it would no longer uphold the Washington Treaty. In March 1935, Alaska's nonvoting delegate, Anthony Dimond, pleaded with Congress to defend Alaska, which he pointed out, bridged "the Great Circle Route"—the shortest distance between the United States and Asia. Attempting to provide Washington-based legislators a brief tutorial of northern geography, Dimond expounded: "In order to grasp the defense problem in the North Pacific, it is necessary to consult proper maps, or, better still, a globe."[7] He explained to lawmakers that the Circle Route lay two thousand miles north of well-defended Hawaii but was only 276 miles south of the Aleutians, prompting the delegate to beg the question: "Is it not obvious that an enemy moving across the Pacific . . . would rather first invade Alaska?"[8] Acknowledging categorically the need for the national defense works at Pearl Harbor, Dimond nonetheless argued it was not nearly enough to defend what he called the Panama-Hawaii-Alaska triangle.[9] He introduced a bill authorizing the appropriation of nearly ten million dollars for what he considered an equally justifiable air base in Alaska. "Establish bases at Anchorage or Fairbanks, also in the Aleutians," urged Dimond. "I say to you, defend the United States by defending Alaska!"[10] Dimond's bill was referred to and later died in the House Military and Naval Affairs Committees.[11]

But as relations between Tokyo and Washington, D.C., continued to deteriorate, it was the military that began to fully grasp Dimond's congressional geography lessons. The War and State Departments realized that the Aleutians were not only stepping-stones *to* Asia but also stepping-stones *from* Asia, which could very well lead the Japanese Navy across the ocean, into British Columbia, and directly into the heart of the Pacific coast of the United States. While congressmen balked at the expense of defending Alaska's sparse non-Native population, noting that the impenetrable span of the Pacific Ocean is mainland America's greatest defense, military experts agreed more and more with Dimond, who warned that the suggestion of geographical safety "ignores the newly developed military arm, the airplane, with its almost incredible speed and immense striking power."[12] Hearings held before the House Committee on Military Affairs during the summer of 1934 attracted consistent military support for a base in Alaska. Aviation experts like Brigadier General William "Billy" Mitchell testified that Japan was "our dangerous enemy in the Pacific" and reasoned that they "will come right here to Alaska." Mitchell famously declared that "Alaska is the most central place in the world for aircraft," and therefore "he who holds Alaska will rule the world."[13]

Undoubtedly pushed by the unequivocal military support, Congress passed legislation in 1935 for six strategic areas, including Alaska, in which each would maintain an Army Air Corps base.[14] The caveat was the bill lacked appropriations for the actual construction of an Alaska base, and consequently plans to defend the Circle Route stalled. Undeterred, Dimond continued to appeal to Congress for both navy and air stations. The delegate ceaselessly fought on the floor and in bill after bill to convince his sympathetic, though stingy, colleagues to fund a national defense program in Alaska.

Dimond reasoned that if Alaska was left undefended in a Pacific war, the enemy would seize and take possession of the coast of Alaska in force. Any thought of dislodging the enemy without massive retaliation was futile. In addition, Dimond warned that the possession of Alaska would bring those hostile forces within 750 miles of the United Sates and would outflank the fortified base at Pearl Harbor, which, as the delegate calculated, is approximately twenty-four hundred miles from the nearest point on the U.S. coast. Hence Dimond, stressing the blatant risk to America's safety, called upon Congress to authorize the construction of first-class defense stations on the coast of Alaska. "If the principle of getting there first with the most men is still good strategy," maintained the delegate, "then facilities for 1,000 fighting planes on the coast of Alaska will be a mighty factor in providing defense of the North Pacific."[15]

"The time to install defense works in Alaska is now," Dimond urged Congress in 1938, but again the bill died. Two years later, with war now engulfing two continents, appropriations for the defense of Alaska was finally secured. Congress passed bills for two naval air stations at Sitka and Kodiak, which expanded, albeit rather slowly, the navy's presence in Alaska. And because the Far North remained "studded with question marks," as the U.S. Army Air Corps chief at the time noted, the construction of Ladd Field near Fairbanks commenced as an experimental station for testing planes in cold weather.[16] That year also brought the first army establishment in Alaska's history for national defense—the Elmendorf base near Anchorage.[17] "Never before," wrote a U.S. Army historian, "not even at the time of the gold rushes, was the Territory so advertised. Americans, who seemed to have forgotten the existence of the northern possession, rediscovered Alaska."[18] Anthony Dimond, however, was not so optimistic. "My only apprehension," lamented the delegate, "is that we are starting defensive measures too late and proceeding with them too feebly."[19]

THE ALASKA-SIBERIA AERIAL BRIDGE

Despite the continued sentiments of domestic isolationism represented in part by congressional inaction, President Roosevelt, like the military, recognized the need to protect America and her Allies with a strong air defense in the Pacific. Yet before the Munich Conference, the entire U.S. aviation industry had produced only about six thousand planes a year. To step up the country's war preparations, though still proclaiming neutrality, Roosevelt ordered the production of nearly ten thousand aircraft in 1938. A year later, legislation passed that authorized the U.S. Army Air Corps to develop and procure six thousand more.[20]

With Nazi Germany and imperial Japan rapidly advancing, America's vast human and industrial resources began a massive national mobilization effort. In 1940 the government developed programs to help build and equip several aircraft assembly plants.[21] The automobile industry halted production of Fords and Chevys to produce airplanes. Inland factories protected from enemy bombing raids filled the president's order for at least fifty thousand planes, more than doubling national production in a year.[22] When much of the country's male workforce went off to war, female aircraft workers, idealized by the image of "Rosie the Riveter," went to work building planes.

Besides the military and industrial leaders, the country's scientific organizations also made vital contributions to the effort, especially in the area of aeronautical research.[23] Preparation for war encouraged enormous technological leaps in aircraft design and performance. Streamlined, all metal fighters quickly replaced wood and fabric biplanes. The Boeing B-29 Superfortress, with its remote-controlled guns, pressurized cabins, and power engines, became the most advanced bomber of the day. The P-51 Mustang, an entirely new plane designed by North American Aviation in 1940 for the British Royal Air Force, quickly became the best U.S. dogfighter of the war.[24] And the P-39 Aircobra, together with its aerial-kin, the P-63 Kingcobra, was the most successfully mass-produced fixed-wing aircraft manufactured by Bell Aircraft Corporation. The Cobra was the first fighter in history with a tricycle undercarriage, the first to have the engine installed in the center fuselage for better maneuverability, and the first to include a cockpit door. The P-39 and the P-63 would later be sent en mass to Russia via Alaska, where the fighter plane was used with great success by the Soviet Air Force on the Eastern Front.[25]

It was in April 1940 that the government's air defense effort also turned its sights toward Alaska. General Henry "Hap" Arnold, chief of the U.S. Army Air Corps, spearheaded an aerial inspection tour across the northern territory to locate both tactical and commercial sites for airfields beyond those being constructed at Fairbanks and Anchorage.[26] While studying the broad aspects of the air defense system in Alaska, General Arnold could not help but notice "how close our Alaskan shoulder, from Nome to Point Barrow, comes to Siberia."[27] Arnold's plan called for the construction of a dozen airstrips that would ultimately support the northern air route from the Canadian border to Nome on the west coast of Alaska.

With war looming, the U.S. Navy and Army concentrated on building stations at Anchorage and soon thereafter in the Aleutians, while the Civil Aeronautics Administration (CAA) focused on the interior network of airfields.[28] These fields eventually included sites in Nome, Cordova, Juneau, Naknek, Bethel, Big Delta, McGrath, Moses Point, Galena, Gulkana, Tanacross, and Northway.[29] According to Arnold, "They [the airfield sites] lie along the logical air routes from the Far East to the industrial centers for the United States. They are," the general stressed, the airways of the future."[30] Thanks in part to the CAB's denial of Reeve's certification, the pilot was one of the few flying freelancers in the territory and was therefore hired by the CAA to survey possible construction sites by air. This unforeseen development in his relationship with the federal government commenced Reeve's unique wartime role as a "one man civilian air force" in spring 1941.[31]

Alaska's airfield construction could not have come at a better time, for Hitler's threat had become even more ominous as the Third Reich swept across Western Europe like a brush fire, claiming Norway, Denmark, the Low Countries, and then northern France. Congress responded by passing the Lend-Lease Act on March 11, 1941, which promised to supply nations fighting the Axis powers with vast amounts of war material, particularly airplanes. When pushed about the legality of Lend-Lease, as well as its cost, Roosevelt defended the aid program, telling the press Lend-Lease was strictly preventative, famously comparing the legislation to a garden hose used to "put out the fire in your neighbor's house before your own house caught fire."[32]

A few weeks later, Germany invaded the Balkan region. Then, in a startling demonstration of blind aggression and ethnic hatred, Hitler's armies attacked Russia on June 22, 1941, directly violating the German-Soviet Pact made in August 1939. By September the German Luftwaffe had destroyed most of the Soviet Air Force.[33] Casualties sustained by the Red Army were so severe that Soviet Premier Joseph Stalin was forced to send British Prime Minister Winston Churchill a letter requesting at least four hundred planes and five hundred tanks per month, to remove "the mortal danger looming over the Soviet Union."[34] Less than a month after Stalin's appeal to the West, the United States, Great Britain, and the Soviet Union signed the Moscow Protocol on October 1, 1941, which extended the Lend-Lease pledge to the communist state.

America shipped the first fighter planes made for Russia across the Atlantic and then flew them up through Africa and the Middle East. An even longer route sent war material around Africa, up the Persian Gulf, and across Iran.[35] The so-called Southern Route was extremely dangerous because scores of Nazi U-boats patrolled Atlantic shipping corridors and consequently sunk several cargo ships at a loss of 584 planes.[36] With America's arctic neighbor a mere fifty-five miles across the Bering Strait now under siege, Roosevelt had to squelch the blaze before, as Delegate Dimond had forewarned, Alaska caught fire too. Although army intelligence officers doubted Japan would join Germany's attack on the Soviets for fear that Stalin's warplanes would strike Japanese cities, some cautioned that imperial Japan might see the German invasion as a sign of weakness and use it as opportunity to destroy the Siberian bases. If Japan invaded Russia's Far East, analysts postulated that the empire of the Rising Sun, in its militant struggle to control the Pacific, might also attack Alaska. The worst-case scenario, warned the Naval War College, was "Germany and Japan might act in concert to occupy Alaska and vanquish the Soviet Union and America simultaneously."[37]

The more urgent and far safer plan of action called for American and Russian aviators to ferry military aircraft and supplies across the Bering Strait by hopping a succession of strategically positioned airfields spanning five thousand miles across two continents, aptly named the Alaska-Siberia Air Bridge Route (ALSIB); to most North Americans, it was simply called the Northern Route. The plan called for American pilots to take off from a staging area in Great Falls, Montana, and fly north into Canada by way of Calgary, Edmonton, Alberta, Fort Saint John, Fort Nelson, and Whitehorse. The ALSIB route then extended across the border into Alaska, to Fairbanks and Nome, at which point Russian crews would take over the planes, flying them across the subarctic wilderness of Siberia to bases in Uel'kal, Markovo, Sysymchan, Oymyakon, Yakutsk, Olekminsk, Kirensk, N. Ilimsk, and Krasnoyarsk.[38] From there the planes would be sent to the Eastern Front for immediate use against the German's Luftwaffe.

The construction of the air bridge across Alaska came at a time when the Russians urgently needed planes to stem the German tide that threatened to engulf Moscow, as it had Rostov and Sevastopol.[39] "That was when Stalingrad hung in the balance," wrote U.S. Army Captain Richard L. Neuberger of the grave nature of ALSIB program, "when German field marshals could sight the Volga through their field glasses."[40] But before aircraft and defense materials could be ferried through Alaska, several intermediate airfields still had to be built.[41]

THE NABESNA-NORTHWAY AIRLIFT

The historic events at Nabesna-Northway during the summer of 1941 seemingly underscored Anthony Dimond's prophecy "that hereafter the fighting will start before war is declared," for the urgent work to build a modern airport in the midst of wilderness was fueled by aerial battles raging on the other side of the globe.[42] In its role to facilitate the ALSIB program, the Civil Aeronautics Administration commenced the first major airfield construction project at the roadless Athabascan village of

Northway, located not far from Canadian border near the confluence of the Nabesna, Chisana, and Tanana Rivers.

The selected site was hardly ideal; aerial hazards and obstacles littered the terrain. The village itself was situated in a boreal forest bordered by the Tanana Hills to the north, the Mentasta Mountains to the west, and the Nutzotin Mountains to the south. In addition to the seasonal flooding of the river, numerous lakes and ponds made the ground perpetually soggy and restricted the construction of a cross-strip in the likely event of poor wind conditions. Nevertheless, CAA planners chose the site for its strategic importance on the map. Many planes had already crashed trying to make it from Whitehorse, British Columbia, to Fairbanks, Alaska, and the Northway site existed halfway in between. An airstrip at that particular spot could serve multiple purposes: as a major stopover for fuel or parts, an emergency landing strip in foul weather, or for a way to fly in supplies if the need arose for an overland road into Alaska.[43] The CAA granted the Idaho engineering firm and builder of the Hoover Dam, the Morrison-Knudsen Company (M-K), the contract for constructing the Northway airport in spring 1941, just a few months before the German invasion of the Soviet Union and, most ominously, Japan's attack on Pearl Harbor. "We are fully aware of the great and emergency need for the rapid completion of the many air bases and their accompanying installations," declared M-K's corporate voice, *The Em Kayan*. "By dint of unceasing effort on the ground and in the air, the Alaskan *Em Kayans* are going all-out to *Keep 'Em Flying*."[44]

Within weeks of the enactment of the Lend-Lease program, M-K construction foreman Pat Walker hired Bob Reeve to fly him sixty miles north of Nabesna Mine into Tetlin, Alaska, the closest landing strip to the selected site.[45] From Tetlin, Walker and Reeve went up the Tanana River by boat to Northway Village, located between the Nabesna River and Skate Lake and named for the village chief, T'aiy Ta, who had adopted the name "Chief Walter Northway" from a riverboat captain around the turn of the century.[46] There, Walker and Reeve hired a native crew of twenty men to cut out from the thick spruce forest a rough one-hundred-foot by eight-hundred-foot airstrip, which they completed in just six days.[47]

Still faced with the problem of how to get the tons of supplies and labor needed to build a modern airport into a roadless area, the Morrison-Knudsen Company decided the best course would be to truck in both men and material as far as possible and then fly the cargo into Northway. The route tracked the Richardson Highway from the port town of Valdez to Slana, and then down the Nabesna Road, built by the ARC back in 1933. CAA planners quickly made arrangements with Nabesna mine owner Carl Whitham to use his landing strip as a staging area. The transit of equipment from Valdez to the mine took roughly four to five days to cover the 234-mile distance.[48]

Before construction could begin at Northway, engineers first had to improve and enlarge Whitham's Nabesna "bush" strip. With Reeve's guidance the contractor built a six-thousand-foot main runway and two two-thousand-foot cross-runways near the Nabesna River.[49] By summer the Nabesna Landing Field had become one of the biggest in Alaska, shorter only than Elmendorf and Ladd Army airfields.[50] As one historian remarked, "What had started as a landing field brushed out by Whitham for Nabesna Mine was now one of the few landing fields in the eastern interior that could handle bombers."[51]

At the end of the road at the Nabesna mine, crated and barreled construction supplies were loaded on athey wagons (flat-track wagons with continuous tractor treads) and then hauled by cat tractors over six miles of muskeg swamp to the river. "The muskeg was so soft that a trail could not be used repeatedly," recalled Reeve. "The athey and cats were soon traveling all over the countryside, the muskeg 'road' becoming miles wide."[52] Once supplies arrived at "Bob's Field," Reeve immediately hauled people and supplies in his Fairchild 71 over the Nutzotin Mountains to Northway.

Besides flying over twenty-eight hundred barrels of asphalt needed for paving the runway, Reeve ferried a variety of other items, many of which were oddly sized or too big for his plane. Even though Reeve's high-wing monoplane was built to transport cargo, a majority of the equipment arriving from Valdez was so big that it had to be cut into pieces by acetylene torches before fitting into the Fairchild's hold and then rewelded at Northway. Everything was flown in except the large, seventeen-ton tractors—the "cats and cans"—that pulled twelve-ton Wooldridge scrapers over the unsurveyed frozen tundra.[53] According to M-K, the only tools to guide the cats were "a rather sketchy series of airplane pictures and an Indian guide."[54] The overland expedition from Nabesna to Northway had to pick its way through dense forests and icy streams. Hazards mounted as the enormous vehicles forded the Nabesna River several times. On one occasion personnel had to build a crude barge to ferry the tractors across the river.[55] Moreover, the abrasive sand and gravel along the river cut tracks and rollers to pieces. "At one time," noted *The Em Kayan*, "replacements of these parts were flown in and dropped from a plane."[56] Reeve recalled that he also dropped food to the crew. Bob was sent to scout for the tardy caravan, discovering that it had not only selected a different route but had "picked up some extra natives along the way."[57] Once the parade of earthmoving equipment finally arrived, contractors were able to lengthen and improve the crude Northway runway so that larger aircraft could bring in even more people, equipment, and supplies.

Another of the many subcontractors hired to build the CAA airstrips was the Iowa highway contractor Lytle & Green Construction Company. Engineer Ralph Green remembered that the necessary accesses to bridges were constructed from local timber. Because few workers were available in the area, Green noted that his work crews hired to cut trees had to be brought up from Iowa. The two crews worked eleven-hour shifts seven days, to capitalize on the long daylight hours. The hectic schedule at Northway attracted local attention. "Sometimes the locals thought we were nuts," recalled Green. "But it was one of those things you did without stopping to think that it couldn't be done."[58]

Although local attention was not the engineer's objective, local information was. According to Green, his work crew sought guidance from the local Native community as to where the landing strips and roads should be built. "Local knowledge combined with the engineers' ingenuity," explained Green, "created a force to challenge the obstacles. Natives informed the crews that where aspens grow, the underlying base would be gravel rather than permafrost. The aspens provided wood needed in the projects, and airstrips and roads rested on gravel underpinnings rather than on the more unstable permafrost."[59] Wartime airfield construction did in fact provide employment opportunities to local villagers, but it came at a cost. Walter Northway, the longtime traditional chief of Northway, earned one dollar an hour working as a laborer clearing brush. "In 1940," Northway recalled in his biography, "they started building the airport. The first plane came in with four guys and they surveyed the ground. . . . They hired local people to cut brush. . . . The airstrip was built right over the Indian cemetery. They dug up the graves and burnt them at the end of the airfield. There are still beads around there at the Moose Creek end."[60]

Meanwhile, back at Nabesna, trucks and busses made their way to Bob's Field day after day, dropping off passengers waiting to be carried across the mountains. Also arriving was Tillie, the children, and Tillie's mother. The family had traveled from Fairbanks to stay with Reeve through the duration of the summer. They lived in a one-room cabin loaned by a local "hunting guide," probably Harry Boyden, while the support personnel lived in tents. The only other structure was built by Morrison-Knudsen as a headquarters to facilitate flight operation. With the near twenty-four-hour light that allowed him to fly well into the night, Reeve at first was able to get the military and construction workers over to Northway as soon as they arrived. But as they flooded in, sometimes twenty at a time, they began to congregate and, to Tillie's dismay, needed to be fed. Reeve's wife thus began to cook hearty meals for the men on a sixteen- by thirty-six-inch Yukon wood-burning stove three times a day throughout the summer.[61]

With his family pitching in to support camp needs, Reeve focused on flying. He and his Fairchild were airborne from dawn to dusk, but Reeve still couldn't keep up with the demand of supplies and people piling up at Nabesna. To expedite the airlift, Morrison-Knudsen ordered a new plane from Boeing, an 80A model, and sent Reeve to retrieve it in Seattle. Dubbed the "Yellow Peril" because of its color and difficulty stopping, the 80A was designed to haul four thousand pounds, but Reeve managed to fly in seven-thousand-pound loads with the aircraft. This routine continued around the clock until the deep freeze of late November, by which time Reeve had transported eleven hundred tons of construction supplies and over three hundred workers in just a few months.[62]

On the eve of America's entrance into World War II, the government considered Northway a "city in the wilderness," consisting of a 5,300-foot by 350-foot runway, nine buildings, radio towers, an office, electrical plant, and six-room houses with luxuries such as bathtubs, draperies, and modern kitchens for airport officials. The thousand-gallon fuel tanks, for which the big door in the Boeing 80A had to be drastically modified, stood behind each of the houses to furnish year-round heating.[63] To honor the bush pilot for his extraordinary service, the federal government officially christened the old Nabesna field "Reeve Field," a gesture made to acknowledge the tenacious bush pilot.

Less than a month after the completion of seasonal work at the Northway strip, the Japanese attacked Pearl Harbor on December 7, 1941, descending America into war. Reeve continued to work for the CAA, flying supplies, construction material, and workers into the new airfields at Big

Delta, Tanacross, Galena, Moses Point, and Nome. In 1942 he worked for the Alaska Communications System (ACS), flying ACS personnel and material throughout Alaska, and eventually to the Aleutians, which would become Reeve's signature air route. During the war Reeve was the only civilian flyer under exclusive contract with the military and the only one authorized to fly in the Aleutian war zone. After the war the pilot continued to serve the island chain, forming Reeve Aleutian Airways in 1947. Unlike most of the Alaska carriers founded by the former bush pilots, Reeve clung stubbornly to his name and independence, making Reeve Aleutian Airways one of the most successful airlines in Alaska history.[64]

Thanks to the dedicated efforts of people like Billy Mitchell, Hap Arnold, Anthony Dimond, Ernest Gruening, Bob Reeve, and hundreds of brave pilots, Alaska's position as an air bridge linking East and West emerged as a vital asset in both the European and Pacific theaters. Still, America's military leadership at the time was all too aware that even though construction had started on a number of air, naval, and army installations, Alaska lacked defenses adequate to hold the vast territory if an efficient force invaded.[65] As an atmosphere of concern turned to near hysteria, airfield construction commenced at Northway in spring 1942. As fellow pilot Rudy Billberg would later put it, the continued effort between Nabesna and Northway was "the biggest [Alaska] airlift of the war."[66]

7

The Last Causalities
of Fog and War

AFTER THE ASSAULT ON PEARL HARBOR, IT APPEARED AS THOUGH
Anthony Dimond's warning had come true. The Japanese military machine
looked to conquer the Pacific by hopping from one island nation to the
next. By early 1942 it had invaded Guam, Indochina, Thailand, Wake, Hong
Kong, Singapore, Malaya, Java, and Burma. After capturing Papua New
Guinea, the Solomon Islands, Fiji, Samoa, and New Caledonia, Japan's next
target was feared to be Australia. By May 1942, less than six months after
Pearl Harbor, the Philippines fell. In June 1942 the war came to Alaska.
The Japanese bombed Dutch Harbor, and shortly afterward they invaded
Attu and Kiska. The invasion resulted in the placing of foreign troops on
American soil for the first time since the War of 1812. The Japanese occupation of the Aleutian Islands was likely meant as a diversion, intended
to draw the U.S. Pacific Fleet northward while consequently weakening
military and naval defenses at Hawaii. The strategy failed. American
intelligence deduced the scheme, and the U.S. fleet defeated the Japanese at the game-changing Battle of Midway. In summer 1942, however,
Japanese occupation in the Aleutians remained unresolved. Alaskans
therefore stayed on high alert, acting as though a Japanese invasion of the
mainland was imminent.

Everyone agreed that the vast span of the Pacific Ocean no longer
served as a protective barrier. While the continuous development of aviation technology played a role in the narrowing, the defending abilities of
the airplane also became the solution. As wartime construction contractor Morrison-Knudsen explained: "Civilians as well as military men have
come to look to the sky for help."[1] Indeed, the war effort in the Wrangells

produced heroes like Bob Reeve, who made enormous sacrifices to support America and her allies engaged in battle half a world away. But the extraordinary engineering and aeronautic endeavor to protect distant nations left casualties here at home. On July 13, 1942, in the heightened atmosphere of war, the U.S. Army 176th Engineer Regiment arrived in the Wrangell region determined to complete its mission: to build an airfield at Gulkana. The problem, at least to the Ahtna Natives living there, was that army engineers planned to build the Gulkana Airfield squarely on their village at Dry Creek. With little or no awareness as to what was to happen, the U.S. Army appropriated their ancient homelands and ordered the Native villagers to vacate.

THE FORCED REMOVAL OF DRY CREEK VILLAGE

At the time of the U.S. Army's arrival, more than a dozen people lived at Dry Creek, and in the winter even more Native people from Copper Center worked trap lines across the surrounding countryside. Oral testimony gathered by historians in the 1980s revealed that U.S. Army officials told the Dry Creek villagers that the land was needed for military purposes and for national defense. Unconvinced by the army's explanation of an imminent foreign attack, the Dry Creek Ahtna refused to meet the arbitrarily imposed schedule to leave their homes. When the army's deadline came, witnesses say the Ahtna were ordered at gunpoint to pack their belongings and leave the site to make way for construction of the Gulkana Airfield.[2]

Ahtna houses were then burned or removed. One resident recalled that when he was out hunting, the army purposefully burned down one of his houses occupying his homestead while the other was dismantled, transported to Copper Center, and deposited in a field beside the highway. When he approached the army to request compensation for his destroyed and appropriated property, he was told that he would have to travel to Fort Richardson, near Anchorage, to pursue the matter—at the time an impossible feat. Other Ahtna and Upper Tanana people recalled similar circumstances at villages such as Tanacross, in which nearly all expressed a lack of due process and protection of their personal property.[3] By August the regiment had constructed two five-thousand-foot and thirty-five-hundred-foot gravel-surfaced runways, an air operations center, an Alaska Communications System facility, an air navigation radio range facility, a motor repair facility, a hospital, and five barrack buildings to house several hundred army troops. Any sign of the onetime Ahtna village remained only in the memories of its former inhabitants.

After completing the Gulkana Airfield, the army prohibited the Dry Creek Ahtna to return. Scores of people lost their houses and ownership of the land on which they were built. They lost personal property, both legal and sentimental, none that could ever be replaced. Cultural activities conducted on their traditional homelands for centuries had suddenly ceased. For enduring so many losses, the Ahtna were nevertheless ignored. They were never reimbursed, even though the army had in place policies and procedures for appropriated lands. No public record or acknowledgment recognized their sacrifices to the war effort. Even the junction of Richardson Highway and the newly constructed road connecting Anchorage with the Alaska Highway, meeting exactly at the site of Dry Creek, received a western name commemorating two nineteenth-century American explorers, Captain Edwin F. Glenn and Lieutenant Henry Allen. The names were merged to form Glennallen.[4]

The people who had lived in the shadow of the Wrangell Mountains since *time immemorial* viewed their wartime experience as a sacrifice, but few saw it as patriotic. Their lands were invaded, homes destroyed, game that was once hunted for food fled to less populated territory. They endured and adapted but were never recognized by their country as heroes for giving up this land. Instead, the U.S. Army's treatment of Alaska Natives living in the way of war reduced them to refugees: "They had a big war there, down in Germany or somewhere," recalled Annie Ewen, an Ahtna Athabaskan whose family had lived at Dry Creek Village for generations. "With the big war came soldiers, to build an airfield. They told us eight families to move. One house was burned down. We moved into a tent for two years and then down to Copper Center."[5]

Within a year, settlers from Outside moved to the bustling new town. They secured title to land north of Copper Center and rapidly began opening private businesses catering to highway travelers.[6] Newcomers enjoyed hunting for sport and competed with the Ahtna for the local game on which their means of existence depended. In the new cash-based economy, the Ahtna struggled to find wage-paying jobs. Most tragically, disruption to their traditional way of life brought extreme sadness to a people forced to deal with everything from poverty to prejudice, stemming from the army's treatment of the Ahtna villagers in 1942. "Operating without sufficient understanding of native culture and perhaps without sufficient sensitivity," wrote historian Stephen Haycox, "Army personnel might not have recognized the significance of the dwellings and activity there. It is clear from their later memories of the events, however, that the natives did regard their dwellings as permanent, their use of the land from time immemorial as valid, and their ejection from land as temporary."[7]

The extraordinary social and economic changes brought about by the war were certainly beneficial for some. Opening the region via roads and airfields would bring opportunity and progress to the Copper Belt. But for the Ahtna, ownership of the land appropriated by the U.S. Army was never restored. After 1942 they became a lost generation, targets of discouragement and disparagement by the newcomers, and strangers to their children's children. Split by fast-paced cultural changes such as truancy laws that required school attendance in the 1950s, fallout from statehood in the 1960s, and the construction of the trans-Alaska pipeline in the 1970s, the next generation of Alaska Natives, presented with tough choices, adapted and passed by the older generation. Although this would be the generation pushing for the passage of the Alaska Native Claims Settlement Act in 1971, the year 1942 left the Ahtna and Upper Tanana of the majestic Wrangells Mountains forever changed.[8]

THE WAR EFFORT AT NORTHWAY

The summer of 1942 remained tense for Alaskans. Air-raid alarms, proceeded by blackouts, sounded regularly. Buildings and vehicles were coated in camouflage paint. Gas masks and firefighting equipment were distributed to a nervous populace, which was undoubtedly shaken by images of London in the aftermath of Hitler's blitzkrieg and wondered if Alaska was next. Executive Order 9066 authorized the forced removal of Alaskans of Japanese ancestry to internment camps in the Lower 48. Even Alaska Natives living in the Aleutians were evacuated from their homes and forced to live in dilapidated southeast canneries for the duration of the war.[9] For fear of attack, civilian transportation came almost to a halt. Military personnel ordered ships to remain in port. Railroad schedules were altered or canceled altogether. And, most significant to Alaska's skyboys, the federal government grounded all planes for civilian service. "When the war broke out," recalled Merle Smith, "the bush pilots offered their services to General Buckner for the defense of Alaska, but they were told they were not wanted in the Army. What they were doing was exactly what was needed."[10] And what was needed in the summer of 1942 was the continued construction of the CAA airports, accelerated now to a frantic pace.

By this time Bob Reeve had moved on to serve the army in the Aleutians and replacing him as Morrison-Knudsen's chief pilot was Harold Gillam. Besides taxiing M-K inspectors around the circuit of airfields the company was in the process of building throughout the territory, Gillam took over management of the Nabesna-Northway operation. In January, he had leased his two Pilgrims to the construction company and then traveled to Cheyenne, Wyoming, to purchase a Lockheed Electra transport plane, equipped for fast speeds and heavy loads.[11] The Electra was a twin-engine monoplane and was Lockheed's first all-metal design. Its length was about thirty-nine feet, its wingspan fifty-five feet, and it had a maximum speed of 202 miles per hour. With a fully enclosed pressurized cabin and extensive instrumentation, the Electra was considered a very modern plane in 1934, the year it was launched.[12] The plane, however, would carry an ominous history—it was the same make flown by Amelia Earhart in her failed attempt to circumnavigate the globe in 1937. Unfortunately, the Electra purchased by Gillam on behalf of M-K would meet a similar fate.

Gillam returned to Anchorage that spring and set out to hire several well-known bush pilots to conduct flights between Nabesna and Northway. The Alaska flyers were paid a salary of eight hundred dollars per month plus keep—a far higher income than they took in as air-service carriers. Many of them went on to become some of the best known pilots in Alaska, including Fairbanks pilot Frank Barr, future Katmai pilot John Walatka, Valdez pilot Jack Peck, and up-and-coming bush pilot Rudy Billberg. Another Nabesna-Northway flyer was Cordova's Merle Smith.

On May 1, 1942, Smith arrived at Nabesna and immediately began flying freight to Northway.[13] Smith inherited Reeve's 80A, the Yellow Peril, joining two crews that alternated flights twenty-four hours a day. Eventually the M-K fleet consisted of the two Pilgrims leased from Gillam, two Boeing 80A Trimotor biplanes, a Travel Air 6000, and a Stinson Trimotor. Pilots referred to the ragtag fleet as the "fatigue run" planes. The company also maintained a Spartan Executive, a Vultee, and the Lockheed Electra 10A flown almost exclusively by Gillam. These planes were used to transport supervisors, inspectors, and other high-profile passengers. Collectively they flew what Nabesna-Northway pilots aptly called the "glamor runs."[14]

By midsummer, construction of Northway had intensified, especially as word arrived that the Japanese had invaded Attu and Kiska and were occupying American soil in the Aleutian Islands chain. While Alaskans across the territory feared an impending invasion, the pilots quickly focused on the task at hand. Hauling construction supplies and personnel became a nonstop process for three months, until the job was done on August 28. Barr, Billberg, Smith, Walatka, and the other flyers were mainly responsible for ferrying the tar and resin for the Northway runway, a strip two thousand feet long, five hundred feet wide, and six inches thick. "They told us, 'Don't get out [of the aircraft] except to eat and for toilet stops,'" recalled Billberg, who flew one of Gillam's leased Pilgrims. "The job took 15,300 barrels of tar. We would haul five barrels of tar and resin in a Pilgrim, which overloaded it. We would have to run three-quarters of a mile down the valley at Northway and then we would sink in soft sand."[15] After completion of the runway, pilots like Smith started flying freight and food runs at Northway. They also ferried boilers, lumber, and fuel tanks. As Billberg explained, the pilots carried "everything necessary for a paved runway with lights as well as living quarters and cooking facilities for military personnel."[16]

Enemy occupation of Alaska seemed especially dire for those pilots with young families, and like most, Smith sent his wife, Bertha, and their sons to Nebraska, where they stayed for the duration of the war.[17] Not all families evacuated, however. On June 2, 1942, the day the Japanese attacked Dutch Harbor and launched an invasion of Attu and Kiska, pilot John Walatka's daughter Johanna was two years old. In July he brought his family with him to Nabesna. A few years later, Johanna and her mother recounted in a journal a hectic scene but perhaps a magical one when experienced by a child:

The first week of June Daddy quit his job to fly for an outfit that was putting in airports to help our army. He came to Lake Clark and got us. We flew to Anchorage and then in a few days flew (in a tri-motored Stinson) to Fairbanks. Everyone was nervous. The Japanese had bombed Dutch Harbor and we were expecting them in Anchorage. We expected to go from Fairbanks to Nabesna with Dad, but women were not allowed at camp. Finally we did get to go the last of July. Boy, were we glad to see daddy! He had a nice tent ready for us. Here we lived in the midst of incomparable scenery, with the air like champagne—no, I mean seven-up—and went fishing for grayling in a beautiful mountain stream every day. Daddy flew a tri-motored Stinson. There were two Pilgrims, two old Boeings and the Stinson. They hauled tar and resin to Northway for the airport. We stayed till the job ended (August 28th) and then flew to Anchorage in a Lockheed Electra, piloted by Harold Gillam.[18]

While the bush pilots continued to haul supplies from Nabesna, a platoon of Company "F" of the 175th Engineer Regiment arrived at Northway in July to increase the airport facilities so that it could accommodate the Air Transport Command, tasked to commence the Lend-Lease ferrying program to Fairbanks. Expansion of the Northway complex that summer included additional barracks, a mess hall, winterized tents, a dispensary and hospital, a latrine, operation buildings, a crew chief building, an AC club oil house, warehouse, power house, bath house, administration building, garage, and well. The runway, thanks primarily to the Alaska bush pilots flying in the needed materials, was extended to seventy-five hundred feet and eventually paved. Extra Quonset huts were used throughout camp.[19]

The combined efforts of the military engineers and the civilian bush pilots resulted in the arrival of the first American-made fighter planes destined for immediate battle at Stalingrad, where fierce fighting raged. "All summer long," recalled Smith, "any time you stood on that airport you could hear one airplane right above, one fading out in the distance toward Fairbanks, and another coming up from Whitehorse."[20] "In the Alaskan . . . solitudes," described an American Army Engineer of the historic scene, "we saw planes come down on makeshift landing fields, planes painted with the red star of the Soviet Union."[21]

Even though eastern Alaska was safe from enemy fire, by September pilots and army personnel fought a bitter battle against the worsening weather. The frigid temperatures encountered during the Northway project that winter were probably more severe than on any other construction job in Alaska. The Air Transport Command pilots who ferried the planes to Fairbanks in wintertime experienced temperatures that often plunged to minus-fifty degrees. A lack of sufficient hangar space sometimes forced mechanics to work outside under difficult winter conditions.

"Sixty degrees below zero was not unusual," wrote military historian James D. Bush Jr. "Permanently frozen ground, poor transportation facilities, and inaccessibility of the site (by air only in winter) caused considerable delay."[22] In the end, the harsh assignment paid off. On June 1, 1943, the Northway project was essentially completed at an estimated cost of $585,340, and it was turned over to the Northwest Service Command.[23] At the time of completion, the number of Lend-Lease combat airplanes delivered to Russia over the top of the world through Northway exceeded one thousand aircraft.[24] By the end of the war, eight thousand planes had been transferred to the Soviet Union via Alaska, including 2,618 Bell P39 Aircobras and 2,397 Bell P63 Kingcobras.[25]

Throughout the duration of the war a total of $11.3 billion worth of supplies were shipped to the Soviet Union across the Alaska-Siberia Air Bridge, yet recently declassified archives suggest that the enormous success of the air route also came at the expense of human lives. At least 113 Soviet pilots, and possibly more, perished while flying missions over the vast Siberian wilderness. Approximately 133 aircraft were also lost in the effort to ferry planes to the Eastern front. The Russian Federation would later recognize these pilots by commemorating the Siberian portion of the ALSIB route as "the Route of Courage."[26] Likewise, a monument honoring the Lend-Lease operation was erected in Fairbanks in 2006. Still, despite the remarkable efforts demonstrated by military engineers, Russian and American aviators, and, of course, the Wrangell Mountain skyboys, the significance of their wartime struggles are seemingly overshadowed by the more well-known Aleutian Campaign.

Indeed, on May 11, 1943, American forces mounted a response to Japanese occupation. Fifteen thousand heavily armed American troops stormed the windswept and fogbound Aleutian Island of Attu. For nearly three weeks soldiers clambered ashore and overcame stiff resistance from twenty-four hundred Japanese defenders. Although troops suffered heavy causalities on Attu, the victorious American command prepared to take back Kiska. On August 15 a massive force of nearly a hundred ships and a force of over thirty-four thousand American and Canadian troops were assembled, but when the armada invaded, the Americans discovered that the enemy force had slipped away covertly several weeks earlier. Military leaders considered the invasion of Kiska a "fiasco" and critics labeled the failed attack as "a ridiculous anti-climax." Kiska became an infamous tactical mistake that tied down enormous resources that could have been better used elsewhere in the Pacific.[27] Ultimately military leaders realized that any major operations of strategic significance lay in the central Pacific and not in the supposed "stepping stones to Asia." In the end the Aleutian campaign—also known to military historians as the "theater of frustration"—did little to ensure Japan's ultimate defeat.

On the other hand, the establishment of the Northern Route and the ferrying of war supplies to Russia dramatically changed the tide of the war in Europe. It was also tactically important in the Pacific theater by keeping key terrain out of Japanese hands. Because Alaska was viewed as a strategically vital air corridor, the United States eventually expended more than one billion dollars in the territory, which not only boosted Alaska's economy but left in its wake a modern aviation infrastructure.[28] The Lend-Lease operation transformed Alaska from a wilderness frontier into a wartime front and has since been praised as the best period in the history of Russian-American relations. "Between the American and Russian aviators in Alaska," wrote Captain Neuberger in 1944, "there is great mutual admiration."[29]

In terms of both geography and politics, the war most certainly reestablished Alaska's role as a "bridge to the Pacific." Nevertheless, despite the ALSIB's game-changing role in World War II, one historian has pointed out that "those who flew the planes and built the air route between the United States, Canada, the Yukon Territory, and Alaska, and eventually across to Russia, [have] received relatively little or no recognition."[30] The lack of public acknowledgment has to do, in part, with the fact that by 1945 America's relationship with the Soviet Union had turned extremely cold. While the Soviets moved to transform central Europe into a buffer zone against the West, dropping the so-called Iron Curtain infamously described by Winston Churchill, technological advances rendered the continental United States a vulnerable target. The perceived danger of a transpolar attack made Alaska a strategic air center for basing and commanding forces prepared for both defense and retaliation against a valiant friend- turned-foe, now considered the "Red Menace."[31]

CASUALTIES AND CASTAWAYS

As the threat of invasion diminished, so did Morrison-Knudsen aviation jobs. In winter 1942, Harold Gillam hired Merle Smith to take over his

Kuskokwim mail run. Then, in January 1943, Gillam pulled Smith off the mail run and sent him to Nome to assist the army in its surveying work on the Seward Peninsula. Smith was still working for M-K when summer arrived, but as Smith recalled, "My job was winding down. The need for pilots and mechanics was not very great, and they were letting people go. . . . It was obviously time to start looking around for something else."[32]

While Smith wound down his workload for the company, he began to hear rumors that Chisana, one of his stops on the Copper Belt Line, had not seen a plane in eight months. No one thought much of it, for the federal government had shut down gold mining during World War II. While Alaska and the rest of the nation were at war, services to the mining communities had declined dramatically. Consequently, Chisana's elderly miners, forgotten by a world in conflict, became indirect causalities of the fog of war.

Hoping to substantiate the stories, Smith borrowed an M-K plane, and after picking up mail in Chitina, flew across the Wrangells to the remote mining camp. Years later, an industry salute to the bush pilot replayed the scene: "The hungry miners stared in amazement at the sight of the huge, yellow plane, as it flashed through the moon-shocked shroud of night fog."[33] On arrival, Smith discovered decrepit miners with no food or supplies, preparing to walk out over Skolai Pass and on to McCarthy. "They didn't know if they could make it, considering their age," explained Smith, "but they knew they had to try or starve when winter came."[34] Smith promptly took the miners' orders and returned to Chisana in another borrowed M-K plane—a much larger 80A, the same plane used by Reeve and himself at Northway.[35] Smith returned to Anchorage to settle up with the company. Ray Shinn, superintendent of M-K in Alaska, told him that he owed nothing for the rescue flight. When Smith protested, explaining that he received payment from the miners for the flights, Shinn nevertheless dismissed him. He knew that he would eventually need to let his pilot go. "You're just getting started up again over there in Cordova," Shinn explained to Smith, "you'll need it [the payment]. So you keep it."[36] And indeed, after the Chisana rescue Smith decided to return to Cordova Air Service and the Copper Belt region for good.

The slowdown at M-K, however, did not seem to affect its chief pilot, Harold Gillam, who continued to fly at a furious pace, freighting and carrying officials around to sites all over Alaska. The innumerable trips in the overloaded Electra worried his fellow pilots. Gillam Airways's former pilot

Oscar Winchell noted that "he was working too hard," even commenting to his daughter, Pat Wachel: "The way he's going, Harold won't live to work out the year for M-K."[37] Winchell's prediction sadly proved true. Harold Gillam was a tragic causality of the war effort, but instead of war it was just the fog that led to the fatal crash.

On January 5, 1943, around the same time Smith went to Nome, Harold Gillam prepared to take off in the M-K Lockheed Electra from Boeing Field in Seattle. His destination was Anchorage, with one refueling stop in Ketchikan. Passengers included Robert Gebo, M-K general superintendent in Alaska; Percy Cutting, M-K airplane mechanic; Dewey W. Metzdorf, owner of the Anchorage Hotel; Joseph Tippets, radio expert of the Civil Aeronautics Administration; and Susan Batzer, a young Idahoan who was on her way to take a job in Alaska with CAA.[38] Though all strangers, everyone chatted casually as packages and people were loaded onto the airplane. According to Tippets, "Harold boarded last and latched the door."[39]

At the time of the doomed flight, Gillam was in many ways at the top of his game. He held a commercial pilot certificate with single- and multiengine 150-856 horsepower, land, sea, and instrument ratings, and had accumulated approximately 7,412 hours of flying time—about 757 of which were in a Lockheed Electra. "He was physically qualified," noted the Civil Aeronautics Board report, "properly rated and certified for the flight involved."[40] Although broken skies made most the flight up the Inside Passage uneventful, dense fog shrouded the coastal town of Ketchikan. Gillam prepared for an instrument landing but then became confused by the radio signals. Confusion led to dread and the realization that the Electra was "temporarily lost." It turned out that Gillam had not obtained a recent chart showing the Coast Guard's most current compass headings for the Annette Island Radio Range. Gebo, who was acting as Gillam's copilot, told the CAB that "both were confused by the radio range signals they were receiving and Gillam was preparing to use his radio direction finder equipment at the time the left engine stopped."[41]

"Suddenly the left engine quit," Gebo told Ethel Dassow in an interview for the *Alaska Sportsman*. "The oil pressure dropped to zero. Gillam put the propeller in high pitch and cut the throttle. Then he put the right engine propeller in low pitch and opened the throttle as far as possible. We were flying at 5,000 feet."[42] A strong downdraft hit the plane, which lost several thousand feet of elevation in just a few minutes. Gillam radioed Ketchikan that one motor was out and that he was in trouble but gave no location.[43] "A crash landing was coming," reported M-K's *The Em Kayan*, which also noted in positive prose that "Harold Gillam was the one to bring it down. No man knew more about the art of 'pancaking' a plane down onto any spot that loomed into sudden view."[44] Gillam cut the right engine throttle, dropping the air speed to about fifty miles an hour. Breaking out of the clouds, a mountain loomed in view. "We could see the trees and the bare patches of snow," recalled Gebo. "That's the last I remember for a few minutes."[45] A tree limb then caught the right wing and the Lockheed Electra hit the mountain.

Gillam's Electra was overdue and unreported at Ketchikan at five o'clock that afternoon. Overcast skies, harsh winds, and torrential rainstorms prevented crash victims from building a signal fire as well as planes from spotting them from above. When word reached Merle Smith that Gillam's plane was missing, he immediately got in his plane and left Nome. "I didn't say good-bye, yes or no, to anybody. I just took my flight mechanic and we filled her up with gas and took off for Anchorage. . . . I told them I had heard that Harold was missing and I came down to get in on the search."[46] On January 8 the *Seattle Times* reported the missing plane. "He [Gillam] is the best pilot in Alaska and has been lost many times," the Pacific Northwest paper wrote optimistically. "If anyone knows that country and can come out of a difficult spot, he can."[47]

Remarkably, everyone lived through the crash landing, though all passengers received numerous wounds. Gebo broke his leg; Metzdorf broke his collarbone. Tippets received several deep cuts and slashes around his face. According to Gebo, "Gillam was drenched with gore from a cut in his scalp, but was otherwise uninjured."[48] The worst injury occurred to Susan Batzer, who had her wrist nearly severed during the crash. Without proper medical treatment, however, the injury proved to be fatal. The young stenographer from Idaho Falls died of blood loss. Survivor accounts say that "they never saw anyone so brave."[49] After Susan died, Gillam decided to seek help. He gathered up a box of raisins, a can of sardines, a few bouillon cubes, matches, a parachute, and some magnesium flares from the plane. He told his passengers that he was going to build a signal fire on top of the ridge. If he saw anything favorable, he would go on. He never came back, and no one ever saw him alive again.[50]

The four survivors remained lost for a period of twenty-nine days following the accident, during which time an extensive air, land, and water search carried on around them. After three weeks, the party was given up for lost and the search was abandoned. But on February 3, nearly a month after the doomed flight left Seattle, Percy Cutting and Joseph Tippets came upon a U.S. Coast Guard patrol boat in Weasel Cove while searching for help. Four days later, the seriously wounded Robert Gebo and Dewey Metzdorf were rescued from their camp by civilian guides and Coast Guard personnel.[51] On Saturday, February 6, a Coast Guard shore party found Gillam's body on the beach of Boca De Quadra Inlet. The forty-year-old Alaskan aviation pioneer was dead. He apparently died of shock, starvation, and exposure. How long he lived after leaving the plane is not known. But those who retrieved his body described the pilot's last heroic effort to save his passengers. Gillam, according to witnesses, had strung his bright-red long underwear in a tree for a signal and extended his boots on high poles to mark the location in case of deep snow. Then, as *The Em Kayan* described, the pilot "wrapped himself in a parachute and accepted his fate—a hero to his last track."[52]

The conclusion of World War II, as well as Bob Reeve's departure from the Wrangells and the deaths of Merritt Kirkpatrick and Harold Gillam, marked an end of an era in eastern Alaska. The brief though monumental moment in history came to a close at Reeve's Field. The CAA reasoned it no longer needed to maintain the Nabesna strip, and over the years the river has gradually claimed the large sand field. Like the strip itself, a generation of Wrangell Mountain skyboys faded away—all except for Merle Smith, who would take advantage of advancements in aircraft technology and airfield expansion and pull Cordova Air Service from obscurity to dominate eastern Alaska's airline industry. The postwar era also attracted a new generation of skyboys, who, as the youngest pilot of the Northway Project, Rudy Billberg, later confessed, would soar over the Wrangell Mountains "in the shadow of eagles."

From Air Carrier
to Cordova Airlines

WORLD WAR II WAS A TRANSFORMATIVE PERIOD IN ALASKA HIS-
tory. Among the numerous changes sparked by the war, in many ways the
most celebrated was aviation. A handful of romantics lamented that the
war brought an end to the "golden age of frontier flight," but most Alaskans were realists, pointing out that the postwar era also brought safe,
efficient, and reliable air transportation to the territory, including eastern Alaska. In addition to regulatory oversight established by the government in 1938, the war produced modern airfields, and thanks to wartime
industrial productivity, more powerful aircraft. The end of global conflict
meant that much of the military's airplane surplus was sold to commercial airlines. In 1947 a writer for the *New York Times* remarked, "During
the war the beat of propellers became commonplace [in Alaska]." The
paper, however, noted an important change: "Now there is reduced military flying and increased commercial aviation, and the trend seems to be
toward even more flying for business and pleasure."[1]

With the exception of Bob Reeve's, individual flying businesses
throughout the territory began to merge their planes, pilots, and pre-
scribed routes after the war to make their services more efficient and,
most important, more profitable. Mergers and incorporation, however,
threatened to eliminate the small local air carriers. And though there
were far more pilots navigating Alaska skyways, far fewer businesses
promoted their operations by the name of the pilots. Rather than being
independent, most flyers worked for a company, and most remained in
the realms of anonymity. By the time of statehood in 1959, eleven intra-
state carriers operated scheduled service in Alaska. One was Merle

Smith's Cordova Airlines. The Wrangell Mountain skyboys who flew for Smith still accomplished great feats, but with the exception of tight aviation circles, the flying public rarely knew their names.

SMITTY TAKES CONTROL OF THE TILLER

While Smith remained occupied during the war flying for Harold Gillam and Morrison-Knudsen, Cordova Air Service (CAS), under the frantic watch of manager and mechanic Carl Baehr, had downsized the fleet to one plane—a Bellanca—and had only one pilot, Herb Haley, on its payroll.[2] Times were so bad for the struggling air carrier that stockholders even tried to sell CAS to Alaska Star Airlines in 1943, but the Civil Aeronautics Board denied the transaction.[3] The road from a waning regional air carrier, which depended on a practically defunct mining industry, to an interstate airline that flew hundreds of passengers and tourists on scheduled regular routes between Anchorage, Juneau, and Bristol Bay on Douglas DC-3s, started near the war's end when Cordova Air Service stockholders asked Merle Smith to return to the failing company.

In July 1944, Smith returned to Cordova Air Service with a plan.[4] First, he bought out all stockholders so that he owned Cordova Air Service outright. Then he purchased an SM8A Stinson from Jack Peck in Anchorage. Smith would later add to his fleet two SR10 Stinsons and a SR9 Gull-Wing Stinson, capable of carrying four passengers. Scheduled services by the end of the war included routes between Cordova and Anchorage four times a week, and Cordova and Fairbanks, with stops at Valdez, Copper Center, Gulkana, Gakona, and Paxson, once a week.[5] In 1945, Smith acquired a Lockheed L-10E Electra from Morrison-Knudsen (M-K) for twenty-five thousand dollars. It was the first all-weather, twin-engine airplane to fly between Anchorage and Cordova. The Electra was kept for a year then sold in Seattle. In its place Smith purchased a DC-3, a plane three times larger than anything he had flown before.

The Douglas DC-3 was a fixed-wing, propeller-driven aircraft that revolutionized air travel for passenger service throughout the nation as well as in Alaska. It was the first airliner to make a profit by carrying just passengers without the support of mail contracts or other forms of subsidies.[6] The ship's enormous size "came in handy," admitted Smith, during the 1948 steamship strike that shut down shipping to Alaska. During the sixty-nine-day strike, Smith flew to Seattle to bring necessary supplies into Cordova and elsewhere. "A ship strike in early Alaska was a disaster," noted Smith. "The territory was dependent on the Alaska Steamship Company for everything. The small Alaskan towns did not, by any means, 'live off the land' as popular conception had it. They were more like an army in the field, dependent upon a long and vulnerable supply line for their survival."[7] But had it not been for the CAA contractor Morrison-Knudsen's building a modern airport at Mile 13 along the old Copper River & Northwestern Railway route in 1941, Smith would not have been able to land such a large aircraft at Eyak Lake and therefore would have been helpless to serve Cordovans and the scattered communities populating the Interior.[8] Not surprisingly, Smith was the first pilot to land on the new Cordova field.[9] It would be appropriately named the Cordova Merle K. "Mudhole" Smith Airport in 1988.

Smith's air service during the strike gained the Cordova carrier recognition from the Civil Aeronautics Board, which certified Cordova Air Service in 1949 to fly passengers disembarking from Alaska Steamship Company vessels. CAB certification also granted CAS air routes linking Fairbanks and Valdez; Cordova, Katella, and Yakataga; and communities throughout Prince William Sound, including Tattlek, Whittier, and Chenega. A brochure from around 1950 touted CAS as a "certificated airline," which invited tourists to "visit or play in the most scenic part of Alaska by air."[10] The subtle message CAS conveyed in the brochure: air carriers transport things, but an airline carries people.

By 1951, Smith's Cordova Air Service maintained ten airplanes, three of which were dual-engine. The company employed twenty-two people, fifteen of them stationed in Cordova. The airline served eighteen communities, including Alaska's largest city, Anchorage. Despite Northwest Flight 4422, which smashed into the western face of Mount Sanford while en route from Shanghai to New York City, killing all on board, the perception of mechanical flight in the Far North had changed its image.[11] No longer did Alaskans view aviation as a mere curiosity, for the combination of federal regulation and military activities had secured aviation a role in the lives of residents. The fear of flying had sharply diminished in the eyes of Alaskans, and like stateside airlines, CAS began to make a profit transporting passengers to speedy destinations, rather than relying solely on the transport of their supplies and mail to keep business in the black.

Nevertheless, Smith recognized that in Cordova's case, technological improvements might just be too much of a good thing. Postwar airplanes had indeed become more powerful and now could fly from Seattle to Fairbanks without refueling in Cordova. In addition, steamship routes had started to stop at the Alaska Railroad port town of Seward before sailing to Cordova, negating for passengers the quicker option of flying into the Interior. Because the commercial fishing industry remained the lifeblood of the coastal town, not to mention most of coastal Alaska, CAS continued its dedication to diverse services, acquiring charter contracts to fly regular mail, passengers, and supply flights to ten canneries three times a week during the summer.[12]

In 1952, Smith saw an opportunity to expand his routes. He merged Cordova Air Service with Christensen Flying Service (owned by pioneer bush pilot Haakon Christensen).[13] In the merger Cordova Air gained the route from Anchorage to Seward, while Valdez and Cordova airports were upgraded to accommodate DC-3 aircraft. With business expanding, Smith reincorporated his air-carrier service in 1953. The new name, Cordova Airlines, matched the postwar air industry's modern image and expectations. He added a second DC-3 to his fleet and moved the headquarters for Cordova Airlines to Merrill Field in Anchorage.[14] Despite the move, Cordova Airlines reinstated service to the neglected interior Copper Belt region. Regular routes included Cordova to Chitina, McCarthy, May Creek, and Chisana. Irregular routes involved trips to Bremner, Copper Center, Gulkana, Gakona, Chistochina, and Nabesna. Mining, however, was not the primary reason Smith returned to the Copper Belt—it was Alaska's fledgling tourist industry's promotion of the "last frontier," which in many ways was made possible by the unlikely combination of the declining gold-mining industry and the rise of modern aviation.[15]

MINING'S GOLDEN AGE LOSES ITS LUSTER

The alchemy of the aviation and tourism industries provided Alaskans with a sense of optimism after the war, but when it came to the territory's pillar industry—mining—its future was not so bright. In the earliest months of America's involvement in World War II, even before the Japanese invasion of Pearl Harbor, enlistment in the armed forces not only drained the region of mining laborers but construction projects, like the one at Northway, which offered better wages and thus drew laborers away from the mines. As the rest of the U.S. economy mobilized for war, Alaska's mining industry experienced a lack of supplies and spare parts. But most significant, the Office of Production Management in Washington, D.C., the agency responsible for the coordination of defense activities, ruled that placer gold mines were not essential to the war effort in September 1941.

The ruling represented a major departure from past wars, during which gold mining was considered a strategic industry that usually bankrolled a nation's war machine. But since the United States abandoned the gold standard and banned the possession of gold bullion by private citizens during the Great Depression, the yellow metal had lost its market value. On the eve of World War II, the U.S. Treasury—the only legal buyer of gold—had stockpiled twice as much as the rest of the world combined. The Office of Production Management reasoned it made no sense to spend precious resources on further domestic production of the precious metal. Thus the deathblow for the gold-mining industry came on October 8, 1942, when the War Production Board declared gold mining a nonessential industry and ordered most placer and lode gold mining on American soil to cease indefinitely.[16]

Not surprisingly, Alaskans, who produced one quarter of the nation's gold, reacted strongly to the "nonessential metal" classification. According to historian Terrence Cole, "Alaskans feared the low-priority ruling would mean the depopulation of interior Alaska and the transformation of the territory into a barren waste of ghost towns and lost hopes."[17] Faced with uncertainty, mine owner Carl Whitham decided to halt production at Nabesna, writing to company director Claude Stuart in March 1942 that "conditions make advisable we close Nabesna Mine for the duration of the war."[18] With the sudden death of mine owner Asa Baldwin three weeks before the War Production Board passed Limitation Order L-208, Stuart took over operations of Bremner's Yellow Band Gold Mines in an atmosphere of doubt. Mining had been suspended for four years, and the future looked grim. Considering the national circumstances combined with Baldwin's death, Yellow Band directors decided to postpone operations at Bremner as well.[19]

Although Congress repealed Order L-208 on July 1, 1945, sufficient money never materialized to reopen the Bremner mines. Market conditions caused the mining industry throughout the territory to decline rapidly. Without government subsidies the Alaska gold industry struggled to compete with the increase of mining operations worldwide that effectively lowered the price of gold. The high cost of gold mining in

Alaska, especially in the high mountain regions, proved far too prohibitive. To prevent the Bremner claims from reverting to the public domain, Stuart paid for assessment work out of his own pocket for years. In the end, a few placer operations along the Bremner River limped along into the 1970s, but none of the Yellow Band claims produced ore in payable quantities again.[20] When Carl Whitham passed on in 1947, employees deserted the Nabesna Gold Mine. Nabesna, along with the community of mines in the Bremner District, joined McCarthy and Kennecott as barren ghost towns—relics of Alaskans' big dreams and lost hopes.[21]

DEVELOPING NOSTALGIA TOURISM

Although World War II marked, as historian Terrence Cole put it, "the beginning of the end of the gold-mining industry in Alaska," optimism still existed for the territory's struggling economy.[22] The massive buildup of aviation during the war years opened new doors for the fledgling tourist industry in the North. Inadvertently, the collapse of mining in eastern Alaska gave way to an aviation empire built on passenger's nostalgic notions of Alaska's gold rush days.

As far back as 1929, Santa Clara University geologist and Jesuit priest Father Bernard Hubbard, who spent many years exploring the Far North by foot and by flight, predicted that "Alaska aviators will soon be taking tourists, by plane, into this remote but interesting region."[23] Sixteen years later, commercial pilots, as Father Hubbard envisioned, were bringing sportsmen seeking a rustic "Boone and Crockett" experience into the northern wilderness. Nearly two decades later, the Alaska Development Board (ADB) echoed Hubbard's belief in tourism as a potential economic spark: "Alaska is one of the great tourist areas of the world," declared a 1946 ADB report, aptly titled "Alaska's Recreational Riches": "So far, its recreational resources have barely been tapped." According to economic planners, "Now that the war is over, the airplane doubtless will play a new role in Alaska as a tourist carrier."[24] Not only would air carriers replace miners with tourists as their major clientele in the postwar era, but some, like Merle Smith's Cordova Airlines, would promote the sagging industry as a source of nostalgia to attract curious visitors to Alaska's mining ghost towns of the Last Frontier.[25] Smith wagered that the mystique and novelty generated by pioneer life on the edge of civilization would fascinate tourists. Alaska's postwar economic upturn shows that Smith's bet paid off. As historian Roderick Nash put it, Alaska sourdoughs and the wilderness itself would become "marketable commodities."[26]

The territory's chief pioneer for flying tourists into Alaska's roadless places started with Merle Smith's friend and fellow flyer Ray Petersen, who had made his mark in Alaska tourism by transporting the nation's angling elite to pristine rainbow trout rivers and streams in Katmai National Monument in southwest Alaska on his airline, Northern Consolidated.[27] Petersen made the case that if Alaska was to ever sever its dependency on the federal government and support itself economically, it would have to develop its most lucrative resource, which he believed was Alaska itself. In 1951, Petersen told outdoor writer Louis R. Huber that "tourists are the biggest thing that Alaska can develop," and further observed that "we [air carriers] are counting on them as our long-range, steady customers."[28]

Under Petersen's leadership, Northern Consolidated Airlines (NCA) opened five fishing camps, collectively known as Angler's Paradise. To attract clients to the remote camps, Petersen consciously promoted a kind of frontier ambiance in his Alaska tours. The camps' elite anglers paid a high price to sleep under single canvas–covered tents in sleeping bags on old military cots.[29] Petersen expertly utilized the media to promote Angler's Paradise by inviting a host of outdoor writers from such papers as the *New York Times*, the *Christian Science Monitor,* and the *Seattle Times*. Each responded with extensive glowing reports and scores of new publicity. *Field and Stream*, *Outdoor Life*, and *Alaska Sportsman* echoed support for the camps.[30] Petersen even hired a local homesteader, trapper, and hunting guide, Rufus Knox "Bill" Hamersley, to publically endorse his camps. During the winter of 1950–51, the Nonvianuk homesteader toured the United States, enticing radio and television audiences with salty tales about life and fishing in Alaska.[31]

This type of promotion appealed to postwar Americans. Contrasted with a decade of unprecedented development and urbanization, advertising campaigns in Alaska harkened back to America's era of the Wild West, where free-spirited pioneers slept in log cabins and cowboys trotted an untouched, endless landscape under big, open skies. The frontier theme appealed to a generation of Americans who watched *Raw Hide* and *Davy Crockett*, 1950s-era television shows viewed by millions on the Wide World of Disney each Sunday night.[32] American television consumers also watched *Wild Kingdom* and at the movies saw the highly praised and

Disney-produced nature documentary *Arctic Wild*, which portrayed Alaska as America's "last wilderness." By the end of the 1950s tourists began to desire an experience that offered more than superior hunting and fishing. This new postwar tourist appreciated Alaska's pristine wilderness—a luxury quickly disappearing on America's new industrial, technological, and progressive frontiers.[33]

Merle Smith's foray into frontier tourism was in part meant as a business scheme, for during his early years at the helm, Smith had to be downright cunning to survive the competitive industry. Local pilot and onetime employee Jo King tells a witty anecdote about Smith's manufactured Copper River "gold rush," which underscored the airline president's wily ways. According to King, routine flights out of Cordova and up the Copper River took Smith's pilots over the Abercrombie Rapids, a familiar landmark, just about every day. On what was a supposedly a typical flight, one of Smith's pilot's noticed that the Miles Glacier had retreated far enough so that it no longer blocked the river's flow. As a result, the Copper changed course, shifting the spectacular rapids to the opposite side of the canyon. Mudhole, "a survivor in a survivalist world," as King described him, figured out a way to take advantage of the dramatic ecological event. He started sending his pilots on "secretive missions," then sent "old prospector friends" up to the site with gold pans to check it out. Rumor had it that he suggested they "salt" the river—or fire shotguns shells peppered with gold nuggets into a promising-looking gravel bank to fool the most professional gold panner. Rumor or truth, word got out: "Gold! Gold! Gold! At the old Abercrombie Rapids!" King recalled that the excitement became so infectious that Cordova Airlines couldn't fly the gold-hungry (or simply adventure-hungry) passengers fast enough to Cordova on Mudhole's DC-3, and then upriver on his smaller charter planes. No one ever found gold, but Mudhole's gold rush was a great success for both business and entertainment value: "Gold or not," observed King, "tourists had an exciting picnic up the canyon."[34]

MCCARTHY-KENNICOTT SOURDOUGH TOURS

When Ernest Gruening visited the Chitina valley in 1938, the soon-to-be governor of Alaska recognized the rich recreational possibilities the region had to offer. Smith, who had flown Gruening and his entourage from the Interior Department over the Wrangells that day, also saw the potential of developing a tourism market in the extremely westernesque ghost towns of McCarthy and Kennecott in eastern Alaska. The mining area was once the greatest copper-milling center in the world that dominated the physical, economic, and cultural landscapes of the Chitina valley. Like so many other western mining camps, once the copper ran out and prices plummeted, the Kennecott Copper Corporation simply cashed in its profits and left the Copper Belt.

Between 1938 and 1955 isolation and solitude shielded the structural integrity of the abandoned buildings, insulating them from twentieth-century change. For all practical purposes, wrote recreational planner Gregory Ringer, the few remaining inhabitants of McCarthy and Kennecott were "encapsulated in their own time zone."[35] Several years later, on a visit to the Wrangell Mountain ghost towns, historian William Cronon agreed: "The thing that initially strikes one about Kennecott is just how western it is. Despite its far northern location, nearly everything about it evokes the West."[36] What also appealed to Merle Smith back in 1955 was the sublime natural setting, which provided a stunning backdrop to the rustic ghost towns and abandoned railway. Commanding the attention of any visitor were three peaks: Mount Blackburn, Mount Atna, and Regal Mountain, each bulging with ice, beckoning a stunned gaze toward the northwestern horizon. Standing in McCarthy, visitors could see two glaciers, the Kennicott Glacier and the Root Glacier, surging from the massif's seemingly impenetrable wall. Running near town on its way to meet the Nizina River was a muddy torrent of ice melt formed by the confluence of the two glaciers.

Radiating from McCarthy is a network of immense rivers, which provided prospectors routes to what they believed were copper-filled mountains. By the 1950s the town of McCarthy was in a state of collapse, a mere scattering of false-front buildings and old log cabins, representing a shell of the town's former glory. Six miles away, perched upon a lateral moraine carved by the converged Kennicott and Root Glaciers, at the foot of Bonanza Ridge, sat the conglomerated mill town of Kennecott. Though faded, the barn red–colored paint covering each of the old company structures could be viewed by the handful of remaining residents in McCarthy. Abandoned since 1938, Kennecott remained a cobbled collection of employee cottages, recreational facilities, carpenter shops, and power plants resembling a kind of fairytale industrial village. Its stacked, fourteen-story mill building, still stoically erect, represented a time when gilded age businessmen lorded over the land. "The red walls and white window trims have faded," noted Cronon, "but one gets little feeling of decay or collapse. It is a ghost factory in a ghost town, yet its haunting could almost have begun yesterday."[37] Perhaps not all that surprising, Smith's inspiration for the McCarthy/Kennecott tour was sparked because it reminded him of another mid-twentieth-century tourist destination—Knott's Berry Farm in southern California, a living ghost town created as a tribute to the history of the Old West.[38]

Knott's Berry Farm, like the world's first theme park, Disneyland, and its constituent part, Frontierland, were landmark American tourist attractions that conveyed a carefully selected message of the "old frontier" that greatly influenced visitors' notions of the West and its history. "When they enter Frontierland," wrote western historian Patricia Limerick, "visitors might ask Disneyland employees for directions but they do not have to ask for a definition of the frontier." As confirmed by a trip to Knott's Berry Farm or Frontierland in the mid-1950s, the Old West, as every tourist knew, existed on the edge of Anglo-American settlement. It was populated by mountain men, cowboys, prospectors, and outlaws, who rode horses and drove stage coaches to conquer rivers, mountains, plains, and all other wide-open spaces. Knott's Berry Farm, as with Disneyland's vision of the frontier, above all conveyed a story of success.[39] "Well, doggone," Smith wondered, "this looks kind of like McCarthy. If they're pulling in tourists here, why can't I do the same thing with tourists at McCarthy?"[40]

With the successful development of frontier tourism in Alaska already established by his friend Ray Petersen, Smith started his tourism flights using the same premise, beginning in 1955. To promote his Wrangell Mountain tours, Smith applied Alaska's last frontier motif, but instead of copper mining, which would have been historically accurate, he evoked a more nostalgic and familiar historical episode, the great Klondike Gold Rush. He even named the collective scheduled flights to McCarthy/ Kennecott and other destination throughout the Copper Belt, the "Sourdough Tours."[41] To accommodate the more urban tourists, Smith bought the Hubrick house in McCarthy and a family named the Browns fixed it up as a lodge. Smith and the Browns eventually purchased a building called the Golden and fixed it up as a hotel and saloon. Finally, he purchased Jack O'Neill's store and converted it into a museum of sorts, filling it with discarded items from around McCarthy. The Sourdough Tours commenced in Anchorage, where tourists were loaded onto a DC-3 airliner. From Anchorage the DC-3 flew over the Chugach Mountains to May Creek. The strip at May Creek was originally built in 1947 by the Alaska Road Commission to support mining along the Chititu River, but it also happened to be the only strip in the region long enough to accommodate that size plane.

From May Creek a Model T truck with wooden benches in the back hauled gawking tourists, astonished by the vast beauty of the country, twenty miles down the Alaska Road Commission–built dirt road paralleling the Nizina River to McCarthy. After a "miner's lunch" at the "ghost town," guests spent the afternoon panning for gold in a nearby stream. Tours of McCarthy's old buildings were also provided. A company brochure, rich with frontier imagery, promised to transport the visitor back in time, boasting that the McCarthy trip was "Alaska's most exciting weekend tour":

> When you take your "Alaskan Style" bus for McCarthy Lodge, you will see a hydraulic placer gold mine now being commercially operated in Alaska. After a hearty "Miner's Lunch" you're panning your very own. What a thrill when you spot those flakes of silver and gold. When the sun is high, it's cocktail time at the lodge, and one takes on the gold baring nuggets and notes. Then, after a fine dinner served family style, join us at the fabulous Golden Saloon where you find yourself in another era. With the playing of 1920s vintage records, your lodge hosts improvising on the violin and mandolin, you're in for an evening of solid music, tasty drinks and interesting chats with the McCarthy Sourdoughs.[42]

On the second day of the Sourdough Tour, visitors made the six-mile trip to Kennecott for a picnic and to hike around. Travel between McCarthy and Kennecott took place on the "Kennicott Express" (referencing the glacier it is paralleling), another Model T automobile mounted on railroad wheels. "We were running Model T speeders, making about two or three mile an hour, and it was a very enjoyable trip for our tourists," explained Smith. "Upon reaching Kennecott's property lines, we had manufactured our own turn table and we turned our vehicle around and proceeded to McCarthy. This made a total of about eight miles of scenic tourist attraction. It was an isolated section, and moose and bear were viewed on practically every trip."[43]

Once there, visitors wandered freely through the industrial buildings, including the fourteen-story gravity-fed ore concentrator building that dominated the skyline above Kennecott; the leaching plant where the syndicate pioneered the use of sulfur ammonia in processing copper tailings; the power plant, with its four huge smokestacks resembling a steamship; the hospital, which saved numerous patients flown into McCarthy by Harold Gillam; the superintendent's office, the only log cabin on site and the oldest building in Kennecott; the multistory bunkhouses; the general store; the two-room school house; the community center that functioned as a theater and indoor gymnasium; and the several private residents for families of the teachers, medical staff, and upper management.[44]

When the Kennecott Copper Corporation pulled out its mining operation, it did so almost in one day, removing all of the town's residents and employees on the last train to Cordova in 1938. Many folks therefore left much of their material possessions behind. In 1955 curious visitors found homes still supplied with bedding and kitchenware, store shelves stocked with supplies, and medical records and x-rays on file in the hospital.[45] In her book *Alaska Bound*, travel writer Kathryn Winslow wrote that during the Sourdough Tour the ghost town evoked an appealing nostalgia. "In some of the homes the curtains still hang in the windows," wrote Winslow. "In the community building, which housed the school and library, the books and periodicals date back over thirty years. The railroad station, jail and general store are ready-made for your camera.[46] Winslow described the abandoned furnished houses in Kennecott as "eerie as those in McCarthy," an experience that many visitors might find appealing. "You walk over to the mortuary and count three coffins stacked for customers," continued Winslow. "You look in at the empty hospital, which still holds a faint aroma of antiseptics. You see a theater, laundry, saloon. The piano is not even dusty; the air here is so clean. You tap on the keys, which are quite out of tune, of course, and think of the people taking the last train out, carrying what they could and leaving the rest behind."[47]

LOCAL RESISTANCE

Not everyone found mining a nostalgic endeavor, however—to them it existed very much in the present. Those who still believed that Kennecott held mineral value and represented a means for men to make money did not go lightly into the past. They resisted the urge by the modern generation to turn their tools, machines, and assembly lines into tourist attractions. Subsequently these miners were determined to repel Smith and his Sourdough Tours from McCarthy and Kennecott, which had hauled over nine hundred passengers into the Copper Belt after just one year of operation.

The first sign of resistance came from the Kennecott Cooperation itself, which worried about the liability of so many tourists rummaging around their property. They posted "No Trespassing" signs and contracted Ray Trotochau, whose copper company, the Sultan Milling and Mining Company, maintained surface rights to the property, to raze the mill town in 1957. Trotochau failed to burn the historic complex but produced his share of damage, nonetheless. He stripped and tore down the superintendent's house and the manager's house, removed all the high-voltage power lines (salvaging the copper wire therein), and systematically pilfered all the brass valves from the buildings.[48]

Although he constantly threatened to burn the rest of the mining complex, Trotochau never fully complied with Kennecott's instructions. In his mind there was still money to be made. The Sultan Milling and Mining Company had fourteen employees picking up high-grade ore in the vicinity of the old Kennecott mine, so Trotochau moved to keep Cordova Airlines and its tourists out of the area by stretching a cable across the right-of-way and track of the old Copper River & Northwestern Railway, about a mile from Kennecott.[49] The action infuriated Merle Smith, who summed up the situation in a letter to Senator Gruening in July 1959: "We still give the 'speeder rides' up to the mining property, which is about four miles," explained Smith. "They [Trotochau and the Sultan Milling and Mining Company] agree that it is a public right-of-way and we are entirely within our rights to proceed up to the mine on this public right-of-way as long as our passengers do not leave the public property; however, they maintain that when they purchased Kennecott they purchased these rails. The Bureau of Public Roads in Juneau also agree with them, which pretty much leaves us out in the cold."[50]

The letter sparked a yearlong letter-writing discussion between Smith, Senator Gruening, and the new State of Alaska on the legal circumstances surrounding Smith's Sourdough Tours and the private mining operation at Kennecott. When Secretary of Interior Fred Seaton concluded that the federal government maintained the property rights of the rails, and that Trotochau and the Sultan Milling and Mining Company had illegally blocked Cordova Airlines from access to the site, tensions only grew worse.

Trotochau, just before the tourist season began in spring 1960, responded by removing nearly two miles of the old railroad rails from the mill site to McCarthy.[51] Both the senator and the federally run Department of Commerce recognized that Sultan Milling and Mining Company was illicit in its actions, but with the achievement of statehood in 1959 the new State of Alaska maintained the right-of-way, and it was now up to the Alaska Department of Public Works to decide what to do.[52]

In September assistant attorney general Norman Schwalb with Alaska's attorney general's office reviewed the Copper River & Northwestern Railway file and determined "there seems to be no doubt that about a mile and one half of rails and ties belonging to the State of Alaska have been removed from the right-of-way grade." He then listed three possible legal actions: one, the state could compel the company to replace the rails; two, serve the company with an injunction to prevent the removal of more rails; and three, sue for damages suffered by the state. Although the attorney general's office conceded that probably all three actions could be brought in one suit, Schwalb recommended against taking any action, reasoning that there was no compelling purpose in replacing the rails, that the Sultan Milling and Mining Company had agreed not to remove any more rails, and that damages to the state were minimal. As far as the State of Alaska was concerned, the use of the railroad bed for trucks and cars as used by the Sultan Company seems to be as practical as any. The attorney general's office therefore recommend letting this whole matter remain in status quo.[53] The commissioner of Public Works concurred, concluding that Trotochau's only crime was to "establish a highway rather than a railroad."[54]

The state's conclusions did not sit well with Merle Smith. Smith argued and fully believed that the state's final decision regarding Kennecott would irresponsibly trump the historic mine's true economic potential—tourism—and at the same time betray the legitimate businessmen who had Alaska's best intentions at heart: "I feel that I have been sold down the river due to your interest in a possible mining venture, which isn't really a mining venture. . . . I believe I am safe in saying that if you investigate that mining operation that you will find no state labor laws being complied with and nothing being done in the way of constructive mining."[55] Admitting the roots of commercial aviation in the Wrangells depended on mining, Smith agreed that "if we can get a mine going in any area that it will be a considerable worth to my company," but he noted that Trotochau and the Sultan Milling and Mining Company was not the company to achieve such a goal.

In a letter to the commissioner Smith had harsh criticism for the state's support of Trotochau, accusing leadership of turning a blind eye to the region's tourism potential. "In the first place you don't have any mining activity and in the second place you have shut your eyes to the tourist development of the area which has been comprised on solely by my airline."[56] At minimum, the pilot insisted that the road Trotochau had blazed on a public right-a-way be made into a public thoroughfare.[57] In concluding his letter, Smith reminded the commissioner that the agreement between Mr. Trotochau and the Kennecott Copper Corporation was for only surface rights and despite the state's hopeful intentions of resuscitating the mining industry at Kennecott, Sultan Milling and Mining could not legally mine the site. He also was quick to point out that any plan to reopen the mine was pure fiction, citing that the Kennecott agreement directed Trotochau to destroy the mine. "If Kennecott had found any deposits worth mining," noted Smith, "they'd have done it decades ago."[58]

When all was said and done, the state's decision of no action essentially killed Smith's tourism business to the popular McCarthy/Kennicott "ghost towns." Smith, meanwhile, had moved on. He began looking for an alternative attraction, eventually applying for and receiving from the CAB an extension of Cordova Airline's route beyond its terminal point at Chisana to the terminal point at Dawson City in Yukon, Canada, via Northway, Alaska. There Smith received a welcomed reception. To stimulate tourism, and thereby attracting visitors numbering in the thousands from the Lower 48, the Canadian government spent over six hundred thousand dollars to restore the historical mining sites. It also constructed a new airport to accommodate jet aircraft in 1967.[59] To Smith's undoubted satisfaction, Cordova Airlines provided the only air service from Alaska.[60] Thus the famed Yukon mining town of Dawson, a name synonymous with the 1898 Klondike Gold Rush, became Smith's new frontier commodity that not only enticed but embraced his vision for a tourist destination with the Midas touch.

CORDOVA AIRLINES SOURDOUGH TOUR
AIR ROUTE MAP

FAIRBANKS

BIG DELTA

MT.McKINLEY

GLENNALLEN

ARC.

CHISANA

CHITNA
McCARTHY

ANCHORAGE   VALDEZ

CORDOVA

PRINCE WILLIAM
SOUND

SEE YOUR TRAVEL AGENT

Cordova Airlines

ANCHORAGE INTERNATIONAL AIRPORT
BOX 6203, ANCHORAGE, ALASKA

92-107-32 A

Cordova Airlines
SOURDOUGH Tours

ALASKA

After Merle Smith reincorporated his air carrier as Cordova Airlines, he started the Sourdough Tours, which used in its advertisements frontier imagery to entice tourists to mining ghost towns such as McCarthy and Kennicott. "Cordova Airlines Sourdough Tours brochure, ca., 1955." Courtesy of the Cordova Historical Museum, Cordova Air Service folder, Aviation Files, 92-107-32 A.

Inspiration for the Sourdough Tours was not the Klondike but rather Knott's Berry Farm in California. Smith's tours commenced in Anchorage, where passengers were loaded onto a DC-3 airliner. From Anchorage the DC-3 flew over the Chugach Mountains to May Creek, which maintained the only strip long enough to accommodate Smith's DC-3. Tourists traveled to McCarthy, where they met the "Kennecott Express," a Model T automobile mounted on railroad wheels, and road the hybrid six miles to the Kennecott mill site. There visitors wandered freely through the industrial buildings, including the fourteen-story mill that dominated the skyline. Travel writer Kathryn Winslow wrote that during Cordova's Sourdough Tours, the ghost town evoked "an appealing eeriness . . . ready-made for your camera." Courtesy of Charles "Bob" Leitzell, Mokelumne Hill, California.

In 1968, Cordova Airlines merged with Alaska Air to become Alaska Airlines. According to Smith, it was his company's exclusive route into Canada that made his Cordova Airlines attractive. With Cordova's newly acquired "Convair-Liner," Alaska Airlines continued the highly popular "Golden Nugget Service" in 1968, which featured a Gay '90s motif, accentuated by an on-board piano bar and flight attendants dressed as can-can girls. Merle Smith Collection, Alaska Airlines, Seattle, Washington.

Surveyors mapped the route for a potential road along the Copper River corridor between 1951 and 1952. The entire project was conducted via air support from Cordova Air Service. Despite the valiant effort by surveyors and pilots alike, the road was never built. The destruction caused by the 1964 earthquake eventually put the project on permanent hold. Courtesy of the Cordova Historical Museum, 02-40-10.

The Alaska Road Commission made preparations to convert the Copper River &
Northwestern Railway into a highway in the summer of 1950. Cordova Air Service
pilot Herb Haley transported survey crews at the beginning and end of each work
day between the base stations and their survey sites. This was accomplished in a
Piper Cub equipped with tandem landing wheels that took off and landed from,
as one surveyor declared, "the most unbelievable places—sandbars." Courtesy
f the Cordova Historical Museum, 2-40-12.

Terris Moore, the University of Alaska's "Flying President," overcame aviation barriers while establishing a research laboratory on the summit of Mount Wrangell in 1952. The lab's scientists initially studied cosmic rays, and with the arrival of the Cold War they studied the physiological effects of living at high altitudes in frigid environments. Such scientific activity, supported entirely by aviation, was the impetus for the university's Geophysical Institute, which transformed the onetime mining college into a world-class research facility. Cordova pilot Herb Haley lands on top of Mount Wrangell at fourteen thousand feet. Courtesy of Charles "Buck" Wilson, Fairbanks, Alaska.

The International Geophysical Year (1957–1958) was a public relations effort designed to bring the earth, atmospheric, and ocean sciences into the classrooms and living rooms of the general public in order to attract more students into scientific careers. The new enthusiasm for the scientific disciplines opened the gates to glaciological and volcanic study and also gave the Wrangell Mountain Observatory a purpose beyond military interests. Scientists on Mount Wrangell prepare to ski down from fourteen thousand feet to seven thousand feet to meet the supply plane. Courtesy of Charles "Buck" Wilson, Fairbanks, Alaska.

Cordova Airlines took over air service to the Wrangell Mountain Observatory in 1953. Lead pilot for the operation was Herb Haley. Independent flyer Jack Wilson also supplied the researchers. In the 1960s Wilson made a record sixty-nine landings on top of Mount Wrangell. Usually uneventful, occasionally a pilot like Herb Haley was reminded that landing on a live volcano was a dangerous endeavor. "Pulling Out Cordova Airlines plane." Courtesy of Charles "Buck" Wilson, Fairbanks Alaska.

By the mid-1970s approximately 250 guides from both sides of the border flew into the Wrangell Mountains to hunt the coveted Dall sheep. Most resident-guides belonged to the group that maintained the sportsmen's fair chase ethic, but a minority group indiscriminately targeted wildlife without regard for fellow guides or the future of their business. In later years Jack Wilson lamented the "quick-get-a-trophy-and-get-out" mentality of the more aggressive guides. "In the Old West men had exploited the riches of the new country with a will, and we were no different." Pilot and hunting guide Howard Knutson displays his clients' trophies during a fly-in hunt in 1976. Courtesy of Gary Green, McCarthy, Alaska.

The airplane gave those living in the shadow of the roadless Wrangell Mountains access to medical services, grocery stores, and the mail. Airstrips became gathering places where residents caught up on the latest local news. Experts who have studied this region have described it as developing an "airplane culture." McCarthy residents waiting for a pickup sometime in the 1980s. Courtesy of Gary Green, McCarthy, Alaska.

In the decades after World War II, more and more Americans escaped the hectic urban life to seek solitude in the nation's remaining empty places. Some visitors to Alaska went to spectacular lengths to reach wild places that had never been touched by human beings. Today airplanes commonly fly over the scenic Kennicott Glacier on flight tours. Courtesy of Gary Green, McCarthy, Alaska.

A new generation of wilderness seekers became the latest conquerors of the last frontier wilderness, and a new generation of Wrangell Mountain flyers took them to their secluded destinations. A lone plane lands on a braided river sandbar surrounded by the Wrangell Mountain wilderness. Courtesy of Gary Green, McCarthy, Alaska.

Bush pilot Gary Green poses with his airplane at an unnamed location, somewhere in the Wrangell Mountains. Courtesy of Gary Green, McCarthy, Alaska.

Soaring Spies, Surveyors, and Scientists

WHILE MOST ALASKA AIR CARRIERS WERE IN THE PROCESS OF extending their reach beyond Alaska and establishing commercial routes primarily for traveling passengers in the decades after the war, an intrepid and fairly unfamiliar few continued to fly the nonestablished air routes into Alaska's most remote areas. The McCarthy-Kennicott Historic Museum described the region's 1950s-era aviators as "unsung heroes" simply "doing their job." But looming in the backdrop—and usually bankrolling much of their day-to-day tasks—was the federal government's monumental effort to protect America's skyways during the Cold War.

In 1943, just two years before World War II concluded, a journalist for *Barron's National Business and Financial Weekly* reminded readers that "in casting Alaska's horoscope one should bear constantly in mind that only eight miles separate Little and Big Diomede Islands, owned respectively by Russia and the United Sates; that the mainlands of Alaska and Siberia are only 54 miles apart."[1] At the time, political and military pundits heralded the short distance between East and West as eminently important to the Allied effort. The skyways over Alaska served as a strategic air bridge underscored by the centerpiece of U.S. and Soviet wartime cooperation, the Lend-Lease program—a program that, by the war's end, would be emphatically denied by both governments.

By 1945, emerging ideological differences between capitalist America and communist Russia began to rapidly polarize the two superpowers. Just one year after the war ended, England's Winston Churchill declared that an "iron curtain" had descended across the European continent, representing a mortal threat to free market democracies worldwide.

Joseph Stalin worsened the situation with reports that he had deployed an army of several hundred thousand to the Chukotka Peninsula "to ensure that Soviet forces could attack the United States" and "to land in Alaska in the event of war."[2] Relations with Washington, D.C., deteriorated further when the Soviets detonated their first atomic bomb in 1949. With the advent of nuclear weapons and advanced aviation systems for delivering bombs over vast continents and oceans, age-old notions of geographic safety had completely vanished. By 1950 the New York Times told Americans what most already feared, reporting that the Pentagon realized Alaska was "vulnerable both to air bombardment and to airborne assault."[3] Heightened were extreme concerns that the Soviets would launch a surprise nuclear attack against the United States and a ground invasion by way of the shortest route: Alaska.[4]

Responding to the idea that the Arctic region itself would become a future theater of war, U.S. commanding generals established Alaska (positioned so close to Russia that geologists could actually register seismic anomalies set off by a fledging nuclear program) as a critical front in the Cold War.[5] According to historian Kathy Price, "the Arctic would serve as a forward deployment zone, and warning area, a listening post, a first line of defense, and a potential resource storehouse." America's most northern territory, Price explained, "became the western anchor for these Arctic and sub-arctic activities."[6] By the early 1950s the transpolar air routes and close proximity to our ally-turned-enemy had transformed Alaska from a bridge to the East to America's "northernmost sentry" and guardian of the West.[7] As retired U.S. Air Force historian John Haile Cloe put it: "The honeymoon, such as it was, was over."[8]

THE COLD WAR COMES TO EASTERN ALASKA'S SKY FRONTIER

At the start of the Cold War, military planners paid particular attention to the unmaintained but quite usable airfields once associated with the Lend-Lease program. Strategic wisdom reasoned that in a premeditated invasion, the Soviets would use our airfields against us. Just a few years after the Nabesna–Northway airlift, the U.S. Army ordered Lieutenant Colonel Ken Sheppard to assess Reeve's Field, among others, to determine if Soviet pilots might target them as staging areas in an attack against the United States. Morrison-Knudsen had enlarged the field twice during the war. Its longest extension measured ten thousand feet. A second cross-wind was added to serve as an emergency strip for larger aircraft shuttled between the Lower 48 and Murmansk.[9] Illustrating the tectonic shift in foreign relations, Sheppard reported that "if the Russians got to [Reeve's] airfield without being shot to pieces, the watchmen at the mine could handle the situation."[10]

The Nabesna "watchmen," to whom Sheppard referred, not only served as actual "caretakers" of the mine but may have been part of a local resistance force called the "Nabesna Faction," organized through a U.S. military counterintelligence program called the "Alaska Project." In March 1950—within months of the Soviet's first detonating of an atomic bomb—the Alaskan Command devised an intricate plan that used Alaskan civilians as secret agents in an underground intelligence-gathering network in the event that the Russians attempted to occupy or invade Alaska. The Air Force's Office of Special Investigation (OSI) and, for a short while, the Federal Investigation Bureau (FBI) jointly oversaw the top-secret mission.[11] The Alaska Project, also known as Operation Washtub, adopted two distinct operational components. The first involved the recruitment and training of Alaska citizens to be assigned the task of Stay Behind Agents (SBAs). Trained in Morse code and photography, their job was to transmit by radio all enemy movements and activities. The second involved the construction and equipping of hundreds of survival caches along escape-and-evasion (E&E) routes flown by Strategic Air Command bombers. Caches—supplied with one year's worth of rations, medicine, weapons and ammunition, clothes, skis, snowshoes, sleeping bags, and blankets—were built for American combat aircrews forced down in the remote Alaskan wilderness. In addition, local residents were recruited and trained to maintain the caches as well as to guide the downed airmen to safety. Many of the E&E agents were bush pilots, hunters, prospectors, and trappers whose job skills made them particularly suited for their role in facilitating aircrew survival and who could go about their daily routine in anonymity in places where new arrivals generally stood out like suspicious sore thumbs.[12]

What ended the cloak-and-dagger activities of the Alaska Project became the catalyst for a far more frightening realization: that long-range bombers, rockets, and missiles reduced conflicts from weeks and months to mere minutes, and were massively more destructive. Conventional command-and-control systems were considered inadequately slow in reacting to a nuclear attack. The U.S. military consequently poured massive funding into developing computer-driven technology that could track and intercept enemy bomber aircraft using information from remote radar stations. Such an early warning communication system was considered vital for over-the-pole defense of the nation. Representing the eastern Alaska link in a much larger chain of Alaska's coastal defense known as Aircraft Control and Warning (AC&W) sites was the U.S. Air Force radar station at Middleton Island. Back in 1932, two prospectors convinced Bob Reeve to fly them 140 miles south of Valdez, over the vast Gulf of Alaska, to the Middleton Island, which supposedly had a fine, smooth wide-open beach good for landing. "Gold was in the beach sand," claimed the enthusiastic prospectors, "just like over at Nome." After badly damaging his Eaglerock while landing on a steep spit strewn with rocks, and using all his resourcefulness and mechanical know-how to get airborne, Reeve swore: "That was my first and last flight to Middleton Island!"[13]

Twenty-three years later, Middleton Island remained just as difficult to access. Nevertheless, the air force established a radar station on its north end with the purpose of seeking out unfriendly aircraft over U.S. airspace. If detected, Middleton's crew would direct American fighters to intercept them.[14] But because the characteristic climate conditions often shrouded the island in fog and storms that disrupted radar communication, the air force installed White Alice tropospheric scatter transmitters at Middleton in 1956. The improved telecommunications system bounced radio signals off the troposphere, connecting the AC&W radar sites along the coast and the Distant Early Warning Line (DEW) system in the north with central command-and-control facilities in Anchorage and Fairbanks.[15]

In 1957 an airstrip was constructed on the island allowing cargo transport and personnel to fly in and out. The CAB awarded Cordova Airlines with the contact to carry the mail and to transport site personnel to and from the island. Although the military could be a lucrative customer for regional commercial carriers, the increasing use of air force and Alaska Air National Guard flights into White Alice stations like Middleton Island made it difficult for scheduled carriers to compete, let alone make a profit.[16] Merle Smith sent the base commander a letter effectively saying as much, notifying him that Cordova Airlines was reducing its scheduled weekly flights from three to one. Smith cited traffic decreases due to competing military aircraft as the reason.

Still, Smith recognized the value of maintaining the military as a regular customer: "We would be glad to step our schedule up any amount,"

Smith offered the base commander, "even to a daily basis." He emphatically maintained that taxpaying Americans "would afford a great saving if [business] would be transferred to Cordova Airlines flights."[17] In 1963, however, the combination of budget reductions and new technologies better employed elsewhere forced the air force to inactivate the Middleton Island station. The decision prompted Smith to request from the CAB an extension of his Northway route to the Interior's Fort Greely, Delta Junction area, where a growing but air transport-less population center hosted the army's Arctic winter training games, headquartered the military's Ballistic Missile Early Warning System, and served as home to Alaska's first and only nuclear reactor. With an approximate six thousand pounds of cargo in addition to six to eight military passengers per week, it was a lucrative route indeed.[18]

SURVEYING THE COPPER RIVER
FOR THE ALASKA ROAD COMMISSION

Fueling the government's approval of Smith's additional route request was the federal government's preoccupation with eastern Alaska's mineral potential to support its growing nuclear industrial complex. Agencies such as the U.S. Geological Survey and the U.S. Atomic Energy Commission targeted an array of geological minerals crucial to Cold War defense that went far beyond the vaunted Kennecott copper ores.[19] Reports of nickel, chromium, silver, lead, tungsten, zinc, platinum, tin, mercury, arsenic, and the atomic element antimony were said to be "hidden in stores of commercial-sized quantities" throughout the old Copper Belt.[20]

Aviation reconnaissance would be used to locate these strategic minerals buried deep within the Wrangell Mountains, but to get supplies in and ore out was a dilemma. The solution, as touted by Cordova's Chamber of Commerce in pamphlet from 1950, was the Copper River Survey. The city's leadership correctly recognized that a road supported by the escalation of Cold War activity would benefit them economically as much as militarily: "In the interest of national defense and to develop Alaska," boasted the patriotic advertisement, "roads are of great importance." Cordova boosters believed that a government-built road would reconnect them to the Interior, and at the same time "reopen a vast area of mineral resources."[21] But this was no ordinary job, nor ordinary road. According to the government's contractor, Aero: "Job 10591 is an invasion of the last frontier, Alaska; it is a contest against cold, wind, snow, dust and mountains in a setting of breath-taking scenery and rich Alaska history." Simply put: "We are mapping the Copper River Canyon for the Alaska Road Commission."[22]

The 1950 Copper River Survey commenced in late summer and was completed by the first snowfalls of autumn. The Alaska Road Commission subcontracted the project to Aero Service Corporation, who brought in Jack Ninneman, an expert in photogrammetry, and Bob Shinaman, an "ace" Trig Traverse man, to lead the survey crew. The ARC furnished other field men as well, including boatmen, cooks, and, most significant, knowledgeable pilots. Their task was to survey the Copper River from Chitina to the so-called Million Dollar Bridge near the Childs Glacier northeast of Cordova—a feat that had not been accomplished since engineers working for the Copper River & Northwestern Railway surveyed the Copper River Canyon, a route Rex Beach famously called the "the Iron Trail" in his 1913 historical romance of the same name.[23] In his book Beach artfully described the ultimate purpose for that first survey: "Every bridge, every skyscraper, every mechanical invention, every great work which man has wrought in steel and stone and concrete, was once a dream. But the promise of Kennicott copper," waxed Beach, "transformed the dream of harnessing the riches of the Last Frontier into reality." As Beach saw it, the man "who gained control of Alaskan transportation would come the domination of her resources."[24] Forty years later, the ARC surveyors' purpose remained pretty much the same—to map a route for a road that would connect Cordova to the Alaska road system, providing a stream of traffic into the heart of the Interior—dreamers still hoping to access, and thereby dominate, Alaska's riches.

The ambitious project's first task was acquiring aerial photographs of the Copper River, from where it plunged through the Chugach Mountains, forming the Copper River Canyon, to the sprawl of glaciers, each calving icebergs into the river from opposite banks, about fifteen miles from Prince William Sound. Project managers hired an "old-time bush pilot" to survey the area by air. In the company's Christmas newsletter, Aero employee Virgil Kauffman described what he viewed as the pilot's "rugged" frontier flying: "The Copper Canyon is like a monster wind tunnel," exclaimed Kauffman, "sharp mountains and glaciers rise on either side." But to acquire the information surveyors needed, the skillful pilot "flew the photographers at an altitude far lower than the tops of the surrounding canyon walls." Just taking the photographs was an admirable achievement. "The turbulence of the area is terrific," remarked Kauffman. "Ask one office yokel who made the trip to tell you how sick a man can get in a plane!"[25]

By September ground crews ascended onto the river. Two section houses built by the Copper River & Northwest Railway forty years ago served as base camps for the surveyors. The Tiekel Section House near Chitina served as the first camp, and as crews made their way down river, the Ginny Section House served as the second. Working from these two field stations, surveyors used the aerial photographs to established set points along the old railway line. They also ran a Trig Traverse along the river that, together with the necessary elevations, was used to control the aerial photographs. A traverse, according to surveyors, is the field operation of measuring the lengths and directions of a series of straight lines connecting a series of points on the earth. Each of these straight lines is called a traverse leg, and each point is called a traverse station. In a traverse three stations are considered to be of immediate significance, hence the term "Trig Traverse." The procedure proved successful: "The compilation of the maps is going according to schedule," reported Kauffman, "and rough as the field job has been the Trig Traverse is again proving its worth in the rapid production of accurate results."[26]

Throughout the summer the survey crew moved from set point to set point along the river in two rowboats, for walking in many areas in the canyon was hazardous. The boats, however, only assisted the surveyors in their daily tasks. The chief transport need was moving field parties at the beginning and end of each workday between the base stations and their survey sites. This was accomplished by a Piper Cub equipped with tandem landing wheels that took off and landed from, as Kauffman declared, "the most unbelievable places—sandbars."[27] Piloting the Piper Cub along the Copper River's endlessly tangled strings of sandbars that summer was Herb Haley, who found a job with Cordova Air Service flying mostly charter flights for the town's numerous salmon canneries in 1942. By 1943, Haley was the carrier's solitary pilot. In the early 1940s most regional bush pilots, including Merle Smith, had left their respective charter businesses to fly for the military contractor Morrison-Knudsen. After Smith returned to Cordova Air Service to serve as company president in 1944, he sent Haley to reestablish CAS's Wrangell Mountain routes.[28] "The pilot is marvelous," wrote Jack Ninneman in his project report. "While the two boats handle the side-shot crews, he takes the forward crew ahead, goes back and brings Bob Shinaman ahead, goes back and brings up the flags—everything but drive the stakes. He can land on a tablecloth!"[29]

Aero crew member Charles "Bob" Leitzell remembered Haley being an excellent pilot but personally "reserved."[30] Leitzell also recalled Haley's flying skills and grace under pressure, especially while taking off from extremely short gravel bars, where piloting a plane became a group effort. "Often it was necessary for the surveyors to hold the plane's wings to assist in a take-off, and at other times, plane, passengers, and equipment barely skimmed the silt-filled river."[31]

As the job progressed into early fall, the crews made note of brown bears feeding on the spawned salmon. But as bears and spawning salmon indicated, the long arctic daylight and seasonal temperatures were quickly vanishing from the Copper River Canyon. Consequently, volatile weather became an increasing concern for the surveyors. As Ninneman put it, the surveyors in 1950 were "in a race with the weather." Attempting to explain the situation in a letter to his superiors, the seasoned surveyor wrote: "I am not trying to get out of a tough job, but that country is impassable when there is snow—and I mean impassable by snowshoes or any other method." By September the sun was setting not long after 3:00 p.m. behind the bright orange, birch-covered mountains tinged with termination dust. Dropping temperatures formed chunks of ice on the river, making boat use too dangerous. In addition, strong storms brewing in the Gulf of Alaska began to blow upriver. Ninneman reported a typical fall day in the canyon: "Today we fought high winds, sand blowing so one could not face it. Winds increased hourly—pilot got report of impeding 80 m.p.h. gale."[32]

By October the windstorms became so bad that crews were stuck at the Ginny Section House for a week, waiting patiently for the grounded CAS plane. Because Haley usually flew in their provisions, food, and fuel, "the question we all asked," recalled Leitzell, was "who do you eat first!"[33] Forced to ration supplies, Ninneman later wrote: "Imagine they are cussing me right now." But then he reassured himself that this crew would be alright. "Aero has an expression—*We hired out tough.*" Snow inevitably came, which forced Herb Haley to replace his wheels with skis. Though extremely cold, the windy weather calmed, allowing Haley to evacuate the stranded men from the last camp. Beyond their rescue, the pilot received praise from everyone involved in the operation. "Without his skill and ability," wrote Kauffman, "the survey would not have been completed before the real snow arrived."[34] In November survey crews reached the Million Dollar Bridge. Despite the cold and stormy weather, the 1950 Copper River Survey had accomplished in about two months what it took surveyors four decades ago to accomplish in three years. Air transportation had replaced mules and hard foot travel, but above all, noted Kauffman, "the aerial photography has resulted in an overall economy of mapping effort."[35]

After the success of the river survey, Herb Haley continued to fly for Smith's newly incorporated Cordova Airlines while stationed at Chitina and at times McCarthy. These airstrips had regained their vitality to the region, because in the end a road connecting Cordova to the wider road system was never built. Obstacles presented by glaciers, avalanches, and the everyday maintenance challenges were proving to be daunting and expensive. Then the 1964 earthquake obliterated the work in progress, and funding for building the road was diverted elsewhere. Even with a flood of oil money into state coffers in the early 1970s, uncertainty about the proposed Wrangell–Saint Elias National Park and unresolved Native land claims in the area made building the road problematic.

When the State of Alaska resumed construction on the Copper River Highway in 1973, the Sierra Club sued the state for failing to follow the proper Environmental Impact Statement process and a federal judge ordered any further work halted.[36] While discussions about whether to build a road and open Cordova to new business and tourism opportunities continued, it was clear that attitudes regarding Alaska's environment and identity had changed since 1911, when corporate railroad builders from Outside first "opened" Alaska's riches to economic development.[37]

By the late 1960s and early 1970s, defining exactly what qualified as Alaska's "riches" had transcended into a battle between Cordova boosters and the town's "no road" faction, which desired to remain independent from that outside world. Aspirations for building a transportation system that would provide access to minerals, agricultural development, and ultimately populated settlements were replaced with aspirations held by a majority of Cordovans, who decidedly felt that being disconnected from the road system had its own value. "Cordova isn't the easiest place to get to in Alaska," wrote journalist Steve Edwards. "That's OK, because the remote setting is one of the community's charms."[38]

Alaska roads have historically provided important economic and physical benefits to communities they connect, but as historian Terrence Cole explained, "the roads in Alaska are psychological as much as anything else." Being cut off from the road system and "the rest of the world" can adversely affect a small-town society, but this was not the case in Cordova. Cole suggests that one reason for the community's acceptance of its isolation was its long-standing association with aviation, which connected Cordovans with the world when they chose to—not the other way around. "Remember the main way that Alaskans got around was by airplane, explained Cole during a recent interview. "The airplane was a lot cheaper and easier [than building roads] and that technology enabled Alaskans to do without roads."[39] Likewise, researcher Holly Reckord recognized the existence of a community triangle between Cordova, Chitina, and McCarthy, noting that for all the residents living in those communities, as well as all the places in between, "the plane seems to have replaced the long defunct railroad as the main means of transportation. The existence of the highway is irrelevant for them and to the way they related to the land."[40] Thus, by directly linking their town's current isolation to Alaska's past image of independence, Cordova's collective psychology helped preserve a sliver of aviation's golden age of frontier flight, which ultimately fed the Wrangell Mountain skyboy image and kept the narrative fresh for decades to come.

TERRIS MOORE, THE FLYING PRESIDENT

Besides servicing White Alice sites or flying surveyors throughout the treacherous Copper River Canyon, pilots like University of Alaska–Fairbanks president Terris "Terry" Moore provided scientists access to some of the Wrangell Mountains' most extreme places. The mastery of high-mountain landings proved to be essential in providing air support for scientific research at the Wrangell Mountain Observatory located atop the active volcano, Mount Wrangell. The successful establishment of the mountaintop observatory gained the interest of the military in 1953, particularly in how high altitudes and frigid temperatures physiologically affect human beings living and working in such environments.[41] As relations between the United States and the U.S.S.R. worsened, and a "hot war" between the two enemies became a distant possibility, such cold weather science took on new relevance in terms of national defense.

Known as "the flying president," Terris Moore was not a typical Wrangell Mountain skyboy. In 1949 he became the University of Alaska's second president. Before assuming the leading position in the university, Moore was a successful investor and businessman and had a distinguished academic career at Harvard University. He was also an avid mountaineer. In 1930, along with Allen Carpe and Andy Taylor, whose work with Bell Laboratories involved cosmic ray research, Moore made the first ascent of Mount Bona, a volcano in the Saint Elias Range and one of Alaska's highest peaks.[42] Though living in Massachusetts, Moore returned to Alaska throughout the decade, climbing Mount McKinley, and later Mount Sanford, with his wife and fellow Harvard man Bradford Washburn in 1938. All the while, Moore cultivated an interest in flying.

By 1948, University of Alaska's first longtime president, Charles Bunnell, was rumored to retire. Because of his activities in Alaska, Terris Moore's name had been mentioned as an excellent candidate for the top job. The university's Board of Regents, particularly Regent William "Bill" O'Neill, worried that a non-Alaskan from the East Coast would ignore and ultimately misrepresent Alaskans' interests. In early March 1949, while the candidate search was in process, Regent O'Neill headed to Dan Creek, near McCarthy, where he had a mining camp. To get there he had to go by bush plane to the May Creek landing field and then walk on snowshoes eight miles along the Nizina River to the camp. O'Neill knew that with the glaciated mountains of the Wrangell Range looming from all sides, Dan Creek was one of the most isolated places in Alaska. "Regent O'Neill was cut off from the rest of the world," wrote historian Neil Davis, "or so he thought."[43] Then, in the stillness of a cold spring, O'Neill heard the buzz of an airplane over his camp. Two hours later, presidential candidate Terry Moore had arrived at his Dan Creek camp, surprising and impressing the old-time Alaskan with his very Alaskan-like determination. But Moore's academic background, mountain climbing, and flying experiences did not convince the practically minded university regent Cap Lathrop, who swayed almost half of the University Board of Regents to vote against Moore. Despite those "who were dragging their heels," Moore overcame his critics. He was hired in 1949 by the other half of the Board of Regents, who wanted to "inject the University with new blood."[44]

As president Moore continued to engage in his favorite activities, such as climbing, and even named "University Peak" in the Saint Elias Range for the University of Alaska on one of his trips. But mostly, he continued flying, at least tentatively at first. Moore's flying tended to bring him unwanted attention from his detractors at the university, who contemptuously referred to him as "fly-boy." An article in the *Saturday Evening Post* published during Moore's first few months on the job only fueled the controversy. "This is a school trying quite desperately to prove that it's more normal than unique," commented the author. But the article was quick to point out that "it still isn't quite an ordinary school. The president is hard to find on sunny afternoons, because he is likely to be out flying around somewhere."[45] Although the article gave the impression that Moore was lackadaisical about his duties and more interested in his flying "hobby," it nevertheless highly misrepresented the flying president. During his first year in office, Moore flew numerous administrative trips to the benefit of the university, including ferrying faculty members to remote parts of the territory to conduct some of Alaska's first significant archeological work.[46] Moore flew Helga Larsen to the Seward Peninsula and Otto Geist to Bettles. As the university's first true academic researcher, Geist contributed greatly to the knowledge of Alaska Native lifeways and secured for the University of Alaska museum one of the largest Inupiaq archeological collections in the world.[47]

Still, disgruntled Fairbankers, including former president Charles Bunnell himself, continued to view Moore's flying with disdain. Despite his naysayers, though, Moore's flying broke new ground in Alaska aviation. His mountain flying feats would place him in the same category as the legendary Bob Reeve. Indeed, it was Reeve who perfected the glacier landing technique, but most of his landings and takeoffs were at relatively low altitudes. Moore's contribution was perfecting high-altitude glacier flying, which advanced scientific research in Alaska and greatly benefited the university. Moore achieved his goals flying a Piper Super Cub, Model PA 18, equipped with combination ski and wheel landing gear. This aircraft was the first Piper of that model to arrive in Alaska.[48]

In 1951, Moore and his friend and colleague Bradford Washburn promoted the idea of a high-altitude research station on Mount McKinley for the purpose of cosmic ray and other research. That year Moore made the first airplane landing on the Kahiltna Glacier at seventy-seven hundred feet.[49] For this he attracted the attention of Dr. Serge Korff, a cosmic ray specialist at New York University. Korff and Moore decided that the Wrangell Range, southeast of Fairbanks, might be more accessible than the Alaska Range. In June 1952, Moore flew over the top of fourteen-thousand-foot Mount Wrangell, a shield volcano, on a reconnaissance flight. Unlike the surrounding cone-shaped volcanoes with knife-like peaks, Mount Wrangell's summit rounds more like Seattle's old Kingdome. Its relatively flat, spacious surface provided scientists an environment in which to work and, perhaps more significant, have room to land a plane. It also presented another appealing feature. Because it is an active volcano, portions of Mount Wrangell's summit are bare of snow and hot enough to provide free heat for a research station.[50]

As the university's president, Moore had three objectives for establishing a high-altitude research station on Mount Wrangell. One was the general advancement of science, along with an expansion of the university's capabilities toward that end. A second was to convince the federal government that the University of Alaska was the logical institution to provide logistic support to federal scientific operations in Alaska. Specifically, he wanted the Office of Naval Research, which operated the Naval Arctic Research Laboratory at Point Barrow, to grant administration of the facility to the University of Alaska. In previous years Swarthmore College in Pennsylvania and Johns Hopkins University in Baltimore had run the Barrow Laboratory. Moore hoped that the establishment of the Wrangell Observatory would prove to the scientific community that his university was capable of superior research and thus persuade the federal government. The usually critical university regents agreed with Moore on this point. The administrative body, as did Moore, viewed the federal agency's practice of using East Coast schools to operate the lab as insulting and another example of federal paternalism in Alaska. Finally, the third goal was more personal. By establishing the Wrangell Observatory, Moore could secure himself a job after he left the position of university president and continue to fly in the name of science.[51]

By June 1953 the cooperative cosmic ray project between New York University and the University of Alaska commenced, with Korff as project director and Moore as chief of logistics. Over a period of several days, Moore used his Super Cub to land four members of the first expedition, two from the Geophysical Institute and two from New York University, at the eighty-seven-hundred-foot level on Mount Wrangell. The men then climbed to the fourteen-thousand-foot summit for Moore's first solo landing on June 16. When Moore took off some minutes later, the university's flying president had established a new high-altitude record for aircraft operation in Alaska. Moore went on to make thirty-six consecutive landings atop Mount Wrangell.[52]

The 1953 Wrangell Expedition consisted of Robert Goodwin, Phillip Bettler, Charles "Buck" Wilson, Hugo Newberg, and Arthur Beisler.[53] That July the Air Force flew a C-124 cargo plane over the peak and air-dropped two Jamesway huts and equipment onto the mountaintop.[54] Once retrieved, the researchers assembled the two huts on the exposed rim of the north crater, known by then as Hut Ridge.[55] One hut housed a five-kilowatt generator and food rations while the other was used for a living space. A major consideration for determining the location of the huts was their proximity to the Gulkana and Chitina airstrips.[56] With air support from Moore, the cosmic ray research station was in full operation. Indeed, the academics atop Mount Wrangell were primarily interested in studying cosmic rays and the interaction of geological features such as glaciers and volcanoes, but physiologists with the U.S. Air Force Arctic Aeromedical Laboratory, Robert Elsner and Frederick Milan, studied the Wrangell Mountain scientists. Their interest focused on the physiologic effects of the extreme environment on the human body. The U.S. military was in fact preoccupied with a wide-range of scientific research and development projects taking place at the Wrangell Mountain Observatory in 1953.

The Wrangell Observatory soundly demonstrated to the scientific community that the University of Alaska was capable of conducting scientific operations in the Far North. Moore therefore successfully convinced the Office of Naval Research that the University of Alaska was capable of facilitating its particular scientific endeavors and to award the university administration of the Arctic Naval Research laboratory at Barrow. Ongoing disagreements, however, between the president of the university and the Board of Regents finally led to Moore's resignation in the midst of the scientific activity in 1953. Although he left the office, Moore fully intended to continue his work overseeing the university's research program at the Wrangell Observatory. In his resignation letter Moore wrote: "I believe that the opportunities in our proposed Mount Wrangell Intra-University Research project are so promising that I can most usefully make my next contribution to the University by devoting full attention to it beginning in the early summer of 1953."[57] In 1954, Ernest Patty not only replaced

Moore but he seized all credit for securing the Barrow research laboratory. Patty made the official announcement of the award the day after he claimed the office of the president, giving little recognition to his predecessor. Even though Moore did as promised—he successfully developed a research facility atop Mount Wrangell, bringing acclaimed recognition to the University of Alaska–Fairbanks—Patty nevertheless informed Moore that the Board of Regents had decided to terminate him from university employment entirely.[58]

In an act likely even more disheartening than leaving his position at the university, Moore turned over the Wrangell Observatory flights to Cordova Airlines's experienced bush pilot Herb Haley. As skilled as Haley was as a pilot, landing on Mount Wrangell was nothing he had attempted before. During one of his first mountaintop landings, Haley's Super Cub's nose hit the snow, flipping the plane onto its backside. With skis and tail facing skyward, Haley reported back to base: "Hello, Gulkana, I have just landed on Mt. Wrangell!!" It took six hours of digging in the snow by the pilot and the observatory crew before the Cordova Airlines plane was turned right side up. Despite crashing at one of the most inhospitable environments in the world, Haley showed no sign of panic. The competent pilot filled the tank with regular automotive gasoline and flew safely off the mountain.[59] Cordova Airlines served the scientists that entire summer, bringing them their mail and other "goodies" from home.[60] But with advancements in balloon technology making it possible to lift cosmic ray measuring instruments to even higher altitudes, the future of the Wrangell Observatory was in doubt. Without Moore—the observatory's champion, ambassador, and logistical administrator—the research project languished after 1954.

In the end, Alaska's flying president left a legacy of scientific administration and promotion from which the opportunities for the development of far-flung facilities in Alaska were wide open. A few years later, in 1959, Moore landed and took off from the summit of nearby Mount Sanford, setting a new high-altitude world record.[61] Although narrow minds chose not to recognize Moore for his efforts, the student newspaper seemed to appreciate their independent, progressive, and altruistic leader, writing: "The spirit of adventure extends to the president of the university, Dr. Terris Moore, who is a member of the Explorer's Club, flies his own plane, and doesn't hesitate to go scouting for lost planes, down somewhere in the Wilderness."

For more than a century, glaciers have attracted scientific attention. Before World War II, activity in North American glaciology focused largely on an orderly approach to understanding the physical properties and behavior of glaciers. Field and laboratory research was carried on by a small group of senior scientists, of whom Walter Wood, president of the American Geographical Society, wrote, "established a firm base on which to build, and whose enthusiasm began to encourage younger men to enter the field."[62] The impact of operations in far northern areas after World War II intensified interest in ice and glaciers especially with the International Geophysical Year, a public relations effort in 1957–58 designed to bring the earth, atmospheric, and ocean sciences into the classrooms and living rooms of the lay public to attract more students into scientific careers. U.S. participation in international science finally opened the gates to glaciological opportunities. Moreover, this new enthusiasm in the discipline gave the Wrangell Mountain Observatory a new purpose.

In 1961, Carl Benson, a glaciologist from the University of Alaska's Geophysical Institute, began conducting research at the site. The observatory was the perfect location for Benson's work. Its high altitude and latitude location, not to mention its central position in the Wrangells and surrounding Chugach and Saint Elias Ranges, gave Benson the opportunity to study more than his share of snowfall. The massive mountain peaks constantly intercept major storms from the North Pacific, for the Wrangells alone have an area of continuous snow and ice cover that exceeds five thousand square kilometers.[63] As Benson put it, the environment surrounding the Wrangell Mountain Observatory has "the most magnificent and extensive array of mountain glaciers outside of the polar regions." But what set the observatory above other research laboratories is that Mount Wrangell is a volcano—a huge, glacier-mantled shield volcano—and the fortuitous location of the observatory provided Benson an excellent opportunity to study glacier-volcano interactions. "On Wrangell alone, outside the Antarctic," explained Benson, "can you study the relation of an active cone to a great ice cap."[64]

Benson spent several summers on Wrangell studying the volcano and the numerous glaciers that flow off its flanks, including Nabesna Icefield, Copper Glacier, and Long Glacier. Benson started with several goals: He wanted to study the effects of volcanic heating on Wrangell's ice cap and glaciers in an effort to learn how much the volcano is actually heating up, and perhaps to warn of a future eruption.[65] In addition, Benson was interested in determining the reasons for Mount Wrangell's flattened dome. Benson speculated that the flat shape may be at least partially the result of subglacial eruptions.[66]

Although gone from the university, Terris Moore continued to support the Wrangell Observatory, both financially and logistically. Support also came from the U.S. Army Cold Regions Research and Engineering Laboratory.[67] Benson and his team of researchers lived and worked from a tent camp established on snow in the North Crater. That first summer the team was forced to chip out a shelter from one of the ice-encased huts from 1953 when their tents were destroyed in a storm. The team constructed another hut farther up the ridge in 1964. Benson and the other scientists designed the hut to be geothermally heated. Unfortunately, in 1964 the volcano began heating up, and by 1973 the hut was uninhabitable.[68]

For flight support the geologists chartered bush pilot Jack Wilson and his Super Cub to fly themselves, their gear, and scientific equipment to the summit of Mount Wrangell. Wilson, who represented a second generation of flyers in eastern Alaska, followed trails blazed by "Glacier Pilot" Bob Reeve and became known as a superb glacier pilot in his own right. As author Gerry Bruder put it, "Valdez's Bob Reeve may have pioneered glacier work, and Talkeetna's Don Sheldon certainly got more publicity for it, but the unofficial title 'Dean of the Glacier Pilots' fits Wilson well."[69] As a kid growing up in Montana, Jack Wilson dreamed about glacier flying.[70] He served as a pilot during World War II, visited Alaska in 1951, liked what he saw, and returned permanently the following year. At the time, Cordova Airlines was looking for a pilot with mountain flying experience to take over the company's bush routes.[71] Within three years, Jack Wilson and his new bride, Jo Edwards (King), joined pilot Herb Haley in Chitina to manage flights into the Copper Belt region.[72]

That first summer, Wilson's efforts focused on the Copper Belt mail run. By the end of summer the pilot knew each peak and valley of the Wrangell Mountains' terrain. At first he studied every map he could find detailing the region between Cordova to Tok. During his cross-country flights, especially when skies cleared and the topography opened below, Wilson spent each minute memorizing the route. After years of deliberate and thoughtful flying, he could navigate the Wrangell Mountains and much of the surrounding landscape without using those charts or maps.[73]

He even learned to land on Mount Wrangell at the observatory by trial and error. "First, I flew up loads of gear alone," wrote Wilson in his memoir *Glacier Wings and Tales*. "This let me find out just about how much weight I could get up there with. . . . I got Carl and his men up there as well, along with plenty of gear and food in case of a long spell of bad weather."[74]

Years later Carl Benson wrote about his trusty pilot: "To fly with Jack at high altitude in the mountains must be like flying with an eagle—he finds and uses thermal updrafts better than anyone else I have flown with."[75] Wilson eventually made sixty-nine ski and wheeled landings at the summit between 1961 and 1965. His extraordinary feat did not go unnoticed. In 1979 the Geophysical Institute, Carl Benson, and Governor Bill Egan honored Wilson at the Copper Center Roadhouse with a plaque that read: "In appreciation to Jack Wilson for 25 years of flying service to research expeditions on Mount Wrangell, Alaska, including 69 ski landings at the summit."

The development of logistic techniques pioneered by Terris Moore and carried on by Cordova Airlines pilots like Herb Haley and Jack Wilson enabled University of Alaska's Geophysical Institute researchers to expand the field of earth science, obtaining for all Alaskans a better understanding of the total environment. Through aerial support, scientists were able to study some of Alaska's most impossible-to-reach places—and that research continues to this day. The Geophysical Institute has maintained the Wrangell facility ever since, using it more or less annually for the valuable study of the interaction between volcanoes and snow and ice. By the 1950s the impact of World War II and the Cold War on aviation was profound. But beyond spies, surveyors, and scientists, this watershed period also brought to Alaska the largest population gain in history. The thousands of military personnel stationed in Alaska came to enjoy the recreational opportunities the landscape afforded, especially sport hunting. One of the most popular destinations for big game trophy hunters in the territory was the Wrangell Mountains. This new market created fresh opportunities for local pilots, and one of the first to take them to their destinations was none other than Cordova Airlines pilot Jack Wilson.

10

Flying Huntsmen

WHILE LEARNING THE LANDSCAPE OF EASTERN ALASKA FOR NAVI-
gational and safety purposes, Jack Wilson became enamored with its
natural, raw beauty. In addition to his regular mail route and random
charters, he flew anglers to the glacially carved Tebay Lakes, near Bremner Mine in the Chugach Mountains, which were part of the Sourdough
Tours offered by Cordova Airlines. Merle Smith encouraged his newest
employee and his wife, Jo Edwards, to establish a camp at the lake to
attract what he called the "well-heeled" fly fishermen. Smith bought a new
125 Super Cub on floats to fly in the customers. "Except for the winter we
spent in the ghost town of McCarthy," explained Edwards, "Jack and I
alternated between living at the scenic, primitive, spectacularly beautiful
Tebay camp and our own rough-hew cabin in Chitina."[1]

When the hunting season began in the fall, Smith moved Jack and
Jo to the CAS cabin at the McCarthy airstrip to cater to the hunters
quickly replacing tourists as the main guests at the McCarthy Lodge. As Jo
explained, "He [Smith] knew that Jack and I had been raised on ranches
and that I was very fond of horses. He reasoned that if Jack were stationed in McCarthy, then I would be available to take care of the lodge
and the six packhorses that he had inherited along with it."[2] While Jo
tended to the horses and ran the lodge, Wilson flew sheep hunters to the
high mountain country in the Cessna 180. It was on these trips that Wilson recognized an emerging niche for pilots in the Wrangell Mountains.
"I was interested in the great Dall rams I was seeing," recalled Wilson. "I
resolved to learn all I could about these sheep and become a sheep guide.
I spent many an hour flying and observing them. I looked for good places
to land a wheel plane and by the time I later went on my own, I had a good

knowledge of the country and the Dall sheep."[3] With Wilson flying most days, Jo did what she could to stay busy, while alone much of the time in McCarthy.

Contemplations about the couple's future suddenly, and rather sadly, became reality. That autumn, Jack's mentor and colleague Herb Haley died in a crash in southwest Alaska. Merle Smith hired pilot Howard Knutson to take over Cordova Airlines management at Chitina. Jack Wilson, however, had other plans. "I certainly missed that good old man," lamented Wilson. "He had been talking of retiring the next year."[4] The loss of Haley likely sparked Wilson to follow his dreams of becoming a hunting guide/pilot. Likely influencing his decision to leave Cordova Airlines was the additional flight time tasked to Wilson after Haley's death. This also caused the disintegration of his marriage. Forced to spend the long winter in McCarthy, Jo decided that this life was not for her. Consequently, Jack and Jo decided to split up. Jo went on to her own bush piloting fame. Besides co-owning an air-taxi service in Chitina, she become an FAA air traffic controller in Alaska, earning the prestigious FAA National Outstanding Air Traffic Controller Award and the Pilots Association award for Outstanding Service for saving a pilot and his passengers by talking them through whiteout conditions.[5] Jo eventually returned to McCarthy, where she married local big-game guide Harley King. For Jack Wilson, he decided to quit his job at Cordova Airlines to strike out on his own. If he wanted to become a Dall sheep hunting guide, he couldn't do it while flying for an airline.

BLAZING HIS OWN TRAIL

Jack Wilson wasted no time. He started Wilson Flying Service early in 1956, basing the small charter business out of Chitina, the same base location of his former employer-turned-competitor Cordova Airlines. "To say that Smitty was displeased with Wilson decision would be an understatement," recalled Smith son, Kenny Smith. "Smitty operated Cordova Airlines much the same as early cattle barons managed livestock in the west. They believed they controlled the respective rangeland, even though it was public, and nobody better intrude. Smitty thought the same way except with the air. Jack had decided not only to fly in Smitty's air but in competition with him and worst of all in Smitty's beloved Wrangell Mountain territory." As the younger Smith put it, "the war was on."[6]

Competition from Cordova Airlines, however, made Chitina a hard place to do business, so in 1959, Wilson expanded his operation to Gulkana Airfield, located just six miles northeast of Glennallen. There, Wilson accumulated a fleet consisting of a used 180 Cessna and a used 150 Super Cub. Both planes would serve him well throughout his independent flying career, a period that would span nearly thirty years. Besides flying exclusively for the university researchers at the Wrangell Observatory who by then were comfortable with his high mountain flying skills, Wilson's first customer as his own boss was the U.S. Geological Survey, there to map the country and place benchmarks in remote locations. During the mid-1940s and early 1950s the returned interest to mining sent exploration teams into the wilderness. Once these federal geologists made the detailed topography maps available to the public, private mining interests quickly followed them like modern-day treasure hunters. By midcentury, geological teams chartered fixed-wing airplanes, which required an appropriate place to land and take back off. This meant that geologists still had to climb the mountains, usually moving from one location to another with the use of horses. After the mid-1950s, however, geologists began to utilize the industry's newest technological tool: the helicopter.

The rising use of helicopters by geologists, and by extension the mining industry, underscored an increasing reliance on aviation generally. As Wilson pointed out, "Even though mining companies started to use helicopters, they still relied upon the bush pilots to bring them fuel, food, and mechanical support. The helicopters needed considerable maintenance to keep them going, which meant flying mechanics and parts back and forth."[7] Still, such advancements in aviation not only complemented but expanded twentieth-century exploration—geologists could now identify an area of interest by referring to aerial photographs taken from a fixed-wing aircraft, and then be dropped off by helicopter to complete more detailed, accurate, yet less time-consuming fieldwork.[8] Being able to land practically anywhere was one reason geologists put choppers to use. The ability to hover in one place for an indefinite period of time proved to be invaluable in aerial surveys, salvage operations, and all levels of aerial reconnaissance.[9] Though still dangerous and costly, helicopters without doubt made access into the most remote wilderness areas easier.

By the late 1950s Jack Wilson began to notice that more privately employed helicopters were appearing in the Wrangell Mountains. Their presence, as Wilson observed, scared the sheep inhabiting many of the mountains geologists were exploring. "The sound of the helicopter coming absolutely terrorized the sheep," wrote Wilson. "They would panic badly and run as far and fast as they could."[10] This created a dilemma for the pilot who made a living servicing the mining companies but was in his heart a sheep hunter and guide. One helicopter pilot told Wilson that he always tried to circle at least once before he came within sight of the sheep to give them a chance to move away from the area he was taking his passengers. As Wilson reasoned, "The helicopter pilots did not want to scare the sheep but they had their jobs to think of and had to perform for the company."[11] Ten years later, nearly every large airport in the region maintained a helicopter landing pad.[12] Wilson, too, had branched into the helicopter business, acquiring a new five-place Alouette utility helicopter to service mining camps in the nearby Wrangell Mountains.[13]

THE START OF FLY-IN TROPHY HUNTS

The Gulkana Airfield was a good match for Wilson's services. The airfield was considered a modern field from the beginning—paved, with gas pumps, underground tanks, and phone service. The FAA had a flight service station there for weather reporting and airport advisories.[14] The Gulkana Airfield was located on Alaska's growing road system, good for bringing in the occasional curious, albeit adventurous, tourist. The field was completed about the same time as the Alaska-Canadian (Alcan) Highway, which connected Gulkana not only to Fairbanks but to the Lower 48 as well. Most significant, Gulkana was centrally located for flying to the nearby Chugach Mountains or the Wrangell Mountains, or even to the unmapped Saint Elias ice fields in the Yukon Territory, which were increasingly becoming target destinations for international scientists and mountain climbers alike. "I knew that boundless, faraway region very well," recalled Wilson, "map or no map."[15] But of all the air services offered in those early days, what Wilson was most prepared for, and liked to do best, was outfitting "fly-in" hunts to the mountain peaks filled with Dall sheep.

Wilson's customers were by no means the first to hunt the big sheep populations of the Wrangell–Saint Elias Mountains. As the last great Alaska gold rush at Chisana passed into history, replacing the hundreds of prospectors en route to the gold fields was a handful of elite big game hunters, primarily from the East Coast, looking for trophy-size mega fauna in the "game fields up the White River behind the St. Elias mountain range."[16] In 1918, John B. Burnham wrote a letter to James McGuire predicting that "if not today, the time is not far distant when in dollars and cents sheep will be the most valuable game in North America. Sportsmen will go farther for sheep than any other game except bears."[17] Burnham's prediction was indeed correct and the year it seemingly proved true was 1959. Fly-in hunts were growing in popularity in the Wrangells, and, as the term implied, bush pilots were hired to fly hunters into choice spots for them to hunt.

Before Wilson started guiding himself, his business served to transport hunters to their outfitters, particularly nonresident hunters. Wilson Flying Service picked hunters up from their flights into Anchorage and ferried them to Gulkana, where they were transferred to smaller planes and flown to their outfitter's base camp in the Wrangell Mountains.[18] Unfortunately for the hunters, many of the local outfits were novices and for the most part unsuccessful. By 1959, however, Wilson had learned from the more experienced pilots about both flying in the country as well as the sheep themselves.[19] He spent much of his time prospecting for good sheep hunting areas in his Super Cub. It also meant looking for natural places to land so that he could bring hunters to the sheep.

Wilson, like most longtime Alaska sheep hunters, considered the particular brand of hunting special, primarily because it was hard. Only the best hunters were successful. Outdoorsmen everywhere viewed sheep hunting an art, which required specific knowledge of "woods lore," a sense of tracking, strong legs, and keen marksmanship. In 1918 big game hunter James McGuire wrote: "The successful sheep hunter must, perforce, have the game vision developed to the very highest order of perfection. He should be a good climber, strong of heart and limb. . . . The prime requisites are a cool head, ordinary ability to judge distances quickly, and good marksmanship qualities." Even with all his hunting experience, McGuire did not profess to be an expert sheep hunter. "If I could consider myself such I would feel that I had reached the very highest pinnacle of hunting proficiency."[20] Even today, only about 40 percent of hunters that seek rams manage to bag a ram each year.[21]

In 1960, Wilson passed his registered guide exam and guided three hunters into the Wrangells from which they took big-trophy Dall rams.

In 1961 he guided Anchorage resident Harry L. Swank into the Wrangells and bagged a world-record Dall ram.[22] Access to Wilson's self-discovered sheep areas required places for him to land his plane and set up a base camp. As a result, he built several airstrips in the Wrangells for the purpose of hunting exploited sheep populations. At first he made a couple of airstrips near the headwaters of the Chitina River, which unlike past big game hunts into the region were located on the southern flanks of the Saint Elias Mountains. He managed to land up in an undisclosed area known as the "Slot" about three miles above the terminus of the Chitina Glacier. Building an airstrip usually meant a lot of brush removal, moving rotten logs and big rocks, and filling holes. Then Wilson became more ambitious. He found his bonanza, known aptly as Sheep Gulch. "It was only a short flight from my base at Chitina to this chosen place," recalled a coy Wilson in his description of the site's exact location.[23] "We cropped our sheep," he explained, "trying to never over-hunt it [Sheep Gulch]. We had some good hunts, both with nonresident guided hunts and with fly-in hunts. Over a number of years we had some easy hunting and there were three directions to go to find sheep in plentiful numbers."[24]

THE SHEEP RUSH AND ITS COSTS

Wilson, however, did not remain the only fly-in sheep hunting guide in the so-called virgin country, for there were other bush pilots attracted to the region after the war. By 1957, Chisana had replaced McCarthy as the hub for regional hunting. Cordova Airlines expanded the bush strip there so that its pilots could fly in food for packhorses in its DC-3.[25] The airline continued to fill its DC-3 with nonresident hunters, ferrying the hunting parties between Anchorage and the strip at May Creek. Howard Knutson, who replaced Wilson at Cordova Airlines, arranged all the fly-in hunting trips for the airline. Flying mostly sheep hunting charters, Knutson would transport groups in the company's Cessna 180 and pick them up in the Super Cub. During the peak of the season, Knutson might have fifty to sixty hunters in the field. Although he earned his guide license in 1959, he rarely used it, for he spent nearly all his time flying hunters around the Wrangell Mountains.

Another of the Wrangell's independent, small hunting businesses belonged to Bud and LeNora Conkles, who in 1951 started a big game hunting lodge on Lake Tanada, located about seven miles from Nabesna

Road. "We were into the beginning of a new era," wrote LeNora, in her memoir *Bush Pilots' Wives*, "when small aircraft was replacing the outfitters who booked thirty days hunts, using pack and saddle horses in their business."[26] Though the Conkles subscribed to the concept of fair chase, not everyone coming to the Wrangells to set up sheep hunting fly-in businesses did. One day in 1964, LeNora recalled that her husband returned from the sheep hills and informed her he was getting tired of the competition from the Anchorage-based pilot-guides crowding the areas where he had his camps and hunters set out: "This particular day had him about as upset as I have ever seen him," wrote LeNora. "Two Super Cubs flying together had deliberately buzzed the rams away from his hunters. Those two clients' camps were on a lake at the base of the mountain they had climbed and almost reached the Dall rams they would shoot. Bud had his special descriptive words to describe the unethical pilots who overbooked clients and were not particular where they set them out to hunt, even if there were other hunters in the same area. Bud was considered a fair chase guide and outfitter. He knew who those pilots were but left them for the Fish and Game agents to control."[27]

Competition among local and outside big game guides continued to worsen. Howard Knutson described hunting guides as "territorial" and recalled incidences of airstrip sabotage, personal threats, and downright physical violence.[28] By the 1970s local guides and pilots had a number of airstrips and adjacent cabin facilities on public lands, intended basically for their own use. Although some were on patented sites, most use was considered trespassing with no legal basis for the hunting operation, but nevertheless use patterns among guides was generally respected. From 1967 through 1976 sixty-eight of the top two hundred listings in the Boone and Crockett Club records were from the Wrangell Mountains, and those taking the trophies were mostly guided nonresidents flown in by plane.[29] With the increase of outside guides into the region, reports of dynamiting strips to block use by competitors, and frequent blocking of strips with barrels to prevent access by the public or other guides, increased.[30]

Whether guides practiced fair chase methods or not, the sheer number of hunters flying into the region caused the abundant sheep populations of the Wrangells to decline. Forty-two percent of all trophy-size rams (harvested animals with horns forty inches or longer) were taken from the Wrangells. And the numbers, according to a study conducted by University of Alaska biologist Frederick C. Dean, had dropped considerably.[31] This led to the deterioration of the quality of the hunts, because guides could no longer assure clients of a wilderness experience or access to a sheep herd that somebody else had not recently disturbed.[32]

It was most decisively the watershed period encapsulated by World War II and the Cold War that reopened the area to sport hunters on a scale never before seen. Renewed interest, however, came at a cost. "Demographic, technologic, and economic growth triggered by the military buildup," wrote historian Morgan Sherwood in his definitive study *Big Game in Alaska*, "marked the beginning of the end of Alaska's frontier innocence and endangered the most fragile part of the wilderness—the big game animals."[33] In the 1950s, the most active period of military buildup in Alaska, activity-duty personnel accounted for 21 percent of the total Alaska population. In 1952 alone the percentage reached 26 percent. When immediate family members of active-duty personnel—Defense Department civil servants and their families, base and commissary employees, Alaska army and Air National Guardsmen, military reservist and their families—as well as military retirees and their families were factored into the equation, the percentage of Alaska's population associated with the military jumped to nearly half.[34]

Unlike centuries of Alaskans who primarily hunted for subsistence purpose, the territory's increasing postwar population embraced the Progressive era's passion of hunting for sport. By the end of the 1940s Ahtna Natives scattered in bands throughout the Wrangell–Saint Elias area were forced to settle in towns like Northway or Chistochina. "We could not live any longer in Nabesna," explained Nabesna Bar resident Jack John Justin Jr., "'cause game commission had too many laws, and not enough food. People moved to the road where they could live."[35] After a brief visit to the region in July 1946 on behalf of the U.S. Office of Indian Affairs, Walter R. Goldschmidt observed several negative impacts on local Native people by increasing military personnel, especially the airmen at the Northway Airfield: "The men of the post engaged in hunting of game which resulted in a serious reduction of the wildlife population," wrote Goldschmidt. "Natives whose very life depended upon the fur and meat animals were filled with resentment at soldiers who shot for mere pleasure, frequently not even picking up the carcasses of the animals so destroyed."[36]

Many of the postwar newcomers lacked the previous generation's sportsman code. Instead, they subscribed to the belief that all sportsmen had the democratic right to shoot wild animals whenever they chose—and to make a living while doing it. Driving the activity's popularity and its egalitarian principles were the record high number of military personnel granted resident hunting rights during the war, including General Simon Bolivar Buckner Jr., who took the Alaska Game Commission to court for the right to hunt on the same terms as any resident Alaskan.[37] The increase in the number of hunters in the postwar years coincided with the reduction of the cost of hunting in remote regions such as the Wrangell–Saint Elias with the availability of small aircraft for transport. By the end of the 1950s, explained NPS historian William Hunt, sports hunting in the Wrangell–Saint Elias Mountains had experienced a complete transformation: "What had been an expensive, elitist venture became a sporting exercise available to almost anyone."[38]

With the rising competition and falling sheep population, guides like Jack Wilson started to outfit moose hunters, flying them into "Jack's Moose Camp" near Mount Drum. As required by law, Wilson used guides to help him with the nonresident hunters. Wilson and his guide chose a spot on the upper Sanford River for their base camp. At the time, the area was virtually unknown and moose were numerous. During a hunt Wilson would land the party on the Mount Drum side of the river. His guide then led the hunters through the timber to above tree line, where he "glassed" the country."[39]

As the 1960s came to a close, sport hunting, despite the declining sheep numbers in the Wrangells, was on the rise. By the mid-1970s approximately 250 guides from both sides of the border flew into the area.[40] These were pilots of experience, many of whom maintained a better sense of the resources than the game mangers. "Most resident guides belonged to the group that established themselves in the region and maintained a proprietary interest by selectively harvesting game for the hunting groups," wrote researcher Michael Lappen in his study of the Wrangell–Saint Elias region.[41] But a minority group representing the so-called rover guides indiscriminately targeted wildlife without regard for fellow guides or the future of their business. Several hunting groups responded by advocating horse hunts as the only "sporting" way to hunt in the backcountry.[42]

Although the State of Alaska established guiding boards and territories in the mid-1970s in an effort to curtail the mindless hunting practices and ensuing conflicts between guides, competition for game nevertheless persisted.[43] In later years Wilson lamented the popular practice of fly-in hunting. "It can be argued that it was entirely wrong and not sporting at all," admitted Wilson. "I knew that was a sound argument with a lot of merit. Yet we did it anyway. In the Old West men had exploited the riches of the new country with a will, and we were no different. As long as there was no law against a lucrative enterprise we did it—whether right or wrong."[44]

11

Creating an Airplane Culture

WITH MERLE SMITH STILL AT THE HELM, CORDOVA AIRLINES OPER-
ated a reliable and professional business throughout the 1960s, serving
the Copper Belt region and beyond. From Anchorage, Smith's airline flew
regularly to Seward. It flew east over the Chugach Mountains to Gulkana,
Chitina, McCarthy, Chisana, Valdez, and Cordova. Tebay, May Creek, and
Glacier Creek were served on a flag-stop basis. From Cordova the airline
serviced Boswell Bay, Katella and Yakataga, then south to Middleton
Island in the Gulf of Alaska, where the military maintained a Cold War-
era White Alice site, and then around Prince William Sound in a circle
route that served a number of canneries and villages.[1] Smith himself no
longer flew; he was grounded in the early 1950s by diabetes.

Smith's airline, however, was by no means the only ride in town. By
the mid-1960s more powerfully manufactured planes coupled with a
postwar corporate business model had commenced the "golden age of the
airline" in Alaska aviation. The much larger Pacific Northern Airlines (PNA)
competed with Cordova Airlines for passengers and freight in towns such
as Anchorage, Cordova, Yakutat, and Juneau. With the rise of the petro-
leum industry in Cook Inlet, Smith attempted to take on his competitor
with plans to expand into the Kenai market. In 1966 he requested from
the Civil Aeronautics Board an extension of its certified Route 124, into
Kenai/Soldotna, arguing that the bigger air carrier neglected the peninsula's smaller communities because of its long-haul service requirements
between Anchorage and Seattle. Because Gulkana Airport served as the
central communications and business areas of the Copper River valley,
Smith also requested that Gulkana, categorized only as a temporary point
on Cordova Airlines Route 124, be designated to an intermediate point

between Chitina and McCarthy. The reorganization would give Smith more operational flexibility in the area and would make the airline eligible for federal subsidy.[2] To determine if indeed amending Cordova Airlines Route 124 was convenient and necessary for the public, the CAB investigated, recommending in 1967 that Gulkana in fact be reassigned. But despite Smith's complaints that his airline had been given little opportunity to keep pace with the expansion of air transportation in Alaska—noting that his contemporaries who started regional airlines such as Wien Air Alaska, Northern Consolidated Airlines, and Reeve Aleutian Airways were two to six times larger than Cordova Airlines—his request to expand into Kenai was denied.[3]

Due in part to the CAB ruling, Smith looked elsewhere for opportunities to grow his airline. His dim prospects appeared to brighten with the chance to help create the largest air carrier in Alaska. The age of the airline—typified by corporations, mergers, and bureaucracy—seemingly flew in the face of Alaska's notion of frontier independence. Yet it was reasoned that incorporation would eventually lead to less reliance on the federal government. In a press release announcing the approval of the latest merger of Cordova Airlines, the CAB even made note that the goal was to achieve financial independence by incorporating a weaker carrier, with a limited route structure and severe financial difficulties, into a stronger carrier. This process, according to the CAB, would lead to self-sufficiency. The board even predicted that a merger with Cordova's routes could ultimately operate without subsidy.[4] Smith, too, saw the benefits that merging with a larger air carrier would bring. Primarily it meant deeper resources and new operational areas. Smith thus decided to merge Cordova Airlines with six other companies in 1968 to become one of the most successful air carriers in the country: Alaska Airlines.[5]

Although Alaska Airlines represented the cutting edge in modern aviation, the company embraced Smith's strategy of nostalgic tourism, promoting frontier tours to its vast clientele throughout Alaska and the Pacific Northwest. In fact, the exclusive route of Cordova Airlines into Canada was the main reason Alaska Air sought the merger in the first place.[6] With Cordova's newly acquired "Convair-Liner," Alaska Airlines commenced the highly popular Golden Nugget Service in 1968, which featured a Gay '90s motif, accentuated by an on-board piano bar and flight attendants dressed as can-can girls. "Even the ticket counters and city ticket offices were dressed up with the Gay '90s look, using special wallpaper and lighting fixtures disguised as nineteenth century lamps," recalled an Alaska Airlines employee.[7] Indeed the new company's direction seemed to align with Smith's own business philosophy and history regarding frontier Alaska and its salability in the modern age.

After Cordova's merger with Alaska Airlines, the company recognized the need to continue bush service in the Copper Belt country. It established a subsidiary called Chitina Air Service that catered to the outlying communities on regularly scheduled routes. Kenneth "Kenny" Smith, Merle Smith's son, served as a pilot and manager for the new company. In 1965 he was the first pilot to land his mail plane on the new McCarthy runway. The event renewed a sense of optimism that echoed the days of 1911, when the Copper River & Northwestern Railway had opened for business and promised access to both mineral wealth and a brighter future.[8] This was not the case earlier that decade, when the new State of Alaska's outlook for economic sustainability, especially in the decade before the Prudhoe Bay oil discovery, was bleak. To simulate growth, Alaska voters passed Proposition 3 in November 1962, approving a $4,175,000 bond for the construction of new trunk airports, which would serve the busiest and most desirable routes across the state.[9] Meanwhile, the private mining company Consolidated Wrangell had recently acquired all the surface property rights at the Kennecott Mill complex and hoped to remove as much of the higher-quality copper ore as it possibly could during the summer season. The plan, according to pilot Kenny Smith, was to fly out the ore.[10]

Wanting to avoid the hassle of flying ore out of the larger May Creek field, Consolidated Wrangell offered to start construction on the McCarthy field themselves in spring 1965.[11] The company persuaded Howard Knutson to leave Cordova Airlines to work for them. Knutson's first job was to determine the direction of the new strip. After flying several angles he marked the best direction by laying out toilet tissue down the center line and the plane followed the tissue. The ideal direction of the strip, however, crossed private property. Knutson approached each of the landholders who eventually donated the land for the new strip.[12] With fifteen thousand dollars for ten thousand gallons of diesel to run the construction equipment, the state engineers, together with Knutson, completed the strip in twenty-two days, using the last barrel of diesel for the grader. (They actually ran out of fuel, so the original runway was higher in the middle.) Tailings from Kennecott were hauled in to surface the original runway.[13]

Knutson recalled that the field was big enough to land a Fairchild

C-119, the so-called Flying Boxcar, and the C-122, which were used transport the copper ore out of Kennecott and made investors "a pretty good profit." The copper was eventually sold in Japan.[14] Once the mining operation was complete, Consolidated Wrangell abandoned its Kennecott claims and, in doing so, left behind the second and significantly larger airfield in the McCarthy townsite. The Alaska Department of Transportation assumed control of the new field while pilots throughout the Copper Belt quickly began putting it to use. By the 1970s general aviation had caught up with commercial aviation and with it, a renewed sense of frontier independence.

The new field proved to be functional enough for Consolidated Wrangell, who finished mining Kennecott's original discovery. The company made numerous successfully landings and takeoffs of a C-122, containing fourteen to sixteen, fifty-five gallon barrels of copper, weighing twelve hundred pounds each. Because the runway alignment at the original airstrip posed a potential hazard to the new airport, FAA's Flight Standards Division recommended that the state abandon (rather than officially close) the old airstrip.[15] Thus the first airstrip to be constructed in the Wrangells, used for so long as a base in the Copper Belt country for skyboys such as Harold Gillam, Bob Reeve, Kirk Kirkpatrick, and Merle "Mudhole" Smith, faded from memory while the new McCarthy airport made way for the future. Specifically, the new McCarthy airport made access into the heart of the Wrangells more obtainable than any time since the abandonment of the Copper River & Northwestern Railway in 1938. Consequently, readily available air travel in McCarthy had an almost contradictory effect: it attracted wilderness seekers hoping to access "untouched" places, while at the same time, it muted residents' desire for roads.

AIRPLANE PEOPLE

Without an airplane McCarthy and its surrounding environs were nearly impossible to reach. The only alternative access into town was by a narrow sixty-mile nail-strewn dirt road starting in Chitina, which followed the old CR&NW railbed route. Even if drivers made it safely over the road, hazards abounded. Most pertinently, McCarthy lacked automobile access from the west side of the Kennicott River. Instead of a bridge, a hand-powered tram trolley car carried individuals across a turbulent and angry river draining the Kennicott and Root Glaciers. But the difficult and old-fashioned nature of accessing McCarthy was an obstacle that many residents actually chose. Although they favored the idea of easier access to the mountains for activities like mining and mountaineering, they nevertheless preferred to make access into their town hard, particularly for the causal automobile driver.

The business community, for example, felt they profited from a bad road because it forced tourists, who might normally drive in with a camper, to fly in and use the hotel facilities available in the town. Others felt that if the road was better maintained and a bridge for road traffic built, it would only attract the undesirable sort: outside hunters who would compete with locals for the scarce resources and potential looters looking to abscond with objects from the area's historic mining sites.[16] For nearly all McCarthy's residents, the town's self-imposed inaccessibility reflected an overall disenchantment with modern life, especially city life, and the community's highly valued self-sufficient way of life.[17]

Central to that independent and unique lifestyle was the airplane, which as one observer described, was used on a "neighborly basis."[18] Conducting fieldwork in the Wrangell Mountain region for the National Park Service in the early 1970s, anthropologist Holly Reckord found evidence of a fully emerged, airplane-dependent culture. Flying over the McCarthy road she counted fifty or sixty residents scattered among fifteen family homesteads. She estimated that over half of them had access to an airplane.[19] It was not unusual for Reckord to observe residents driving pickup trucks to the Kennicott River, then "hopping" over to McCarthy by plane. "Air travel makes Kennicott and McCarthy the communities what they are," noted Reckord. "Without airplane access, most of the people would not live in this area."[20]

The resident population of McCarthy in the early 1970s had burgeoned from five or six to almost thirty. McCarthy's "airplane people," as Reckord called them, consisted of two lodge owners, a couple of local prospectors, and a handful of townspeople. In her study Reckord describes friends "airhopping" from one fishing hole to the next or attending social gatherings held in distant valleys. Even the "non-plane people," Reckord noted, had access to airplanes. Chitina Air Service or the Kennecott Lodge airplane provided charters to Chitina or to any of the small airstrips around the upper Nizina, Chisana, or other areas of the Wrangells. One McCarthy woman told Reckord that she made crafts and other items to barter for airplane rides.[21]

In summer, area pilots made four round-trip flights to Anchorage each week to bring in groceries. The mail was also flown in weekly by pilots like Jim Edwards. On hearing the familiar hum of Jim's engine, nearly all the town's residents ventured out from their cabins to greet the plane. They picked up their packages and letters and, above all, they socialized. Folks often took hours catching up with neighbors, discussing local news, and commenting on the continued growth of children.[22] During the hunting season, airplanes constantly buzzed the town, bringing in hunters from outside. Some of these hunters stayed at the lodge but most continued on to hunting camps located throughout the Wrangells.[23] Residents also relied on airplanes for personal use or subsistence hunting. Because so many people flew airplanes, reports on game sightings between Chitina and McCarthy were commonly circulated throughout the community. But as competition from nonresident hunters rose and available game declined, the use of airplanes reassured McCarthy families that they could still stock their pantries with store-bought goods. No one in McCarthy doubted the airplane was the central feature of life in their town. The machine served as a safety net and tied them to the land and together as a community.

Reckord found that airplane use was even more necessary in the isolated communities scattered throughout the Copper Belt. Residents living along the Nizina River utilized the developed airfields at Dan Creek and May Creek, but many also had their own strips or cleared off a strip on a nearby gravel bar. Airplanes gave residents a sense of freedom when it came to hunting and fishing, purchasing store-bought food, or simply enjoying the land. Plane people could hunt caribou in Chisana, fish at Chitina and Tebay Lakes, trap at Hanagitna, and even fly to the Gulf of Alaska to take advantage of the marine environment's abundant seafood. One air taxi operator and registered guide reported providing local residents with air transport to and from hunting areas in exchange for "gas money."[24] Families with airplanes also had a modicum of access to medical facilities. Some residents even maintained homes in places like Cordova, where they could more easily enter the cash economy and support their airplane-dependent lifestyle during the off-season.

The airplane, then, made access possible to several homesites claimed by residents in the Wrangell region. In 1978 nineteen-year-old Paul Claus spent his first winter in the Wrangells, trapping and flying throughout the Chitina River valley, while building a home at his family homestead near the head of the Chitina Glacier. Paul's father, John Claus, came to

Alaska after the war and worked as a schoolteacher in Anchorage and a part-time hunting guide. While flying sheep hunters throughout the Wrangells, the senior Claus came across what he considered a "great camping site" on the expansive Chitina River, with stunning views of the Wrangells, Saint Elias, and Chugach Ranges. Claus staked five acres under the Homestead Act in 1960, and he, his wife, Eleanor, and two Inupiaq friends built the family's first cabin. There his son, Paul, developed a passion for flying over what the family called a "mountain kingdom."[25]

From their five-acre parcel near Bear Island on the Chitina River, the family's Claus Outdoor Adventures provided a variety of recreational activities for visitors, including mountain climbing, ice climbing, mountaineering, glacier travel, rafting, kayaking, cross-country skiing, hiking, horseback trips, photography, and just about any other activity clients desired to do. The family's dream of a wilderness oasis was almost washed away, however, when a geologist who had contracted Paul to fly him into the field asked Paul if he was worried about building his lodge on a floodplain. Although the Chitina River appeared far from the family's five-acre homestead, Paul took to the air for a look. "Sure enough," Paul admitted, "upriver the water level was higher than at my place. It was only a matter of time."[26]

The Claus's solution resulted in a private land exchange with the federal government of mining property located in designated wilderness for the Hubert's Landing property, located and staked by Martin Harrais in 1926.[27] The land deal gave the Claus family a 97.7-acre tract consisting of a two-room log cabin constructed by Harrais, a water reservoir and aqueduct, an elevated cache, a horse corral and associated outbuildings, and a rail fence. About a quarter of a mile away, Martin Harrais had scraped out an airstrip, which the family of flyers would put to good use. Martin's wife, Margaret Harrais, accompanied her husband to the site in June 1927. In her memoir Margaret recalled how it felt to arrive after a five-day hike from McCarthy. "On up the valley until it seemed we must stub our toes against the great Chitina Glacier," she wrote, "we were home for the summer." Their "dear little home in the wilderness," had a perfect view of Mount Saint Elias and was, according to Harrais, "completely in harmony with its environment." Years later, the Claus family would share the same sentiment.[28]

To the north of the Wrangell Mountain massif the airplane served as the mainstay for another family's lifeway: the hunting-guiding business. Making the hard decision to retire from flying, Jack Wilson sold his Gulkana-based Wilson Air Service to Lynn Ellis in 1978. The Ellis family in turn established Ellis Air, moving the business to Mile 42, not far from the Nabesna mine, at the end of the Nabesna road. Even though they were in theory connected to the road system, Cole Ellis explained he became interested in flying because, quite frankly, it was the "best way to get around."

Cole's family arrived at Nabesna in 1957, when he was just a small child. Longtime resident Harry Boyden sold some of his property to his parents, Bill and Lorene Ellis, who moved with their children to live year-round at the site in 1960. To earn money, Bill worked as a pilot and hunting guide, spending months away from the family. Lorene, who had grown up on a Texas ranch, raised the kids often on her own. With dangerous animals, extreme weather conditions, and stream crossings always a potential threat, Lorene remained mindful that the nearest hospital was one hundred miles away. Consequently, she taught her children to be resourceful, prepared, and aware of their surroundings. Bill Ellis encouraged Cole and his brother, Kirk, to learn to fly when the boys were in their teens. The survival skills engrained in them by their mother paid off. While flying they paid close attention to factors such as altitude, wind direction, and depth perception. The boys soon developed the expertise needed for landing on hillsides and mountainous terrain present throughout the Wrangells.[29]

As with the Claus family, it was the plane more than anything else that gave the Ellis family appreciation for the land. Airplanes allowed residents to access remote areas that were otherwise inaccessible, and that was a significant virtue. Besides flying and guiding sport hunters, Cole Ellis also flew his children out to what he called the "near quiet," places where the silence caused your "ears to start buzzing."[30] And while airplanes gave local pilots ways of reaching extraordinary levels of isolation, they also provided residents with the means to come together. McCarthy resident Jim Edwards explained that people flying over to a friend's homestead in a remote location just to talk and have a cup of coffee was fairly common in the 1970s. Not only were airplanes a vital link for communities choosing to live at the edge of the managed world, but in terms of function and distinctiveness, airplanes provided the essential cohesive quality that gave the Wrangell Mountain communities their frontier identity.[31]

12

Seekers of the Inaccessible

DESPITE MCCARTHY'S NEW AIRFIELDS AND THE LACK OF GOOD roads, the 1970s saw an increase of intrepid newcomers who, like the trophy hunters and even the new generation of mountaineers, hoped to experience Alaska's unique places. But these visitors were not so welcomed by Alaskans, nor the local aviation community. These newcomers proselytized change, and as Wrangell Mountain hunting guide Kirk Ellis acknowledged, "Giving up the old lifestyle is hard."[1]

At McCarthy's Fourth of July celebration in 1972, traveler Josephine Gordon recalled in her journal that everybody in town, including visitors, prepared for the picnic. "40 to 45 people, kids and dogs, beer and food and friendliness," observed Josephine. But Josephine had also encountered an assembly of outsiders at the midsummer celebration the local residents called the "long haired." "Students from USC," snarled Josephine, "subsidized by [the] Sierra Club who were there for the summer making reports on why Alaska should have no roads or recreational areas for its people."[2] The so-called long hairs were in McCarthy advocating for the environmental movement, led by such national organizations as the Sierra Club, Friends of the Earth, and the Wilderness Society. The activists, who indeed perceived their movement more as a crusade, fretted that the same type of political and economic forces that fenced the West during the nineteenth century were similarly in place to transform the Far North.

In the 1970s in Alaska that transformative force was big oil. Four years before Josephine's McCarthy visit, Atlantic Richfield Company (ARCO) had discovered the largest oil deposit in North America in one of the harshest and most isolated places on earth: Prudhoe Bay, Alaska. Lease sales brought nine hundred million dollars to the state's nearly bankrupted coffers and instantly made Alaska one of the richest states in the union. But to get Prudhoe Bay oil to thirsty markets around the world, oil companies needed to construct an eight-hundred-mile pipeline that would cross both public and Native lands, and bisect the Chugach and Wrangell ranges on its way to its terminus point in Valdez.

Prospects for building a pipeline crossing the entire length of Alaska was made even more improbable with the Interior Department's "Land Freeze" policy resulting from disputes over Native land claims in 1966. The federal land freeze prevented the state of Alaska from selecting coveted lands provided under the 1959 Statehood Act. In 1969 environmentalists and nine Native villages filed suit in federal court to halt pipeline construction. The winter prior to Josephine's summer visit to McCarthy, President Richard Nixon had resolved the Native claims issue to hasten pipeline construction. In December 1971 the president signed into law the Alaska Native Claims Settlement Act (ANCSA). ANSCA not only created Alaska Native regional corporations and granted them almost one billion dollars but the law also gave Alaska Natives forty-four million acres of federal land. With the passage of the landmark legislation, the Interior Department and Native groups along the proposed pipeline right-of-way gave their blessings, making it possible for the federal and state governments to grant licenses and permits to the construction companies. Meanwhile, the ongoing oil embargo crisis in the Middle East profoundly shaped the controversy by heightening demand for oil, which ultimately swayed public opinion in favor of domestic oil production and caused prices for crude to skyrocket.[3]

The most contentious legacy of ANCSA, and one that would greatly influence Alaskans and their relationship with the federal government in the ensuing nine years, were two provisions of the law known as (d)(1) and (d)(2). ANCSA's Section 17 (d)(1) called for a review of all unreserved public lands in Alaska "to insure that the public interest in these lands is properly protected." Section 17(d)(2) authorized the secretary of interior to recommend to Congress the designation of up to eighty million acres of land for use as national parks, forests, and refuges. The presence of the so-called long hairs at McCarthy's Fourth of July picnic, not to mention Josephine's disdain for them, marked the arrival of the modern environmental movement to the Wrangells and the beginning of a decade-consuming battle over what was called at the time the Alaska lands bill.

Environmentalists in support of the Alaska lands bill legislation (and who were still smarting over the passage of the Trans-Alaska Pipeline Authorization Act in 1973) wanted to restrain mining, sport hunting, and other unregulated development in the pristine wilderness areas throughout the state. Like resident Alaskans, they too viewed America's northern territory in terms of a frontier. To them, its vast tracks of primitive wilderness served as windows to a time before the coming of white men. This wilderness frontier ideology proselytized that human happiness meant living in harmony with nature. Alaska, according to the rising tide of conservationists, should not be a place to conquer nature, but rather a place in which to commune. Moreover, Section (d)(2) offered Americans a second chance. Pundits in 1975 lamented that "mistakes that were made 'Outside' with the Indian tribes, with the division of territories irrespective of natural resources, with the devotion to progress regardless of environmental consequences—all these errors of the past are being avoided in Alaska."[4] As the director of the National Park Service (NPS), Gary Everhardt at the time proclaimed: "We still truly have a chance to do it right in Alaska."[5]

WRANGELL MOUNTAIN SKYBOYS
ON THE NEW WILDERNESS FRONTIER

Because previous generations had viewed pilots as "gatekeepers" to mineral wealth in Alaska's own version of the Manifest Destiny narrative, it is not surprising that environmental sponsors voiced strong arguments against the use of mechanized access into wilderness places. Conservationists argued that experienced backcountry pilots utilizing tundra ridges, lakes and ponds, snowfields, and gravel bars, instead of established airstrips, had detrimental consequences for wilderness. By transporting people to places that before had been deemed inaccessible, environmentalists saw bush pilots as playing a primary role in expanding the human footprint into those untouched areas.

Without doubt, floats and skis exponentially increased landing options. Rocks and low brush presented no problems for Super Cubs with oversize "tundra tires." Rough terrain no longer proved to be an obstacle. Moreover, the nimble aircraft was capable of rising from the ground within fifty feet and required only about two hundred feet after touchdown.[6] Although environmentalists admitted that wilderness flying rarely impacts the land permanently—float planes left no trace of their landings, repeated snowfall and ice melt hid tracks of glacial landings, and the gravel bars commonly used by wheeled aircraft were periodically scoured by high water—the real problem environmentalists had with planes in wilderness, explained historian Roderick Nash, was that they viewed the airplane as a product, indeed a symbol, of the highly sophisticated technological world that people sought wilderness areas in order to escape.[7]

By the 1970s environmentalists had understood the phrase "Last Frontier" to mean "unexplored territory." This echoed the view of the previous generation's conservation icon Robert Marshall, who believed that "one of the great values of exploration is in pitting oneself without the aid of machinery against unknown Nature."[8] The presence of the new technology dispelled for Marshall the sense of discovery and exploration back in 1929. Environmentalists in later decades shared Marshall's opinion. They advanced the notion that experiencing nature was something to be earned through physical exertion. Backcountry travel required skill and toughness. In the minds of these new twentieth-century explorers, air travel was a purchased comfort and a poor substitute for personal achievement.[9]

Such was the perspective of many Wrangell Mountain visitors, who came in search of a wilderness experience in the 1970s. "I love the wilderness; especially where there are no people," remarked a backpacker from the Netherlands. "What attracted me to the Wrangells is the expansiveness. I've been in the Alps on glaciers, but nothing compares to what goes on in the Wrangell Mountains." Some visitors reported a transcendental or even spiritual experience in the Wrangells: "When I'm alone in the natural world I find that I'm most myself," recalled a visiting backpacker. "I need that time and space away from everything. I need a place to be free from other worries so as to let my mind wander. To me this is the last great wilderness, and I want to experience it and get away from people."[10]

So for the same reasons that Alaskans tended to celebrate the bush pilot—Alaska's skyboy—environmentalists feared him: "The role of aviation in the development of the Alaskan frontier has given pilots there a heroic stature that the 'outside' may find hard to understand," wrote Nash. In other words, environmentalists considered Harold Gillam, Bob Reeve, Mudhole Smith, and subsequent flyers who followed their sky trails typical frontier cowboys, unintentionally helping to cement the skyboy narrative in public discourse. And it wasn't just that they symbolized the coming of civilization. According to Nash, the consequence of the Alaska pilot's role as frontier hero "is his tendency to resist regulation, particularly by government."[11] Moreover, it wasn't just the environmentalists who recognized a rebellious quality in bush pilots. Resentful residents who were worried that distant, non-Alaskan policy makers in Washington, D.C., were "locking-up" the region and controlling Alaska's destiny identified with the cowboy-pilot. The tendency to resist was reflected in the popular 1970s-era bumper sticker: "Alaska for Alaskans: Yankee Go Home." This was a warning of sorts to the federal government and environmentalists from the Lower 48, that many Alaskans, rather symbolically, placed near their gas-guzzling tailpipe. The idea of saving Alaska's primitive wilderness from those who supposedly wanted to destroy it became a battle cry for a generation of conservationists and federal stewards intent on doing "things right the first time."[12] And in the mid-1970s preservation advocates convinced congressional supporters to introduce legislation that would create a national park containing much of the Chugach, Wrangells and Saint Elias ranges and be closed to both mining and sports hunting—two activities local pilots highly depended upon.

AVIATION AND THE NEW NATIONAL PARK

Although nearly thirty years had passed, Alaska Senator Ernest Gruening refused to give up the dream of opening the Wrangell–Saint Elias region to Alaskans and the American people. On November 17, 1966, he asked Secretary Stewart Udall to request that the National Park Service study the establishment of a "National Parkway" starting at Cordova and continuing up the Copper River valley through the Wood and Abercrombie canyons and into and around the Chitina valley. Along the planned route was the unmatched scenery that had entranced the soon-to-be territorial governor during his aerial flight flown by Merle Smith back in 1938.[13] "Since the suspension of the Copper River and Northwestern Railway, coincidental with the closing of the Kennecott mine a generation earlier," Gruening later explained, "the region was no longer accessible." The senator believed that a national parkway would open the region's natural wonders to the public and stimulate private tourist enterprises to accommodate visitors.[14] In 1967, Gruening even patronized Fred Machetanz—one of Alaska's up-and-coming landscape painters and resident of the Matanuska valley—to record some of the Wrangells great peaks on canvas, just as Sydney Laurence had painted and glorified Mount McKinley. "I visualized a future Interior Department brochure in which some of Machetanz's paintings would reveal the region's scenic superlativeness," Gruening later recalled.[15]

Gruening's plans for a national parkway never came to fruition, but the Wrangell Mountains and their outstanding scenic beauty were eventually preserved in perpetuity. Back in 1965 the National Park Service had previously singled out the region for its potential recreational resources as part of the agency's program Operation Great Land, which looked to increase the agency's role in Alaska.[16] Ten years later, NPS sent "keyman" Gerald Wright from its Denver Service Center to assess the eastern Alaska region.[17] At (d)(2) planning hearings in Copper Center, Cordova, Yakutat, and Northway, nearly all testifying residents agreed that places such as Tebay Lakes, parts of the Chugach range, and the Bremner River area warranted protection on some level but voiced concern with the National Park Service becoming the principal land manager. Some pilots saw the agency as too restrictive and a threat to their livelihoods. They wondered if the agency would follow the Lower 48 style of management policies.

Others, ironically, saw the NPS mission—"to preserve unimpaired the national and cultural resources and values of the national park system for the enjoyment, education, and inspiration of this and future generations"—as a threat to the Wrangells unique lifestyle qualities and environment by making the park into a major tourist attraction. Howard Knutson's testimony favored a national park only if it were on lands above ten thousand feet. Bush pilot and guide Al Lee worried that under NPS "there will be six lanes of highway in the Wrangells that will destroy the area." Other pilots like Jack Wilson expressed fears that his business's bread and butter—mining exploration—would be threatened. Moreover, like the other flyers, he worried that the agency would restrict nontraditional landing areas that would prevent pilots from activities such as flying in climbers and skiers to Mount Stanford.[18]

In 1977, Congressman Morris K. Udall introduced H.R. 39, the first bill to be called the "Alaska National Interests Lands Conservation Act." But unlike parks in the Lower 48, H.R. 39 would allow Alaska parks to remain open to consumptive activities associated with traditional, subsistence lifestyles. H.R. 39 included the Wrangell–Saint Elias region among a litany of scenic areas, which according to the proposals would be split into two National Park Service management units: a park and a preserve.[19]

Secretary of Interior Cecil Andrus introduced a bill suggesting additional revisions, including allotted acreage per unit, sports hunting in the preserve (but not in the park), and confining subsistence activities to specially designated "management zones," which would be jointly managed by the state and federal governments.[20] After months of pounding out the bill's specific details with the Interior Department and the environmental lobby, congressional legislators confronted their steepest challenge: Alaska's powerful delegation, which threatened to "kill" any bill that limited resource development in Alaska.

Facing a December 1978 congressional deadline, Secretary Andrus, unwilling to let the Alaska lands bill be defeated, came up with a plan. He advised President Jimmy Carter to use the Federal Land Policy and Management Act (FLPMA) to withdraw 110 million acres that temporarily shielded them from both mineral entry and state selection. President Carter then invoked the Antiquities Act, signing a proclamation that established seventeen new national monuments and permanently protected fifty-six million acres on December 1, 1978. The proclamation included a 10,950,000-acre Wrangell–Saint Elias National Monument.[21] With the most valued lands now in federal protection, at least temporarily, Congress continued to hammer out the specifics for passage of an Alaska lands bill. The National Park Service, with the flourish of Carter's pen, took over ten new monuments and three expanded ones. The agency's priority, then, was developing guidelines for its new acquisitions that would, as directed by Carter's proclamation, continue to allow "local residents to engage in subsistence hunting."[22] The United Nations, meanwhile, had declared the Wrangell–Saint Elias National Monument and Canada's bordering Kluane National Park a World Heritage Park. The designation, although mostly ceremonial and nonbinding, underscored Parks Canada's focus on wildlife protection and its desire to eliminate hunting in the Wrangell–Saint Elias region altogether.[23]

Despite the conflicting management policies between Canada and the United States, central to the formulation of the 1979 NPS regulations were discussions regarding the airplane—specifically, where and to what extent aircraft would be allowed for subsistence hunters. Aware of the increasing tensions between Alaskans and the federal government, the Interior Department attempted to develop regulations that supported local conditions and eased residents' concerns. "In keeping with that philosophy," wrote park historian Geoffrey Bleakley, "it [the Interior Department] allowed visitors to carry firearms and access the park with aircraft."[24] The exception being—and it was a big exception—the 1979 NPS regulations prohibited sport hunting in the monuments, which effectively eliminated an important means in which many residents made a living.

Historian Michael Lappen characterized the Wrangell area residents' attitudes following the monument designation as becoming "aggressively hostile."[25] Infuriated Alaskans staged protests in communities surrounding the new monuments, including Wrangell–Saint Elias.[26] At the Tonsina Lodge, about fifty miles west of Glennallen on the Glenn Highway, an NPS aircraft was mysteriously destroyed.[27] Fueling hostilities was the agency's Alaska area director, John Cook, who felt that NPS should pursue an "aggressive, selective enforcement of sport hunting" in the Wrangells.[28] In the summer of 1979 he recruited rangers from outside NPS regions to patrol for illegal hunting, including Charles A. Budge, who served as the first ranger-in-charge at Wrangell–Saint Elias National Monument.[29] Still, the understaffed Wrangells' ranger team could not realistically administer a monument nine times the size of Yellowstone.[30]

By August 1980 the Senate had finally passed its version of the Alaska lands bill. Preservationists hoped that the bill might still be strengthened to include more wilderness acreage, such as the Malaspina Forelands. They were also frustrated by the bill's unrestrictive stance on mechanized access into wilderness areas for subsistence purposes, pointing out that in the Lower 48, parks ban aircraft landings in the backcountry. They worried that the bill lacked consideration for the number of persons who might gain access to parks by air.[31] All hopes for more restrictive legislation were dashed in November 1980, however, when voters elected Ronald Reagan and a slate of national candidates who opposed the legislation. A few days later, Udall asked the House of Representatives to approve the Senate's version, whether all were in support or not.

On December 2, 1980, Carter, then a lame-duck president, signed the Alaska National Interest Lands Conservation Act (ANILCA) into law. The act set aside roughly one hundred million acres of federal land across the state as national parks, wildlife refuges, recreation areas, preserves, and national forests. Among the areas designated was the twelve-million-acre Wrangell–Saint Elias National Park and Preserve.[32] ANILCA abolished the 1978 national monument and permitted sports hunting in the preserve—but not in the park. And to the ire of many outfitters, subsistence hunters and trappers were allowed to access the park, hunt any animal without restrictions on age or gender, with the caveat that plane-use be prohibited.[33] Americans everywhere applauded the environmental movements' historic achievement. "It may turn out that in Alaska," projected *National Geographic* journalist Joseph Judge, "that magnificent land where the American frontier finally ran out of ground, the American future took root."[34] But to a large number of Alaskans they, like their Wrangell Mountain skyboys, chose to hold on to the lifestyle for which they worked so hard and sacrificed so much. Indeed, the nine-year battle over Alaska's national interest lands was over, but the heated controversy over frontier values and local identity had only just begun.

SPORT HUNTERS' FRUSTRATION PEAKS

After the passage of ANILCA and the establishment of Wrangell–Saint Elias National Park and Preserve, owners of a lodge located midway between Glennallen and Copper Center tacked a sign on their door that read: "We reserve the right to refuse service to anyone. Due to our beliefs in freedom we prefer not to serve the National Park Service." A similar sign was situated on the door of a Glennallen hardware store.[35] Chitina District ranger Jim Hannah explained that in 1981 residents saw the park service as a threat to their independent lifestyle, noting that they were clearly "venting their frustration."[36]

Many of the non-Native residents living in the Wrangell Mountain region feared the proliferation of the federal government. They subscribed to the viewpoint that the presence of institutions like the National Park Service threatened their individual freedom. More to the point, they saw the increase of regulatory demands dictated by ANLICA as an affront to "old-time American values." Part of the problem, according to researcher Holly Reckord, was that most people did not understand why their lifestyle had suddenly come under attack. "After all," noted Reckord, "when they were in school, the frontier life and the enterprise of the frontiersmen were held up for admiration in school textbooks and new accounts."[37] Others resented the characterization of being an exploiter of the land and expressed concern over potential regulations that would restrict flying and landing in wilderness: "I've flown all my life; I love it," explained a Wrangell Mountain pilot in 1980:

I soloed on my sixteenth birthday and my daughter soloed on her sixteenth. This kind of flying, wilderness flying, is the only kind that interests me. Airport to airport is like driving a bus, but here it's really interesting. I get a little thing going with Mother Nature. I fly over and see the caribou herds, the sheep, and the mountains and it's my way of being part of the country. I have a real respect for the land and it bothers me to see a candy wrapper out there. As far as protecting the land, I am probably more concerned about it then ninety-nine percent of the people who are behind the parks.[38]

For many longtime residents it felt that the government and the American people had abandoned them. As one resident, bracing for an army of tourists to arrive, reportedly put it: "There goes the wilderness."

Given the region's big game hunting reputation, it was not surprising that the bitterest arguments between residents and park staff focused on future access to Dall sheep. In 1980, ANLICA established the boundaries to delineate the park from the preserve based on data provided by University of Alaska biologists Edward Murphy and Frederick Dean, who had just completed an exhaustive study of local hunting for the agency. General Wright, the National Park Service's local keyman, contributed information as well, analyzing the harvest statistics for most local drainages to help differentiate between sport and subsistence hunting areas. Park planners felt they had accommodated hunters, leaving about 60 percent of the sheep in the preserve and available for sports hunting.[39]

Moreover, in spite of local thinking, the park typically supported big game hunting. In the words of one park planner, "it is a legitimate quest." What worried the National Park Service and wilderness advocates was a "quick-get-a-trophy-and-get-out" mentality, in which the hunter deprives himself that ability to deepen his relationship with nature and the insights it provides. "He may get his horns for this den and his ego may be satisfied," wrote a park planner in 1974, "[but] little of what the wilderness has to offer rubs off on him. His is not a true 'park experience.'"[40] But despite reopening large parcels of the Wrangells to sport hunters, the decision to eliminate them from the established park areas, especially the Exclusive Guide Areas, which had been granted to individual hunters by the state's Guide Licensing and Control Board, made many furious. "All I can do is bitch," lamented a local guide in the early 1980s. "They've cut forty-five percent of my business, and when you lose that much, life gets tough."[41] A guide in a similar situation agreed: "The Park Service has cut my guiding by eighty percent and my flying by forty percent. The closure has strained our finances and put us in a real bind. I've built my business on trying to be honest and I am not about to let Carter make a crook out of me, so I abide by a law that I don't like. It hurts my family. It is really frustrating."[42]

Residents such as LeNora Conkle, who had owned and managed a lodge and fly-in guide service in the Wrangell Mountains with her husband, Bud, since the 1950s, voiced even stronger criticism of the new park regulations, arguing that they infringed upon Alaskans' right to make a living. In her memoir *Hunting the Way It Was in Our Changing Alaska*, Conkle explained her side of the story:

> We sold our horses and the cabins at Wolf Lake to Doc and Phoebe Taylor of Grizzly Lake Ranch, after Bud was awarded an exclusive guiding area in the Chugach Range. Wolf Lake is located within the Wrangell–St. Elias National Park and Preserve and Doc can't sell his investments where he now hunts, nor will his sons be able to take over the business and guide hunts there. As I understanding it, Doc is limited to the number of horses he can put on the nonrenewable grazing lease we also turned over to him. There are a limited number of hunters he's allowed each hunting season. The insurance required to hunt in the Preserve is outrageously expensive. So, he is working for . . . what? His own pleasure? Well, he can do that on his own time, without the hard work involved in outfitting for big game hunts with horses and airplanes.[43]

Perhaps more frustrating to Conkle than economics was the changing views that Alaska's idealized skyboys was a threat to wilderness. "Whims of nature are frequently unforgivable, in the arctic vastness, or on top of a great mountain," wrote Conkle in a defense of Wrangell's flyers. "Inventiveness is a tool of survival, and more than once, a pilot/guide has brought himself, his aircraft and his client safely back because he was capable of inventing the method." Conkle described the pilot-guides she knew as persons of individualism, innovation, and audacity. Believing that the National Park Service was "underhanded" and that the agency intended to "eliminate hunting in 'their' parks," Conkle warned readers that the true endangered species in the Wrangells was the bush pilot.

NPS ranger Jim Hannah, on the other hand, was not swayed by such arguments. New attitudes held mainly by pilots from outside the region showed no respect for fellow hunters, the game, or the environment. They used balloon tires to ride over a sensitive ecosystem, and the occasional pilot buzzed sheep away from the competition. "Guides need to get into the twenty-first century," retorted Hannah. "If they want to stay in business they need to be a professional. The 'good old boys' think the land is theirs. Intimidation, chasing sheep, 'the Wild West' show," warned Hannah. "That's in the past."[44]

Issues swirling around aviation and hunting became even more controversial when Byron Mallot, Alaska Native leader and twenty-two-year-old mayor of Yakutat, testified in front of a congressional panel. He said that the people of Yakutat living where the southeast side of Yakutat Bay meets the Gulf of Alaska traditionally and customarily accessed the Malaspina Forelands, located directly across the Yakutat Bay, with aircraft for subsistence hunting purposes because the area's harsh unpredictable weather often made a water crossing unsafe. Congress agreed, making the Malaspina Forelands an exception to the rule but noted the decision was not meant "to invite additional aircraft use, or new or expanded use in parks and monuments where such uses have not traditionally and regularly occurred."[45]

Disputes between residents and the federal government flared even hotter in the summer of 1985, when members of the Wrangell–Saint Elias Subsistence Resource Commission (SRC) squared off with NPS and other federal officials over whether subsistence users could legally access the park by airplane for subsistence purposes, arguing that far more areas in the park had been traditionally and regularly accessed with planes.[46] Despite the Yakutat ruling, however, the park took the stance that the use of an aircraft to directly access fish or game for subsistence purposes in the park or monument or to indirectly access fish or game in the park for subsistence was to remain prohibited. The Subsistence Resource Commission, led by Chairman Bill Ellis, was resolutely opposed to this position, arguing that hunters had been using aircraft to harvest wildlife for personal use for years prior to ANILCA's passage. The group responded by recommending that aircraft should be considered the primary means of "reasonable access" for subsistence hunting and trapping due to the lack of available road access.[47] Federal officials, however, rebuffed the SRC's recommendations, claiming that they were inconsistent with congressional intent on airplane use and, in doing so, effectively eliminated aircraft access for subsistence purposes in Wrangell–Saint Elias.[48] Despite the clear decision made by federal government, the local population responded with a letter-writing campaign that lasted into the early 1990s. "To judge by the number and intensity of these letters," wrote NPS historian Frank Norris, "aircraft access appeared to be one of the most unpopular polices applied to Alaska's newly established national park units."[49]

Hunting controversies brewing in the 1980s placed many pilots in a bind. Cole Ellis, son of Bill Ellis, saw the issue as more than a strictly "us" verses "them" dynamic. Rather, the younger Ellis voiced concern that the new regulations failed to prevent the decline of the region's wildlife. "Wolves howling and grizzly tracks began disappearing," noted Cole Ellis during a 1992 interview. He, like many longtime hunters, worried that less experienced subsistence hunters were adding pressure to the Wrangells' sheep population. The park's one sheep rule allowed subsistence hunters to take ewes and lambs—not just the largest ram from one area, as fair chase practices dictated to ethical sport hunters. The law also granted those who recently moved into the area the right to hunt in the park, as long as they didn't use planes for subsistence proposes. With so much competition and pressure on the animals, admitted the soft-spoken Ellis, "it was harder to make a living."[50]

Moreover, Cole Ellis, like ranger Jim Hannah, recognized the unsportsmanlike attitudes and activities exhibited by a handful of not-so-ethical big game hunters in the preserve, conceding that "wild game was easy access to too many hunters." He described increasing situations such as air taxi businesses promoting trophy sheep hunts that drop hunters off and pick them up if clients could not walk out on foot. As such overconsumptive practices continued, sheep populations weakened, causing the hunting seasons to shrink, not to mention the size of the animals themselves, which made finding a full curl harder for sportsmen and their guides. Ellis knew that, from drainage to drainage, the region had too many hunters. But even worse, he worried that resident hunting guides were receiving a disproportionate share of the blame. "It's hard for people [those employed as hunters] to talk publically [sic]," admitted Ellis. "But the [unsportsmanlike activities] makes us [longtime guides] all sad. . . . We use the animals and they've been our way of life. And they've made our living for us and it's been good here. It's been a good life; I've really enjoyed it, but I don't want to be the one killing the last sheep."[51]

Longtime McCarthy resident Jim Edwards flew the Copper Belt mail route for Cordova Airways in the 1970s. His homestead, not far from the confluence of the Nizina and Chitina Rivers, contains his plane, airstrip, hangar, and large garden. Anyone who talks with Jim quickly understands how proud he is of his wilderness oasis. "This is my home in every sense of the word." Jim, who built his McCarthy home from the ground up, has an entirely efficient and sustainable philosophy. Nothing is wasted. Although it is challenging keeping up with the basic necessities—cutting fire wood, growing food, and maintaining his nineteenth-century-era waterwheel in a nearby creek that allows for running water to his house— Jim emphatically contends that his wilderness lifestyle is important. As Jim put it, "This is hard country; there's an art form to living out here." It has been "twenty years of tough going to get to where we are now," he recalls. But much of the old-timer's appreciation for the Wrangells wilderness came through years of struggle early on. "Summer after summer after summer, I went away from my wife to work at industrial jobs I didn't like, jobs that gave me no satisfaction. We saved. We slept in the bushes behind Merrill Field with the kids." Jim's city-life experience taught him significant lessons. An engineer by training, he viewed cities as energy wasters, and that the urban dweller lifestyle was, in his words, "grossly inefficient." Jim's early interest in aviation got him out of the city, eventually over to the Wrangells. "It took only one flight for me realize that this was where I wanted to be for the rest of my life." In McCarthy, Jim explained, there were no traffic lights regulating your life!"[52]

With the establishment of Wrangell–Saint Elias National Park and Preserve in 1980, however, regulation had made its way to the wilderness regions of eastern Alaska. As park restrictions made it harder to make a living hunting, a number of resident pilots turned to nonconsumptive recreational tourism to compensate. They recognized that they needed to work positively with park officials and, in doing so, provided a necessary service: they catered to the high volume of wilderness seekers arriving in the Wrangells. The first service of its kind was McCarthy Air, established by Gary Green in 1988. Green had moved to McCarthy in 1973. He became familiar with the country as a miner and hunting guide. Two years later he acquired his pilot's license. Green started flying friends around the Wrangell Mountains, and then he offered his services to the rising number of hikers, mountaineers, and rafters visiting the national park. Likewise, pilot Kelly Bay came to McCarthy in 1976. There he met his future wife, Natalie, herself a pilot from the Australian outback, and together they established Wrangell Mountain Air in 1992. Basing the operation in McCarthy, like Green, the Bays equipped visitors hoping to glimpse the park's natural wonders from above with scheduled and regular flightseeing and adventure tours.

The Claus family also made a living in nonconsumptive recreational tourism. But where Green and the Bays concentrated on volume, the Clauses catered to those truly seeking the inaccessible, offering an exclusive wilderness experience from their private inholding near the terminus of the Chitina Glacier. Paul married his wife, Donna, in 1982. They moved to the Chitina River site permanently, where they raised three children and built a lodge and air service business called Ultima Thule, a Greek expression used to describe the unknowable realm beyond the northern bounds on their maps. As Paul explained: "I wanted to land people in untouched places, to go places never sought before." Wilderness flying was what Claus loved to do most and Ultima Thule gave him the opportunity to do it for a living.

Even though Martin Harrais was likely disappointed with the production value of his five Darling M. claims, the Claus family intimately understood the property's worth. And they were likely not alone. Back in 1931, when aviation first came to the Wrangell Mountains, the region's sole skyboy, Harold Gillam, had flown Margaret Harrais to the Chitina River strip known as Hubert's Landing while her husband, Martin, made the trek on horseback. Assuring Gillam she was fine on her own, Margaret spent the next several days exploring the country. "I took a long survey of the mountainous horizon," she later wrote. "North, east and south the mountains tower eighteen thousand feet in height, on their crowns and sides glacial snows that are older than history—to the west lay McCarthy, five days distant on horseback and utterly impossible on foot on account of deep water. It was not exactly a rest-cure sanatorium for a nervous person, so I decided I must not be a nervous person."[53]

Margaret Harrais was a competent person who chose to embrace the world around her. The story of her life-affirming experience—made possible by a reliable pilot and an airplane—convinced Paul Claus that Margaret Harrais had discovered, unbeknownst to her husband, the tract's true value during those wandering days in 1931. Surely Martin hoped to find the mother lode, but for Margaret she sought something bigger: Mother Nature.[54] Six decades later, the site remains the Claus family's "dear little home" and through Ultima Thule, and a practical permitting system that allows them to conduct business in the national park while at the same time protect resources, they continue to provide people with life-affirming experiences with the world around them. "Airplanes," as the Claus family website asserts, "are the physical expression of the love of wilderness."[55]

Conclusion

WHERE HAVE ALL THE SKYBOYS GONE?

WHEN BOTH MERRITT "KIRK" KIRKPATRICK AND HAROLD GILLAM died in plane wrecks in 1939 and 1943 respectively, Alaskans everywhere felt a sense of shock and sadness for the fallen flyers. "Dear old Kirk," lamented the editor of the *Cordova Daily News*. "How we shall miss him." Not all the Wrangell Mountain flyers died young, however, for many went on to have long and rich careers. And when these territorial giants— men synonymous with bush flying—passed away, newspapers across the state bemoaned that Alaska had moved one step farther from its pioneering roots.

When Reeve died on August 25, 1980, the editor of the *Anchorage Daily News* reminded readers that men like Bob Reeve carried what writers for decades had described as the spirit of frontier Alaska.[1] An estimated six hundred mourners attended Reeve's funeral service at the Sydney Laurence Auditorium in Anchorage on August 30. His wife, Janice "Tilly" Reeve, flanked by family and friends, accepted the precisely folded flag in honor of Reeve's military service in World War I. Reeve was buried at Anchorage Memorial Park, his pall bearers included Alaska's political and economic elite. Alaskans recognized Reeve for his aviation accomplishments and rightly inducted him into the Alaska Aviation Hall of Fame. But just as when he was alive, Reeve's talents captured attention beyond the Far North. In October 1980 he was named to the International Aerospace Hall of Fame for his role in the development of civil air transportation over what the rest of the world considered the "Last Frontier."

When Merle K. Smith passed away a year later at age seventy-two, on June 16, 1981, the staff writer for the *Seattle Times* wrote: "Now it is our turn for tears. Mudhole Smith is gone."[2] News writers throughout Alaska and the Pacific Northwest remembered Smith for his many feats: saving Chisana gold miners forgotten during the war, his airlifting food to Cordova from Seattle during the Alaska Steamship Company strike, and of course, how he got his famous nickname. Scribes recalled Smith's emergency flights, the basketball flights, and the Champagne flights. His transportation of everything from dog sled teams to athletic teams to elementary-aged kids on a trip to the circus. "Mudhole was a feisty character with a big heart," enthused Susan Bramsteadt, former public affairs director with Alaska Airlines whose own career began with Cordova Airlines in 1963.[3] Two years before he died, Smith told the Cordova Chamber of Commerce that "these forty-three years I have been doing what I wanted to do." Still, his commitment to others was what defined much of that career. After Smith died in 1981, former Alaska CEO Bruce Kennedy saluted the pilot in an editorial published in the airline's inflight magazine. "He was one of a kind in a profession that attracted unique and strong individuals," affirmed the head of Alaska Airlines. "He laid the foundation for what is today one of the largest and most respected names in commercial aviation."[4]

With the exception of Herb Halley—Cordova's stalwart, sandbar flying bush pilot, who died in a crash near Lake Illiamna in 1955—the second generation of Wrangell Mountain flyers also had long and fulfilling careers. After Terris Moore left the presidency of the University of Alaska, he worked as a professor at Colby College, a private liberal arts school in Waterville, Maine, where he spent several years as a business and research consultant.[5] He never forgot Alaska, however, keeping ties to the Far North through serving for a few years on the advisory board of the Geophysical Institute. He remained generous to the university over the years by donating more than thirty thousand dollars in gifts and grants toward what he called his "sentimental objective" of repaying the entire salary he received during his four years as president.[6] In 1967 the university honored Moore with an honorary doctorate. He was named president emeritus in 1973. Moore died in his home in Cambridge, Massachusetts, on November 7, 1993.

Jack Wilson passed away on December 18, 2003, in Fairbanks, Alaska, at age eighty-two. After selling his Gulkana-based air service to the Ellis family, Wilson retired from flying and penned two books, *Glacier Wings and Tales* and *The Quest for Dall Sheep*. The handful of newspapers that published his obituary failed to fully recognize his many flying accomplishments, but the aviation community remembered. Kenny Smith recalled that when he crossed paths with Wilson, the old pilot was always gracious, even though they were competitors at the time. "I'll never forget Jack coming over to me toward the end of that first season and telling me that he had been watching me all summer and had observed how much my flying had improved," wrote Smith. "A very much appreciated and kind lie."[7] Pilots who appreciate Wilson's flying contributions in the Wrangell Mountains recognize him as an elite aviator. "In my opinion," wrote Smith, "history should and probably eventually will give Jack much more credit for his glacier flying achievements." Although Smith places Wilson side by side with Reeve and Don Sheldon as Alaska's premiere glacier pilots, he thinks Wilson is generally forgotten because of the little-known geography over which he flew his entire career. "So at Happy Hour tonight," proposed a pilot from Dillingham on hearing of Wilson's death, "hoist one in memory of Jack Wilson, WWII veteran and Super Cub pilot extraordinaire! I think he would appreciate that."[8]

While many of the Wrangell Mountain flyers who made history above the Copper Belt are now gone, some are alive and thriving. Howard Knutson still flies a 185 Cessna after sixty years. Although his once jet-black hair is the color of a metal aviation fuel can, Knutson is handsome, sharp, and fit. His tanned skin reflects the retired life of a snowbird. After constructing the McCarthy airfield and flying out the last of Kennecott's copper for Wrangell Consolidated in 1965, Knutson earned a living fishing for salmon in Bristol Bay, and about ten years ago flew his Cessna over the North Pole. As much as he enjoys life on the water, Knutson feels his place is in the air. "I couldn't imagine life without an airplane," admits the pilot. While flying he reads the country below him like a history book, "the geology tell the story of Alaska going back one hundred, five thousand or five million years."[9] When asked where his favorite destination is to fly, Knutson's clarifies there is none. "I don't just fly to put holes in the sky," he explains. "I fly because I'm going someplace."

Indeed, what all these aviators have in common is that they flew with purpose. Gillam flew in dangerous conditions not because he was a maverick, but because he hoped to sway government support for airmail delivery. Instead of escaping civilization, Kirk's Cordova Air brought twentieth-century services to the isolated Copper Belt region. Even Bob Reeve, whose antigovernment rhetoric, risk-taking, and independent spirit made him the quintessential skyboy, still made smart decisions based on his knowledge of and respect for the mountain environment. Simply put, he took risks to put food on the table. "Yeah, we did have some cowboys," conceded Knutson. But most would not have described themselves as such. More important, as the pilot stressed, "We had jobs to do."

THE SKYBOY NARRATIVE SINCE 1980

Although aviation represents a modern, twentieth-century industry, aviators are meaningful to Alaskans precisely because they reflect values indicative of the Last Frontier. Like the western cowboy or sourdough miner (occupations often identified with the nineteenth century), work in nature commands a high level of respect from Alaskans. A pilot's work, if successful, requires expertise equal to that of climatologists, biologists, and glaciologists. From pilots like Gillam, Reeve, Kirkpatrick, and Smith who entered the economic scene in the 1920s and 1930s, to pilots like Moore, Halley, Wilson, and Knutson, the second generation of Wrangell Mountain flyers, work in nature was the bush pilots' raison d'etre.

In the years leading up to and even after the passage of ANILCA in 1980, an opinion gained momentum among Alaskans that Outsiders were busily transforming Alaska's natural workplaces into arenas of amusement and leisure. Although the local sentiment was often times strongly distorted, the creation of Wrangell–Saint Elias National Park and Preserve in 1980 and the subsequent discontinuation of certain aircraft and aviation-related activities from the park did force many people to modify or change how they made a living. Opposition to the park effectively pitted frontier Alaskans who worked in nature against those who "played" in nature: in other words, visitors who desired to recreate—backpack, camp, and sightsee—in the Last Frontier.[10] Such attitudes effectively reinforced the skyboy narrative for both sides.

For residents like LeNora Conkle, the Wrangell Mountain skyboy became a manifestation of Alaska populism fueled by longtime insolent attitudes toward the federal government, an echo of Buffalo Bill's manifestation of Buck Taylor. "These men [pilot-guides] had more to fear from the Sierra Club, the Friends of Animals Clubs, and similar environmentalists groups," fumed Conkle, "than from all of Alaska's bears, wolves, or natural elements."[11] By invoking Cody's plainspoken western cowboy Buck Taylor, or later the rebel of government regulation Bob Reeve, Wrangell Mountain residents who identified with the defiant skyboy narrative took the position that those who carved out a living on the northern frontier were somehow more authentic Alaskans than the purported pampered "Outsiders." Even the McCarthy townsite they inhabited maintained a western look, which included false fronts, a western-style bar, and brothel-turned-hotel—a far cry from the all-American community of the 1920s and 1930s.

Meanwhile, a growing constituency of park proponents and environmental scholars from mostly Outside saw local inhabitants and their bush pilots as exploiters who, with their "mechanical horse," threatened to open Alaska's pristine wilderness to development, just as early capitalists commodified natural resources and transformed the wilderness of the American West. Although they characterized aviation as a modern creation, these groups also equated Alaska pilots with cowboys, blaming them (and their irresponsible flying) for eliciting resentful sentiments toward the government.[12] The idea of saving Alaska's primitive wilderness became a battle cry for a generation of conservationists and federal stewards intent on doing "things right the first time."[13] In the late 1970s preservation advocates convinced Congress to create first a national monument, then a national park, containing much of the Chugach, Wrangells, and Saint Elias ranges and closed to both mining and sports hunting—two activities local pilots historically depended on for work. A backlash from the isolated communities resulted, people became contemptuous of rules drafted by distant bureaucrats, which in their minds overreached and unnecessarily cut off the lifeline of their far-flung region.

More than three decades have passed since the passage of ANLICA, and still the entrenched skyboy narrative continues to affect the relationship between residents who straddle the park boundaries and its federal staff. A handful of federal or Outside critics still fail to recognize the bush pilots' accumulation of environmental knowledge as valuable and are blind to the fact that most pilots cherish the skyscape in the same way a fisherman values the ocean or a farmer values the land—this is their life blood, the place that gives their lives meaning, and they truly love it.[14] This generation of Wrangell Mountain pilots also recognize that if they are to continue flying, it makes no sense to relate to the park only as an adversary. At the same time, they grow tiresome of being branded by some as the enemy.

Conversely, what local residents often forget in their criticism of the government is that early aviators benefited from federal road and airstrip construction, regulation, and subsidization. Entrepreneurial pilots initiated the rise of fly-in tourism in the Wrangells that attracted the likes of the National Park Service, rather than the other way around. They even repackaged and sold, via the most sophisticated Madison Avenue–like advertising campaigns, a rescripted narrative of Alaska, one that better matched tourists' expectations of life on the Last Frontier. Even young McCarthyites (quite commonly kids from places far away from Alaska, who return to the Wrangells each summer for seasonal jobs) obtain their pilot's license—a skill they do not use for work, however, but for fun, using their pilot identity as an accessory to convey their exceptionality. They may believe they are identifying with history, but little do they know they are tapping into a narrative—a facade—as false their storefronts. This side of aviation history in eastern Alaska was either overlooked, misunderstood, or simply ignored.

Emeritus historian Stephen Haycox has argued that to explain aviation in terms only of bravado—whether celebrating it or criticizing it—is problematic. Society's creation of the skyboy narrative has made it difficult to get a clear view of the real context in which the courageous deeds of early aviation in Alaska actually took place. According to Haycox, "It has contributed to the sense that aviation was a natural development in the north, and its coming was somehow inevitable." Such a view, argues Haycox, destroys perspective. The skyboy narrative feeds an Alaska version of Manifest Destiny, which "causes us to forget the uncertainty, tentativeness, and confusion which surrounded the birth of aviation in Alaska."[15] Author and pilot Colleen Mondor has written pointedly that problems with the skyboy narrative go far beyond distorting history. "Pilots don't crash in Alaska because they are foolish or crazy or stupid, and they never have—not to anyone who matters." As Mondor makes empathically clear in her book *The Map of My Dead Pilots: The Dangerous Game of Flying in Alaska*, in all the stories, memoirs, and news reports covering aviation over the decades, "they [Alaska pilots] have always been brave in the Far North; they've always been courageous." This image, she argues, is downright deadly, for the desire to mimic the legendary aviators Gillam and Reeve has propelled young flyers to take unnecessary, reckless, even outrageous chances. "Modern rules were not what kept planes in the air in Alaska; decades of aviation history was."[16]

Even the Seattle-based Alaska Airlines ingrained the skyboy legacy in its corporate culture. In the past the carrier took every opportunity to evoke the bush pilot's swagger and scorn of regulation. Alaska's "whatever-it-takes-to-get-the-job-done" ethic helped the airline to become the nation's tenth largest by the end of the twentieth century. But after investigations by the National Transportation Safety Board determined that mechanical failure had caused Flight 261 to crash into the Pacific Ocean on January 31, 2000, killing all eighty-eight people aboard, including multiple families with children returning from holiday in Mexico, Alaska Airlines made sweeping changes to its maintenance program, replacing its heritage of sidestepping government safety regulations with one committed to them.[17]

MOVING BEYOND THE SKYBOY NARRATIVE

In the end, this book is not meant to cover the complete history of aviation in eastern Alaska. Rather, the stories herein represent a history of the evolving cultural perspective of Alaska as the nation's "Last Frontier." This shared viewpoint has swung like a pendulum over the decades, shifting orientation from the past to the future. The study of aviation as it developed in the Wrangell–Saint Elias Mountains gives us the opportunity to better scrutinize this phenomenon. For example, when aviation first came to eastern Alaska, it was the "grounded" miners and air-minded businessmen of the Progressive era who looked up and dreamed big. Brothers Pete and Lee Ramer, along with attorney Tom Donohoe, and banker O. A. Torgerson, followed a business pattern established by the Kennecott Copper Corporation that built an empire by monopolizing regional transportation. They also cooperated with and benefited from the federal government's effort to supply the region with airstrips. Although they failed to successfully develop a profitable mining organization, their decisions were farsighted. By buying up aviation real estate, building hangars and airfields, and most of all, backing Cordova Air Service and being themselves important advocates of the fledgling industry, the Ramer brothers, along with visionaries Donohoe and Torgerson, supported the early careers of Gillam, Kirk, Reeve, and Smith and left a practical aviation legacy that continues to serve the remote region today. An achievement that flew beyond their wildest golden dreams.

But faith in the future came to a screeching halt as the nation descended into the Great Depression. The outlook for Americans, as reflected in the literature, art, and journalism of the day, became a perspective cloaked in a frontier blanket that comforted weary, down-on-their-luck men and women with nostalgic narratives of the past. In Alaska, where the passage of the Gold Reserve Act made aviation an affordable option for miners, the bush pilot replaced the sourdough in western lore, and thanks to a multitude of news writers, became a hero of the Last Frontier. When World War II broke out, bush pilots retained their hero status, but the outlook was to the future. The declaration of gold as a nonessential metal severed aviation's dependency on mining, an activity considered by many a relic of the nineteenth century. Alaska aviation took off as wartime engineers assembled an aviation infrastructure, while American industry produced modern aircraft for the jet age. Individual carriers merged and corporate advertising convinced people to fly en masse, making tourism a mainstay of the economy. Instead of being viewed as the final extension of western migration, Alaska became a northern air bridge, linking air routes around the globe. The focus on science, such as the establishment of the Wrangell Observatory and surveying and mapmaking efforts throughout the 1950s, reflected a perspective on the future that harkened more toward President Kennedy's New Frontier rather than the old-fashioned narrative of the Last Frontier.

Undermining the postwar confidence in the future, however, existed a great deal of apprehension about communist infiltration and the threat of nuclear annihilation. When the Soviet Union successfully detonated an atomic bomb in 1949, journalist Edward R. Murrow observed that "seldom has the end of a war brought the victors so much fear and anxiety." Reflecting a kind of nervousness in 1950s society was a return of the resolute cowboy and the popularity of the Western genre in books, film (think John Wayne), and on television. In Alaska, Merle Smith's ingenious Sourdough Tours flew tourists, rather paradoxically, to old mining ghost towns on modern DC-3s, promising not only to fly them northward but back in time. Similarly Beth Day's 1950s-era *Glacier Pilot* painted Bob Reeve as pioneer, a portrait the pilot exemplified until the day he died. "Mr. Reeve did it the hard way," extolled the editor of the *Anchorage Daily Times*. "There was no subsidy. He built his business with his own hands, the sweat of his own brow and the strength of his own body." By the 1950s popular writers and scholars had characterized the Far North as a bastion of rugged individualism, thereby securely fixing an exceptional quality of the frontier image in the American mind.

In the decade spanning the statehood movement, the skyboy narrative was used more and more to separate Alaskans from the "Outside." As with the American West, the commodification of natural resources made Alaska dependent on absentee capitalists. This seemed to contradict Alaska's pioneer spirit embodied by the central figure in the frontier drama—the bush pilot. Dependence, however, was neither an American nor an Alaskan characteristic.[18] To resolve such contradictions, Alaskans simply linked rugged individualism to capitalist individualism. To those pioneers who came north for gold and copper, then for fish and later for oil, they had to first conquer Alaska's formidable wilderness. To succeed in their quest, such industries would need to seek the courageous and self-reliant—skills necessary to battle the cold and brutal natural environment from which those valuable natural resources came. Just as personal independence became central to national identity, rugged individualism and the pioneering spirit became central to the Alaska identity *and* the aviator identity, despite the fact that both the Alaskan economy and the aviator was entirely dependent on both Outside capitalists and the federal government.[19] Thus in the skyboy narrative success came when the aviator soared independently, not so much from corporate giants or big government but defiantly from nature itself.[20]

By the 1960s and 1970s economic development, urbanization, and frightening advancements in nuclear technology appeared to threaten Alaska's natural and cultural places once thought safe due to isolation. Environmentalists mobilized: they gained legislation for the establishment of the Alaska National Wildlife Refuge, they lobbied to stop construction of the Rampart Dam on the Yukon River, and circumvented the federal government's nightmarish plans to detonate atomic bombs in the Arctic. As if from a B-list monster movie, conservationists warned that scientists, boosters, and politicians had gone mad in their intent to control nature. Reflecting conservationists' fears of this sci-fi horror story was their use of "bygone rhetoric" in their argument against development—rhetoric that embraced Alaska as the Last Frontier.

Although conservationists positioned themselves on the other side of the frontier spectrum, they seemed similarly stuck in the past. They viewed Alaska as a natural world untouched by white man, a remnant of a precontact America, and most significant, as the last chance for the environmental community to save it.[21] Historian Theodore Catton has noted in *Inhabited Wilderness* that Alaska's vast tracks of sublime wilderness "fulfilled a cultural need associated with the closing of the frontier: they were windows to America's past, keepsakes of a once-virgin land."[22] The conservationists relished the idea of Alaska as a permanent frontier where Americans could visit their past both in person and as an idea. Consequently, the conservationists' image of Alaska saw the skyboy as a symbol of industrialization and development and a very real threat.

Although it may seem as though the two versions of Alaska—perceived by frontier residents as a place to conquer or by conservationists a place to commune—were contradictory, they in fact represented two competing views that merged and eventually formed Alaska's Last Frontier myth from which the skyboy narrative was born. The melding of rugged individualism and incredible scenic beauty translated into a very powerful and multifaceted image of man (for women were rarely acknowledged on the Alaskan frontier) and his relationship to the natural world. Both sides differed, almost diametrically, in how the landscape over which aviators flew should be valued, but each viewed Alaska as exceptional and as a symbol of hope, rebirth, and as a second chance. In the past few decades, however, explaining the significance of the frontier in Alaska aviation has been just as problematic as explaining its importance in Alaska history. In fact, the perception hurts Alaska economically. Despite the fact that Anchorage is closer to the West Coast than it is Florida, some merchants classify Alaska as an "international" destination. Others refuse to even ship items northward. In their mind Alaska is too far, not so much in terms of distances but imagination.

Perhaps back in 1948, Anchorage's International Airport was considered a small outpost on the outskirts of town. Romantic, yes, but Alaska's frontier image can be bad for business. According to a 2012 study conducted by the Alaska Economic Development Council, it turns out that the Anchorage airport is far from being a remote outpost. Fifty different carriers from around the world land at Anchorage, including FedEx and UPS. Anchorage serves five million passengers a year but, as too many merchants are unaware, the airport's mainstay is cargo, representing 80 percent of the business in Anchorage. Not only that, Anchorage is the fifth largest airport in the world in terms of cargo and the second largest in the United States for landed weight of cargo aircraft. Most important, Alaska, from the perspective of the global community, is not the end of civilization, as those usually living far from Alaska envision. Anchorage is no farther from Tokyo than New York, which means that a carrier is only a bit over nine hours by air from 90 percent of the industrialized world, providing unmatched access to the world's markets.[23] Needless to say, the questions remains: why does the image of Alaska as America's Last Frontier remain such a powerful influence on a modern-day, globally reaching society?

Despite lingering concerns that the federal government is "locking out Alaskans" to create amusement parks for environmentalists, today's bush pilots continue to make their living flying in Wrangell–Saint Elias National Park and Preserve. They have adapted to a changing market, and consequently they continue to do what they love. Pilots still fly over a wilderness landscape where technology requires superb human know-how and skill. Hunting is still allowed in the preserve and represents big business for many pilot and guides. Numerous local pilots maintain commercial operator permits with the National Park Service, giving them authorization to fly visitors into and out of the park. Although helicopters are prohibited in the park for commercial purposes, they remain the aircraft of choice for park rangers, biologists, geologists, archeologists, and historians who depend on those skilled pilots to provide access to the park's hard-to-reach places to study, manage, and preserve the park's natural and cultural resources. A telling sign that the two sides are seeking middle ground is the employment of Nabesna aviator Lynn Ellis, a onetime hunting guide who now serves as the pilot for Wrangell–Saint Elias National Park and Preserve.

No longer demanding access with new roads as they did in the 1930s, many of the Copper Belt residents (many of whom are pilots themselves) appreciate the wilderness value of the Wrangells and are content to remain connected to the "Outside" as well as to each other through the region's local air routes. Just as Gillam, Reeve, and Smith had done eight decades ago, today's bush pilots continue to provide isolated communities access to economic systems, commodities, and medical care while at the same time allow residents to maintain a "frontier" ethos and wilderness lifestyle. Perhaps former Cordova Airways secretary and Alaska Airlines representative Susan Bramsteadt put it best: "Whether they were operated by single bush pilots like Gillam, Reeve, or Mudhole or major corporations like Alaska Airlines, Alaska pilots are important because "planes connect people."[24]

This book strived to highlight eight decades of aviation history that took place over the mountain region of Wrangell–Saint Elias. It never endeavored to lessen the historical significance of the Alaska bush pilot— perhaps to lessen the embellishment but most important to change to our orientation of aviation in Alaska. I hope the book challenged readers to think about the relation between history, popular culture, and Alaskan identity, Alaska's relationship to the rest of the country, and why the stories of these sky cowboys resonate so strongly among residents of the Wrangells as well as the rest of us. This suggests that, although it is impossible to extract it entirely, we should move beyond the frontier in explaining aviation. By understanding Alaska's bush pilots more broadly, we gain a better appreciation for their feats and their failures. Rather than conquerors, they become students of nature. We see them not only as pilots but as husbands and fathers too. By placing them in a historical context, we have more opportunities to return Alaska to its former "bridging role," so that instead of perceiving Alaska as a last frontier— the end of the road, the bridge to nowhere—we see how aviation has and continues to link us to the larger Pacific and circumpolar world, making Alaska *the* bridge. Perhaps the historical narrative becomes less romantic, but to all us nonflyers the story becomes far more complex, historically grounded, and arguably just as thrilling.

NOTES

NOTES TO INTRODUCTION

1   The term "American Century" was used by *Time* magazine's editor to describe America's political, economic, and cultural dominance during the twentieth century.

2   Robert J. Serling, *Character and Characters: The Spirit of Alaska Airlines* (Seattle: Documentary Media LLC, 2008), 15.

3   Alaska Department of Transportation and Public Facilities, "Alaska Roads Historic Overview: Applied Historic Contexts for Alaska Roads," Alaska Department of Natural Resources, Anchorage, 2014, 101.

4   "Alaskan Air Pioneers," *New York Times*, October 24, 1920.

5   Lawrence E. Davies, "Alaskan Obligated to Travel by Air: Territory Has Only 5,000 Miles of Roads—But Gain Is Seen," *New York Times*, July 15, 1958.

6   Ibid.

7   Ernest Gruening, *The State of Alaska* (New York: Random House, 1954), 433.

8   Willis Camp, "Alaska—the World's New Crossroad," *Alaska Life* (May 1943): 19–23.

9   "Great Anchorage Today: Air Crossroad of the World," Anchorage Chamber of Commerce, Anchorage Alaska, 1965.

10 From the Bookstore With Too Many Details, an online rare bookseller based in Alaska, specializing in signed books on bush pilots and World War II history.

11 Jean Potter, *The Flying North* (New York: Macmillan Company, 1945).

12 "Beth Day, 1924–present," *Something about the Author* 33 (1983): 55.

13 Kathryn Winslow, review of Day's *Glacier Pilot*, *Chicago Sunday Tribune*, July 14, 1957.

14 Review of Day's *Glacier Pilot*, *Book Review Digest* (1957): 237.

15 M. S. Watson, review of Day's *Glacier Pilot*, *New York Herald Tribune*, June 16, 1957.

16 Beth Day, *Glacier Pilot: The Story of Bob Reeve and the Flyers Who Pushed Back Alaska's Air Frontiers* (New York: Henry Holt and Co., 1957), 55–56.

17   Buffalo Bill tended to say during his Wild West show that the bullet was the "pioneer of civilization," where the day's scholars usually credited the plow. For more information on Buffalo Bill, see *The Frontier in American Culture*, essays by Richard White and Patricia Nelson Limerick (Berkeley: University of California Press, 1994).

18   "Cats over Alaska," *Em Kayan* (April 1942): 8–11.

19   "Sky King TV Show," *Crazy about TV.com*, online at www.crazyabouttv.com/skyking.html.

20   E. L. "Bob" Bartlett wrote the introduction of Pat Wachel's *Oscar Winchell: Alaska's Flying Cowboy* (Minneapolis: T. S. Denison & Company, Inc., 1967), 10.

21   Harmon Helmericks, *The Last of the Bush Pilots* (New York: Alfred A. Knoff, Inc. 1969), xi.

22   Roderick Nash, *Wilderness and the American Mind* (New Haven: Yale University Press, 1982), 276.

23   Steven C. Levi, *Cowboys of the Sky: The Story of the Alaska's Bush Pilots* (Anchorage: Publications Consultants, 2008), 12.

24   Kim Heacox, "Bold Pilots and the Great Beyond," *Alaska Magazine* 55 (July 1989): 30–35.

25   David T. Courtwright, *Sky as Frontier: Adventure, Aviation, and Empire* (College Station: Texas A&M University Press, 2005), 6.

26   Ibid., 9.

27   Stephen E. Mills and James W. Phillips, *Sourdough Sky* (New York: Bonanza Books, 1969), 5.

28   Ibid., 10.

29   For more on the region's geology, see U.S. Geological Survey, "A Geological Guide to Wrangell–Saint Elias National Park and Preserve, Alaska; a Tectonic Collage of Northbound Terranes," by Gary Winkler et al., Professional Papers 1616, 2000.

30   Walter A. Wood, "The Icefield Ranges Research Project," *Geographical Review* 53, no. 2 (1963): 163–84.

1. COWBOYS, SOURDOUGHS, AND ALASKA BUSH PILOTS

1   Frederick Jackson Turner, "The Significance of the Frontier in American History," in *Annual Report of the American Historical Association for the Year 1893* (Washington, D.C.: Government Printing Office, 1984), 199–227.

2   Ibid.

3   Richard White and Patricia Nelson Limerick, *The Frontier in American Culture*, edited by James R. Grossman (Berkeley: University of California Press, 1994), 1.

4   William W. Savage Jr., *Cowboy Life: Constructing an American Myth*, 2nd edition (Niwot: Colorado Press, 1993), 8.

5   Ibid., 5.

6   Richard White, "Frederick Jackson Turner and Buffalo Bill," in White and Limerick, *Frontier in American Culture*, 49.

7   Ibid., 46.

8   See Richard W. Etulain, "Origins of the Western," *Journal of Popular Culture* 5 (Spring 1972): 799–805. Theodore Roosevelt claimed a frontier identity in the preface to his four-volume *Winning of the West*, xiv.

9   Pierre Berton, *The Klondike Fever: The Life and Death of the Last Great Gold Rush* (New York: Carroll & Graf Publishers, Inc., 1958), 95–96.

10   Susan Kollin, *Nature's State: Imagining Alaska as the Last Frontier* (Chapel Hill: University of North Carolina Press, 2001), 5.

11   Stephen Haycox, *Frigid Embrace: Politics, Economics, and Environment in Alaska* (Corvallis: Oregon State University Press, 2002), 5; Peter A. Coates, *The Trans-Alaska Pipeline Controversy: Technology, Conservation, and the Frontier* (Fairbanks: University of Alaska Press, 1993), 30.

12   Elizabeth Lauzen, "Marketing the Image of the Las Frontier," *Alaska Journal* (Spring 1982): 13–19.

13   "Frontier Flight," *Alaska Geographic* 25, no. 4 (1998): 8.

14   *Chitina Leader*, July 29, 1913 (originally published in the *Cordova Daily Alaskan* on July 22, 1913).

15   Ken Smith, "Airplanes in the Wrangells," *Wrangell St. Elias News* (March and April 2000), (January and February 2002).

16   U.S. National Park Service, report written by Geoffrey Bleakley, "The Development of Air Transportation, 1929–1955," report date unknown, Wrangell–St. Elias National Park and Preserve (WRST) Historical Files, Copper Center, Alaska.

17   Ibid., " Development of Air Transportation, 1929–1955," 1–4.

18   R. C. Reeve, "Statement before the Civil Aeronautics Board, in the Matter of the Application of Reeve Airways, Valdez, Alaska, for a Certificate of Public Convenience and Necessity, Exceptions to Examiners Reports, Docket No. 340," Civil Aeronautics Board, Washington, D.C., August 1939.

19   Calvin S. White, "Alaska Has Many Wings: Plane Has Become Motor Car of Far North—Its Varied Services," *New York Times*, November 8, 1936.

20   Leo P. Bott Jr., "Observations on Strange Alaska," *Nation's Business*, September 16, 1928.

21   White, "Alaska Has Many Wings."

22   Ibid.

23   In the chapter titled "Flying Machine," coauthors Gay Salisbury and Laney Salisbury explain why planes were not used to deliver the serum to Nome during the diphtheria epidemic in 1925. See their book *The Cruelest Miles: The Heroic Story of Dogs and Men in a Race against an Epidemic* (New York: W. W. Norton & Company), 79–108.

24   Ibid., 79–108.

25   "Capt. Martin Gave Lecture: Lectured to Small Audience on Aeronautics Last Night," *Fairbanks Daily News Miner*, June 27, 1913.

26   Reeve as quoted in Day, *Glacier Pilot*, 34.

27   Winchell as quoted in Wachel, *Alaska's Flying Cowboy*, 59.

28   Michael S. Kennedy, "Arctic Flying Machines and Alaskan Bush Pilots: A Synopsis of Early Aviation History," in *Transportation in Alaska's Past*, Office of History and Archaeology Publication No. 30 (Anchorage: Alaska Historical Society, 1982), 183–238.

29   Steven Kesselman, "The Frontier Thesis and the Great Depression," *Journal of the History of Ideas* 29, no. 2 (April–June 1968): 253–68.

30   Franklin Roosevelt expressed the idea of a limited frontier in a speech he delivered at the Commonwealth Club in San Francisco on September 23, 1932. This was one of the underlying reasons for sending Midwestern farmers to Palmer, Alaska, in 1935.

31   Orlando W. Miller, *The Frontier in Alaska and the Matanuska Colony* (New Haven: Yale University Press, 1975), 2.

32   W. P. Webb, *Divided We Stand: The Crisis of a Frontierless Democracy* (New York, 1937).

33   Robert E. Riegel, *America Moves West* (New York, 1930).

34   Miller, *Frontier in Alaska and the Matanuska Colony*, 2.

35   Ibid.

36   Leo A. Kieran, "Resourceful Air Pilots of Alaska," *New York Times*, March 6, 1932.

37   Writers in the 1930s contributed to a literary genre that fictionalized life on the western frontier, as described by frontier scholars Robert E. Riegel and Robert G. Athearn in *America Moves West,* 4th edition (New York: Holt, Rinehart and Winston, Inc., 1964), 609–10.

38   Paul Lien, "Angels in Furs: A Cavalcade of Alaska Aviation," *Alaska Life* (1940).

39   "Flying Is Different in Alaska," *Los Angeles Times*, July 28, 1929.

40   "Planes Supplant Dog Teams in Alaska, Flying over 55-Day Trails in a Few Hours," *New York Times*, November 29, 1936.

41   "Hearings before the Subcommittee of the Committee on Appropriations," U.S. Senate, on HR 5779, April 9, 1937, cited in Gruening, *State of Alaska,* 303.

42   Alaska had seventy-nine planes in regular service and ninety-four airfields; the number of passengers carried had increased to 16,982 by 1937. These numbers reflect an increase in Alaskans flying in planes by the end of the 1930s. Records cited on April 9, 1937, Hearings before the Subcommittee of the Committee on Appropriations, U.S. Senate, on HR 5779, in Gruening, *State of Alaska*, 290–91; 303.

43   Terrence Cole, "Golden Years: The Decline of Gold Mining in Alaska," *Pacific Northwest Quarterly* (April 1989): 62–71.

44   Vernon L. Parrington, *Main Currents in American Thought,* vol. 3 (New York, 1930), xix–xx.

45   Dick Douglas, *In the Land of Thunder Mountain: Adventuring with Father Hubbard among the Volcanoes of Alaska* (New York: Brewer, Warren and Putnam, 1932).

2. MINES, MAIL, AND MERCY FLIGHTS

1   Ken Smith, "Airplanes in the Wrangells," *Wrangell St. Elias News* (March and April 2000).

2   According to biographer Arnold Griese, Gillam's family accidently threw away his boxed records after his death in 1943; see Griese, *Bush Pilot: Early Alaska Aviator Harold Gillam, Sr. Lucky or Legend?* (Anchorage: Publication Consultants, 2005).

3   Dermot Cole, *Frank Barr: Bush Pilot and Alaska and the Yukon* (Edmonds: Alaska Northwest Publishing Company, 1986), 80; and Jim Rearden, *Alaska's First Bush Pilots, 1923–30: And the Winter Search in Siberia for Eielson and Borland* (Missoula: Pictorial Histories Publishing Company, Inc., 2009), 203.

4   Day, *Glacier Pilot*, 22.

5   Cole, *Frank Barr*, 80.

6   June Allen, "Harold Gillam: A Tragic Final Flight," *Sitenews.us.org*, August 17, 2004 online at www.sitnews.us/JuneAllen/HaroldGillam/081704_final_flight.html.

7   Quoted in Pat Wachel, "An Alaskan Fearless Flier: Harold Gillam," *Alaska Northern Lights* 1, no. 2 (1966): 18–20.

8   Samme Gallaher and Aileen Gallaher, *Sisters: Coming of Age and Living Dangerously in the Wild Copper River Valley* (Kenmore, WA: Epicenter Press, 2004), 156.

9   Rearden, *Alaska's First Bush Pilots*, 203.

10   Kennedy, "Arctic Flying Machines and Alaskan Bush Pilots," 211.

11   Quoted in Day, *Glacier Pilot*, 134–35.

12   Robert H. Redding, *The Young Eagles: The Story of the Alaska Road Commission* (Valdez: Camprobber Publishers, 1977), 7–9.

13   Ibid., 7–9.

14   The Copper River & Northwestern Railway was constructed between 1907 and 1911.

15   After Alaska became a territory in 1912, the Territorial Legislature repealed the 1904 road tax law and replaced it with a flat four-dollar tax. Between 1920 and 1933, Congress paid approximately 60 percent of the ARC's annual budget, while 40 percent came from Alaskans.

16   Alaska Historical Commission, report by Claus-M. Naske, *Paving Alaska's Trails: The Work of the Alaska Road Commission,* Studies in History No. 152 (Juneau: Alaska Historical Commission, 1986), 1.

17   Ibid., 135.

18   Ibid, 124.

19   Board of Road Commissioners for Alaska, "Annual Report of the Alaska Road Commission, Fiscal Year 1923, Part II," Juneau, Alaska, 1923.

20   M. J. Kirchhoff, *Historic McCarthy: The Town That Copper Built* (Juneau: Alaska Cedar Press, 1993), 34.

21   "Nizina Bridge," *Historic Structures Inventory, WRST*, Alaska Regional Office, Anchorage, Alaska, ca. 1991.

22   Griese, *Bush Pilot*, 30–31.

23   Ibid., 31.

24   Ibid., 55; and Mills and Phillips, *Sourdough Skies*, 23.

25 Griese, *Bush Pilot*, 70.

26 Ibid., 68; and "Local Men Will Take Up Flying," *Fairbanks Daily News-Miner*, August 15, 1928.

27 Joseph M. Dunn, "Problems of Alaska Aviation," *Farthest-North Collegian* (June 1929): 15–17.

28 "Spinning Biplane Falls to the Ground Here—Gillam and Danforth Are Hurt," *Fairbanks Daily News-Miner*, September 10, 1928.

29 Rearden, *Alaska's First Bush Pilots*, 204.

30 According to Jim Rearden (in *Alaska's First Bush Pilots*), some reports claim that Gillam only had forty or fifty flight hours, which is minimal for even today's pilots.

31 Dirk Tordoff, *Mercy Pilot: The Joe Crosson Story* (Kenmore: Epicenter Press, 2002), 76.

32 See Griese, *Bush Pilot*; and Tordoff, *Mercy Pilot*.

33 Mills and Phillips, *Sourdough Skies*, 23.

34 The source of this information comes from Ken Smith and the Alaska Aviation Heritage Museum, but it should be noted that the story of Gillam and Marvel being romantically linked remains unconfirmed and has been questioned by numerous sources. Kenny Smith, "Airplanes in the Wrangells, Harold Gillam Update," *Wrangell St. Elias News* (May and June 2001): 12.

35 For a detailed history of the derby, see Gene Nora Jessen's *The Powder Puff Derby of 1929: The True Story of the First Women's Cross-Country Air Race* (Naperville, IL: SourceBooks, Inc., 2002).

36 Ibid.

37 In Tordoff, *Mercy Pilot*, 101.

38 Ibid.

39 "Gillam Will Fly for His New Company," *Fairbanks Daily News-Miner*, November 22, 1929.

40 *New York Times* as cited in Cole, *Frank Barr*, 79.

41 "Gillam Flying Swallow Plane," *Fairbanks Daily News-Miner*, May 6, 1930.

42 Robert W. Stevens, *Alaskan Aviation History* (Des Moines, WA: Polynyas Press, 1990), 880. ARC Records.

43 Gillam passed his airman's examination on June 2, 1930. Rearden, *Alaska's First Bush Pilots*, 207.

44 "Gillam Making Success Air Venture," *Fairbanks Daily News-Miner*, September 6, 1930.

45 Naske, *Paving Alaska's Trails*, 142.

46 "Gillam Will Fly for His New Company," *Fairbanks Daily News-Miner*, November 22, 1929.

47 Gruening, *State of Alaska*, 290–91; and Naske, *Paving Alaska's Trails*, 144.

48 Naske, *Paving Alaska's Trails*, 145.

49 Ibid.

50 William Sulzer's brother, Charles August Sulzer, was Alaska's nonvoting delegate from 1917 to 1919. Mount Sulzer near Skolai Pass was named for him.

51 Bleakley, "Development of Air Transportation, 1929–1955," 1–4.

52 Charles C. Hawley and T. K. Bundtzen, "William Sulzer," Alaska Mining Hall of Fame, online at http://alaskamininghalloffame.org/inductees/sulzer.php.

53 *Chitina Leader*, January 21, 1918.

54 U.S. National Park Service, report by Geoffrey T. Bleakley, "A History of the Chisana Mining District, Alaska, 1890–1990," Wrangell–Saint Elias National Park and Preserve, Copper Center, Alaska, 1996, 14.

55 To Gen. James G. Steese, from William Sulzer, February 18, 1927, Alaska Road Commission, Bureau of Public Roads—Project Correspondence, 1916–1959, RG 30, Box 33 SP1 Chisana, NA-RA.

56 To Aaron F. Nelson, U.S. Commissioner, from William Sulzer, circa 1927. Aviation Files, Wrangell–Saint Elias National Park and Preserve Headquarters, Copper Center, Alaska.

57 Ibid.

58 Kirk Stanley, *Nabesna Gold: And the Making of the Historic Gold Mine and Town on the Frontier of Alaska's Territory* (Anchorage: Todd Communications, 2002), 71.

59 Fred Moffitt, *Geology of the Hanagita-Bremner Region Alaska*, U.S. Geological Survey Bulletin 57617, 1915.

60 "Bremner River District Mecca for Prospectors; Ramer Original Locator," *Alaska Weekly*, March 8, 1935.

61 Description of Chisana–Nabesna Aviation Fields, Alaska Road Commission, Bureau of Public Roads—Project Correspondence, 1916–1959, RG 30, Box 33/10/05/14(4) SP1 Chisana, NA-RA.

62 Board of Road Commissioners for Alaska, "Alaska Road Commission. Annual Report 1930, Vol. II" (Juneau, 1930), 53; and Bleakley, "Development of Air Transportation, 1929–1955," 1–4. Description of Chisana–Nabesna Aviation Fields, Alaska Road Commission, Bureau of Public Roads—Project Correspondence, 1916–1959, RG 30, Box 33/10/05/14(4) SP1 Chisana, NA-RA.

63 U.S. Park Service, report by Paul J. White, *Bremner Historic District, Cultural Landscape Report Wrangell–St. Elias National Park and Preserve, Alaska* (Anchorage: Alaska Regional Office, 2000), 27; and "Nabesna Mining Corporation, Article of Incorporation, October 25, 1929," Alaska State Archives, Juneau Alaska. The names of the original directors are Carl F. Whitham, R. J. Sheppard, Thomas S. Scott, D. H. Kelsey, A. E. Moore, John Coasts, and Frank Shipp.

64 "Gillam Will Fly for His New Company."

65 "Gillam Making Success Air Venture," *Fairbanks Daily News-Miner*, September 6, 1930.

66 Board of Road Commissioners for Alaska, "Alaska Road Commission. Annual Report 1932, Vol. II" (Juneau, 1932), 26; and "Plane Can't Rise from Small Field: Cordova Pilot Makes Good Landing But Will Have to Call on ARC to Enlarge Field," *Fairbanks Daily News-Miner*, June 9, 1931. To Mr. Wm. A. Hesse, Highway Engineer, from Charles T. O'Neill, McCarthy, Alaska, October 14,

1931, Alaska Road Commission, Bureau of Public Roads—Project Correspondence, 1916–1959, RG 30, box 32, SP1 Bremner, NA-AR.

67 To Mr. Wm. A. Hesse, Highway Engineer, from Charles T. O'Neill, McCarthy, Alaska, October 14, 1931, Alaska Road Commission, Bureau of Public Roads—Project Correspondence, 1916–1959, RG 30, box 32, SP1 Bremner, NA-AR.

68 Griese, *Bush Pilot*, 176.

69 "Thomas J. Donohoe, Leading Cordova Citizen for Many Years, Passes Away Today," *Cordova Daily Times*, January 17, 1934.

70 Bremner Gold Mining Company, Articles of Incorporation, Alaska State Archives. Juneau, Alaska.

71 Each strip had been entirely supported with the ARC's territorial funds, and all were built to support the regional mining industry: Board of Road Commissioners for Alaska, "Alaska Road Commission. Annual Report 1932, Vol. II" (Juneau 1932), 26. Other funding sources came through private contributions, from mining companies such as Nabesna Mining Corporation or the Kennicott Mining Corporation, and from roadhouse operators such as Florence Barnes, while other sources included the aviation companies themselves. Gillam Airways and, later, Cordova Air Service both made monetary contributions to specific ARC projects throughout the 1930s (see Alaska Road Commission's Annual Reports, 1930–1941).

72 Board of Road Commissioners for Alaska, "Alaska Road Commission. Annual Report 1929, Vol. II" (Juneau 1929), 63, 65, 67; and Alaska Road Commission, "Annual Report 1930, Vol. II, 53.

73 "Gillam Will Fly for His New Company."

74 Board of Road Commissioners for Alaska, "Alaska Road Commission. Annual Report 1931, Vol. II" (Juneau 1931), 40–42.

75 Pilot A. A. Bennett convinced the Zenith Company to design and build a rugged biplane, starting in 1929. Only seven of the Zenith models were ever built—Gillam's was probably number five. The Great Depression halted production, and the company went back to making farming implements (see Rearden, *Alaska's First Bush Pilots*, 205).

76 "Harold Gillam Landed Yesterday," *Chitina Herald*, January 18, 1931.

77 Stevens, *Alaskan Aviation History*, 870.

78 P. S. Smith, *Mineral Industry of Alaska in 1931 Administrative Report*, USGS Bulletin 844–A (1933): 21; U.S. Park Service, report by Margie Steigerwald, "Pioneer Pilots of the Wrangell-St. Elias" (1996), WRST Park Files, Copper Center, Alaska; and Stanley, *Nabesna Gold*, 78.

79 Territorial Mining Report, by B. D. Stewart, "Mining Investigations and Mine Inspection in Alaska, Including Assistance to Prospectors" (March 31, 1933): 76–77.

80 Mills and Phillips, *Sourdough Skies*, 33.

81 Alaska Territorial Report, by Earl Pilgrim, "Upper Nabesna, Chisana and Snag River Area," MR-078-02 (1930): 5.

82   Gallaher and Gallaher, *Sisters,* 146.

83   Stevens, *Alaskan Aviation History,* 880.

84   Margaret Keenan Harrais, "Alaska Periscope" (unpublished manuscript), 162–63, copy located at Alaska Regional Office, Anchorage.

85   L. B. Gatchell, William R. Alley, and J. G. Johnson, eds., "Alaska Pioneer Flights," in *American Air Mail Catalogue: Reference Listing of the Air Posts of the World* (American Air Mail Society, 1940), 293–97.

86   Rearden, *Alaska's First Bush Pilots,* 10–11. "Del. Dimond Fighting for Airmail Service in Alaska," *Cordova Daily Times,* February 12, 1934.

87   "Report to the Second Assistant Postmaster General on the First Trip of the Alaska Air Mail Service," by C. B. Eielson, 1924.

88   Dorothy Page, *Polar Pilot: The Carl Ben Eielson Story* (Danville, IL: Interstate Publishers, Inc. 1992), 157.

89   Sutherland as quoted in ibid., 77.

90   Rearden, *Alaska's First Bush Pilots,* 12.

91   Division of Legislative Finance for the House Finance Committee, "Air Service to Rural Alaska: A Study in Inadequacy," by Walter B. Parker, Patricia I. Parker, and G. Michael Harmon (October 20, 1979), 48.

92   "Del. Dimond Fighting for Air Mail Service in Alaska."

93   Alaska Territorial Chamber of Commerce, "Alaska: Its Needs for National Defense and Airmail Service," Juneau, 1934.

94   "Air Mail for Alaska," *Anchorage Times,* September 8, 1934.

95   Griese, *Bush Pilot,* 146.

96   Ibid., 149.

97   *Cordova Daily Times,* April 21, 1934.

98   "Gillam Airways Gets Copper River Mail Trips," *Valdez Miner,* November 29, 1935.

99   "Gillam Brings Large Plane to Cordova," *Cordova Times,* July 5, 1935.

100   Tordoff, *Mercy Pilot,* 123.

101   Rearden, *Alaska's First Bush Pilots,* 200.

102   Mills and Phillips, *Sourdough Skies,* 50.

103   Reeve as quoted in Day, *Glacier Pilot,* 135.

104   Robert W. Stevens, "*Spirit of Valdez,* Owen Meals, and the First Airplane in Valdez," *Alaska Journal* (Spring 1985): 46–48.

105   Stanley, *Nabesna Gold,* 101.

106   Ken Smith, "Airplanes in the Wrangells," *Wrangell St. Elias News* (March and April 2000): 9. "Plane Rushed to Aid Injured Man," *Fairbanks Daily News-Miner,* October 3, 1929.

107   Jean Potter, *Flying North* (New York: Macmillan Company, 1945), 150.

108   "Carl Whitham Dies from Recent Fall," *Valdez Miner,* December 14, 1934; and "Carl Whitham Still Alive and Improving Fast," *Valdez Miner,* December 21, 1934.

109   Reeve as quoted in Day, *Glacier Pilot,* 119–20.

110 Jean Potter, *Flying Frontiersmen* (New York: Macmillan Company, 1956), 109.

111 Wachel, "Alaskan Fearless Flier," 75.

112 Potter, *Flying North*, 144–45.

113 Watchel, "Alaskan Fearless Flier," 71.

114 Winchell as quoted in ibid., 76.

115 White, *Bremner Historic District*, 28.

116 *New York Times* as cited in Stanley, *Nabesna Gold*, 60.

117 White, *Bremner Historic District*, 28.

118 Winchell as quoted in Wachel, "Alaskan Fearless Flier," 76.

119 "Davies Flys for Gillam," *Valdez Miner*, March 12, 1937.

120 "Bub Seltenriech," in National Park Service, *Kennecott Kids: Interviews with the Children of Kennecott*, vol. 2. (Anchorage: Alaska Support Office, 2001), 254.

121 "Incorporation Papers, Cordova Air Service," Alaska State Archives, Juneau, Alaska; and LeahDean Kirkpatrick Ross, *Some of My Experiences in Alaska* (Newton, KS: Mennonite Press, 1998), 4.

122 Griese, *Bush Pilot*, 170–71. Gillam Airways established an office in the Donohoe Building in downtown Cordova.

123 "Gillam Injured in Fall from Plane," *Valdez Miner*, April 28, 1934.

124 Reeve as quoted in Day, *Glacier Pilot*, 82.

125 Griese, *Bush Pilot*, 137.

126 Potter, *Flying North*, 144–45.

127 Merle Smith as quoted in Kennedy, "Arctic Flying Machines and Alaskan Bush Pilots," 211.

128 Frank Barr as quoted in Cole, *Frank Barr*, 93.

129 Wachel, "Alaskan Fearless Flier," 18–20.

130 Kennedy, "Arctic Flying Machines and Alaskan Bush Pilots," 211.

3. MUDFLAT TAKEOFFS AND GLACIER LANDINGS

1   Day, *Glacier Pilot*, 17.

2   Potter, *Flying North*, 166.

3   Karen Hartsfield, "Reeve's Unique Family Airline," *Alaska Industry* (January 1973): 34–35.

4   Kennedy, "Arctic Flying Machines and Alaskan Bush Pilots," 184–238.

5   Reeve as quoted in Day, *Glacier Pilot*, 31.

6   David Roberts, *Escape from Lucania: An Epic Story of Survival* (New York: Simon & Schuster, 2002), 14.

7   Day, *Glacier Pilot*, 34.

8   Roberts, *Escape from Lucania*, 15.

9   Meals as quoted in Beth Day, "He Looked Like a Tramp," in *Early Air Pioneers: 1862–1935*, edited by Major James F. Sunderman (New Work: Franklin Watts, Inc., 1961), 248.

10 Reeve as quoted in Day, "He Looked Like a Tramp," 252.

11 Ibid.

12 Reeve as quoted in Stan Cohen, *Flying Beats Work: The Story of Reeve Aleutian Airways* (Missoula: Pictorial Histories Publishing Company, 1988), 12.

13 Leo A. Kieran, "Resourceful Air Pilots of Alaska," *New York Times*, March 6, 1932.

14 Helmericks, *Last of the Bush Pilots*, 96–97.

15 Reeve as quoted in Cohen, *Flying Beats Work*, 12.

16 Gallaher and Gallaher, *Sisters*, 153–54.

17 At one particular dance at the Copper Center roadhouse, Harold Gillam was caught dancing with another man's wife. "Slim really beat up on Gillam, in spite of the several men who tried to stop him." Ibid., 157.

18 Day, *Glacier Pilot*, 72–73.

19 G. Bradley Koontz, "Alaska's 1930s Bush Pilots: Remarkable Fliers and Creative Mechanics Keeping the Engine Oil Warm at 60 below," *Aircraft Maintenance Technology* (April 2007): 36–41.

20 Day, *Glacier Pilot*, 77.

21 Reeve as quoted in ibid., 73.

22 Ibid., 77.

23 Koontz tells Pat O'Conner's story in his article; see Koontz, "Alaska's 1930s Bush Pilots," 39–40.

24 Day, *Glacier Pilot*, 77.

25 Kieran, "Resourceful Air Pilots of Alaska," 22.

26 Reeve as quoted in Day, *Glacier Pilot*, 78–79.

27 Stanley, *Nabesna Gold*, 95.

28 Roberts, *Escape from Lucania*, 26.

29 Stanley, *Nabesna Gold*, 105.

30 Reeve as quoted in Day, *Glacier Pilot*, 72.

31 Pat Wachel, *Oscar Winchell: Alaska's Flying Cowboy* (Minneapolis: T.S. Denison & Company, Inc., 1967), 76.

32 Cohen, *Flying Beats Work*, 12.

33 Reeve quoted in Day, *Glacier Pilot*, 134.

34 Ibid., 55.

35 Reeve quoted in Cohen, *Flying Beats Work*, 13.

36 Day, *Glacier Pilot*, 46.

37 Advertisement in *Valdez Miner*, February 25, 1933.

38 Paul J. White, *Bremner Historic District, Cultural Landscape Report, Wrangell–St. Elias National Park and Preserve, Alaska* (Anchorage: Alaska Regional Office, 2000), 27–28.

39 John Troy as quoted in Cole, "Golden Years," 62–71.

40 Rex Beach, "The Place Is Alaska—the Business Is Mining," *Cosmopolitan* (January 1936).

41 Day, *Glacier Pilot*, 113.

42 "Valdez Alaska: The Key to the Golden Heart of Alaska," *Valdez Miner*, December 14, 1934.

43 "Development Is Speeded Up by Airplane: Pilot R. C. Reeve Tells of Advan-

tages over Former Methods of Transportation," *Valdez Miner*, February 22, 1935, previously published in the *Denver Mining Record*.

44   Reeve Airways Advertisement, *Valdez Miner*, February 24, 1934.

45   "Mining Activity Keeps Pilot Bob Reeve Busy," *Valdez Miner*, March 31, 1934; "Pilot Reeve Sets Record in Freighting This Winter," *Valdez Miner*, May 5, 1934; and "Valdez Pilot Makes Many Trips, Interior," *Valdez Miner*, June 2, 1934.

46   Day, *Glacier Pilot*, 108.

47   William Poy as quoted in "Parachute Drops Heavy Machinery Supplies Safely: Air Transport Plus Parachute Delivery Gets Supplies, Fuel, Food to Camp in Eight Days," *Valdez Miner*, March 15, 1935.

48   "Pilot Reeve and Mechanic Egan Back From Trip," *Valdez Miner*, December 14, 1934.

49   Roberts, *Escape from Lucania*, 18.

50   Ibid., 22.

51   Cohen, *Flying Beats Work*, 15.

52   Rex Beach, "Alaska's Flying Frontiersmen," *American Magazine* (April 1936): 42–43, 96–101.

53   Reeve as quoted in Day, *Glacier Pilot*, 112.

54   Roberts, *Escape from Lucania*, 15

55   Ibid., 20.

56   Day, *Glacier Pilot*, 113.

57   Beach, "Place Is Alaska."

58   Ibid.

59   Rex Beach, *Valley of Thunder* (New York: Grosset & Dunlap, 1939), 190–91.

60   Beach, "Alaska's Flying Frontiersmen," 98.

61   Ibid.

62   Ernest N. Patty, "The Airplane's Aid to Alaskan Mining," *Mining and Metallurgy* (February 1937): 92–94.

63   Haycox, *Frigid Embrace*, 4.

64   Reeve as quoted in Beach, "Alaska's Flying Frontiersmen," 42–43, 96–101.

65   Robert Bates, *The Love of Mountains Is Best* (Portsmouth, NH: Peter E. Randall Publisher, 1994), 71.

66   "Walter Wood's First Ascent of Mount Steele," *Life Magazine* (November 30, 1936).

67   Roberts, *Escape from Lucania*, 4, 12.

68   Cohen, *Flying Beats Work*, 30.

69   Washburn's letter as quoted in Roberts, *Escape from Lucania*, 17–18.

70   John E. Barrett, "Reeve Lands Freight on High Mountain: Pioneers Flight over One of Alaska's Unexplored Mountain Areas," *Valdez Miner*, May 14, 1937.

71   "Pilot Bob Reeve Holds World Record for Highest Landing: Local Man Lands on Glacier 8500 Feet up on Mt. Lucania," *Valdez Miner*, June 25, 1937.

72   Barrett, "Reeve Lands Freight on High Mountain."

73   "Reeve and Dow Return from Mt. Lucania Trip," *Valdez Miner*, May 14, 1937.

74 Washburn's journal as quoted in Roberts, *Escape from Lucania*, 21.

75 Ibid., 19–21.

76 Ibid., 21.

77 Cohen, *Flying Beats Work*, 18.

78 Bates, *Love of Mountains Is Best*, 76.

79 Roberts, *Escape from Lucania*, 35.

80 Ibid., 36.

81 Ibid.

82 Day, *Glacier Pilot*, 166.

83 "Most Hazardous Trip in Career; Says Pilot Reeve," *Valdez Miner*, June 25, 1937.

84 Bates, *Love of Mountains Is Best*, 77.

85 Quoted in Roberts, *Escape from Lucania*, 159.

86 "From a Mountain Climber's Album: Bradford Washburn Is First To Scale Mt. Lucania," *Life* (September 27, 1937).

87 Roberts, *Escape from Lucania*, 31.

88 Ibid., 178.

89 Cited in Day, *Glacier Pilot*, 196.

90 Reeve's letter as quoted in Bates, *Love of Mountains Is Best*, 97.

91 Ernie Pyle, "2000 Glacier Landings Made by Adonis of Alaskan Aviation," *Washington Daily News*, August 11, 1937, page 13.

92 Ibid.

93 Reeve as quoted in Cohen, *Flying Beats Work*, 35.

4. THE COPPER BELT LINE

1 "Historical Sketch of Cordova Airlines," *Cordova Daily Times*, July 18, 1958.

2 William H. Liebe and Chester T. Davis were also on the original board of directors of Cordova Air Service; see CAS Incorporation Papers, September 13, 1934, Alaska State Library, Juneau. John Rosswog, manager of a novelty store, and G. Earl Means, neighbor, became members of the board of directors at a later date, 1930 U.S. Census, ancestry.com; and "Historical Sketch of Cordova Airlines."

3 Ross, *Some of My Experiences in Alaska*, 4.

4 *Chitina Weekly Herald*, November 20, 1932.

5 "Historic Sketch of Cordova Airlines."

6 Ross, *Some of My Experiences in Alaska*, 31; and "Historic Sketch of Cordova Airlines."

7 "Five Ships on Field Yesterday Largest Group of Planes Ever Assembled at the Cordova Airport," *Cordova Daily Times*, April 2, 1934.

8 "Planes on the Go," *Cordova Daily Times*, January 30, 1934.

9 "Returns from McCarthy," *Cordova Daily Times*, January 27, 1934.

10 "Supplies by Plane," *Cordova Daily Times*, April 2, 1934.

11 "President Plans to Fix Price of Gold," *Fairbanks Daily News-Miner*, January 13, 1934.

12   "Bremner Nearing Producing Stage: Says Returning Owner," *Cordova Daily Times*, January 30, 1934.

13   Ibid.

14   Property records show that McCarthy homesteader Alfred Doze sold some property to local merchant J. B. O'Neill, who turned around and immediately sold the land to the Bremner Gold Mining Company. Unfortunately, the deeds for these transactions were burned in fires in Chitina, McCarthy, and Cordova that destroyed all record from 1925 to 1944, so there is no way of knowing the exact tract sold. Chitina Historic Books, Index General, 1915–1944, Film Roll 745, Book 24, pp. 401–3.

15   BGMC (short for Bremner Gold Mining Company) was stenciled on one of the support beams used to build the McCarthy Hangar, suggesting the company's involvement in building the hangar.

16   "Eastern Mine Firm to Back Bremner Mill: M. E. Erdofy of New York, and Others Here to Verify Bremner Report," *Cordova Daily Times*, July 9, 1934.

17   *Cordova Daily Times*, July 16, 1934; and Ross, *Some of My Experiences in Alaska*, 40.

18   Ross, *Some of My Experiences in Alaska*, 40.

19   *Cordova Daily Times*, August 17, 1934.

20   "Bremner Is Perfect Location for Mine; Good Airfield Is Most Crying Need at Present," *Cordova Daily Times*, August 18, 1934.

21   Ibid.

22   Ross, *Some of My Experiences in Alaska*, 40.

23   Mayor Chase's dedication as quoted in "Ceremonies Land Evening Dedicated New Airport; Entire Town Attends Function; Gillam First Pilot to Land," *Cordova Daily Times*, June 22, 1934.

24   Ibid.

25   *Cordova Daily Times*, August 30, 1933; and *Cordova Daily Times*, November 8, 1933.

26   Ross, *Some of My Experiences in Alaska*, 40.

27   *Cordova Daily Times*, September 9, 1935.

28   "Cordova Has Good Prospects, in Opinion of Capt. Lathrop," *Cordova Daily Times*, February 1, 1934; and Elizabeth Tower, *Alaska's First Homegrown Millionaire: Life and Times of Cap Lathrop* (Anchorage: Publication Consultants, 2006), 75.

29   "New Airplane Is Enroute for Local Concern: Cordova Air Service Purchases Bellanca Pacemaker; Employs New Pilot," *Cordova Daily Times*, September 29, 1934.

30   "Local Air Firm to Provide for Gear Exchange; Local Airfield Found Excellent Place for Changing Type Landing Gear," *Cordova Daily Times*, August 23, 1934; and "Novel Landing Gear Proves Successful: Cordova Air Service Announces Wheel-Ski Combination Solves Problem," *Cordova Daily Times*, nd, cited in Ross, *Some of My Experiences in Alaska*, 43.

31   "Designated as Repair Station: Cordova Air Service Gets Its Certificate from Govt." *Cordova Daily Times*, May 1936.

32   "Historical Sketch of Cordova Airlines."

33   Lone E. Janson, *Mudhole Smith: Alaska Flier* (Anchorage: Alaska Northwest Publishing Company, 1981), 46.

34   "New Service Is Offered by Air Company," *Cordova Daily Times*, June 29, 1935.

35   Ross, *Some of My Experiences in Alaska*, 40.

36   "Kirk and Geologists at Yakutaga," 99-2-4, and "Kirkpatrick Folder," Aviation Files, Cordova Historical Museum, Cordova, Alaska.

37   Ross, *Some of My Experiences in Alaska*, 40.

38   Janson, *Mudhole Smith*, 64.

39   Ibid., 44.

40   "A Friendly Message," *Cordova Daily Times*, October 7, 1934.

41   "Chamber to Back Field in Chistochina," *Cordova Daily Times*, February 21, 1935.

42   "Bremner Mine Asks for Enlargements to Its Airfield There," *Cordova Daily Times*, May 13, 1935.

43   To Cordova Chamber of Commerce, from Bremner Gold Mining Company, Inc. May 8, 1935, in Alaska Road Commission, Bureau of Public Roads—Project Correspondence, 1916–1959, RG 30, box 32, SP1 Bremner, NA-AR, Anchorage, Alaska.

44   White, *Bremner Historic District,* 54; and "The Bremner Gold Mining Company Offers 1,000,000 Shares of Preferred Stock at 10 Cents a Share," *Valdez Miner*, June 18, 1936.

45   "Pilot Reeve Tells Anchorage Friends of Valdez Mines," *Anchorage Times*, January 11, 1935.

46   Warranty Deed, Bremner Gold Mining Company and the Alaska Road Commission, February 10, 1936.

47   V. G. Vance was a Cordova banker who initially granted the company its loan to construct the mill for the 1934 season.

48   "The Bremner Gold Mining Company ad," *Valdez Miner*, June 18, 1936.

49   "Time Flies So Should You!" advertisement for Cordova Air Service, circa 1936, in "Kirkpatrick Folder," Aviation Files, Cordova Historical Museum, Cordova, Alaska.

50   Advertisement for Cordova Air Service, Inc., *Cordova Daily Times*, circa 1930s, in "Kirkpatrick Folder," Aviation Files, Cordova Historical Museum, Cordova, Alaska.

51   "Kirkpatrick Lands on Lake Last Evening," *Cordova Daily Times*, May 7, 1935.

52   "Time Flies So Should You!" advertisement for Cordova Air Service, circa 1936.

53   Janson, *Mudhole Smith*, 39–42.

54   Ted Spenser, "Stearman Saga," *Alaska Flying*, nd; and "1928 Stearman C2B," Alaska Aviation Heritage Museum Files, Anchorage, Alaska.

55   Janson, *Mudhole Smith*, 33, 43, 67, 57, 44–49.

56   Bleakley, "Development of Air Transportation, 1929–1955," 1–4.

57   L. Jo King, *Bird in the Bush* (Anchorage: KwiE Publishing, Ltd., 2008), 33.

58   In her scrapbook (now in the McCarthy Museum, in McCarthy, Alaska) Bertha Ramer kept an article titled "Cordova Gains 'Mudhole' Airport," which talked about how Merle Smith received his famous nickname. On

a sticky note, Bertha wrote "Error: Pete Ramer named Smitty 'Mudhole.'"
Reeve, who has long been given credit for the nickname, likely heard it first
from Ramer, who had witnessed the crash.

59 "Merle K. 'Mudhole' Smith, 1908–1981," *Alaskafest* (August 1981): 4.

60 The *Valdez Miner* ran both ads next to each other on June 28, 1935.

61 Smith as quoted in Janson, *Mudhole Smith*, 59.

62 Ibid., 54.

63 Cole, "Golden Years," 62–71.

64 White, *Bremner Historic District*, 28.

65 Quoted in Janson, *Mudhole Smith*, 69.

66 Ibid., 50–54.

67 "Washburn Ends Summer's Work in the Area: Aerial Photographer Departs
Today after Several Photo Flights," *Cordova Daily Times*, October 3, 1938.

68 Bradford Washburn, "Aerial Exploration of the Great Glaciers of the Alaskan
Coast and Interior (abstract)," *American Geological Society Bulletin* 52, no. 12
(December 1, 1941): 1937.

69 Bradford Washburn, "A Preliminary Report on Studies of the Mountains and
Glaciers of Alaska," *Geographical Journal* 98, no. 5/6 (November–December
1941): 219–27.

70 Ibid., 224.

71 Bradford Washburn, "Says St. Elias Range 'Climbed' to Heights," *New York
Times*, August 24, 1938.

72 "Washburn Ends Summer's Work in this Area," *Cordova Daily Times*, October
3, 1938.

73 Janson, *Mudhole Smith*, 69 (quotation); and Michael Lappen, "Whose Promised Land? A History of Conservation and Development Management Plans
for the Wrangell and Saint Elias Mountain Region, Alaska, 1938–1980," (commissioned report) (1984): 114–15.

74 Lappen, "Whose Promised Land," 36.

75 Ibid., 36–37.

76 White, *Bremner Historic District*, 5.

77 Cole, "Golden Years," 62–71; and "Yellow Band Gold Mines Submit Annual
Report," *Alaska Weekly*, December 22, 1939.

78 Cole, "Golden Years," 62–71.

79 Janson, *Mudhole Smith*, 78.

80 "Kirkpatrick—Flyer, Gentleman," *Cordova Daily Times*, April 1939.

5. TAMING THE "WILD NORTH"

1 Nick A. Komons, *Bonfires to Beacons: Federal Civil Aviation Policy under the Air
Commerce Act, 1926–1938* (Washington, D.C.: Smithsonian Institution Press,
1989), 3.

2 Kenneth John Button and Roger Stough, *Air Transport Networks: Theory and
Policy Implications* (Northampton: Edward Elgar Publishing, 2000), 86; and
John R. M. Wilson, *Turbulence Aloft: The Civil Aeronautics Administration amid*

Wars and Rumors of Wars, 1938–1953 (Washington, D.C.: U.S. Department of Transportation, 1979), 4–5.

3 Komons, *Bonfires to Beacons*, 3.

4 Quoted in *Aero Digest*, January 1924, 42.

5 Komons, in *Bonfires to Beacons*, points out that that the plea for regulation by hardheaded businessmen was an uncharacteristic twist for a period in American history noted for its sermons on self-help. See *Bonfires to Beacons*, 8.

6 Ibid., 91.

7 Serling, *Character and Characters*, 18.

8 "They Died Flying the Mail," National Postal Museum, online at http://www.postalmuseum.si.edu/airmail/pilot/pilot_old/pilot_flying.html.

9 Page, *Polar Pilot*, 36.

10 Dunn, "Problems of Alaskan Aviation," 15–17.

11 Ibid., 15–17.

12 Rearden, *Alaska's First Bush Pilots*, xv.

13 Reba Neighbors Collins, *Will Rogers and Wiley Post in Alaska: The Crash Felt "Round the World"* (Claremore, OK: Will Rogers Heritage Press, 1984).

14 For more on the crash that killed Will Rogers and Wiley Post, see Bryan B. Sterling and Frances N. Sterling, *Will Rogers and Wiley Post: Death at Barrow* (New York: M. Evans and Company, Inc., 1993); and John Evangelist Walsh, *When the Laughing Stopped: The Strange, Sad Death of Will Rogers* (Fairbanks: University of Alaska Press, 2008).

15 Pat Reeder, "Remember When or As I Recollect," *WillRogers.com*, online at www.willrogers.com/writers/stories/recollections/remember.html.

16 "Will Rogers, Wiley Post Die in Airplane Crash in Alaska; Nation Shocked by Tragedy," *New York Times*, August 17, 1935.

17 Rex Beach, "Will Had All Alaska Laughing, Then Came Crash, Leaving Sourdoughs Stunned," in Collins, *Will Rogers and Wiley Post in Alaska*, 27.

18 Collins, *Will Rogers and Wiley Post in Alaska*, 72.

19 Wilson, *Turbulence Aloft*, 9.

20 Button and Stough, *Air Transport Networks*, 86.

21 "CAB Examiner Warns of 'Destructive Competition' in Alaskan Aviation," *American Aviation* (January 1941).

22 Button and Stough, *Air Transport Networks*, 86.

23 "CAB Examiner Warns of 'Destructive Competition' in Alaskan Aviation."

24 Ibid.

25 Ibid.

26 Button and Stough, *Air Transport Networks*, 85.

27 Quoted in Janson, *Mudhole Smith*, 87.

28 Griese, *Bush Pilot*, 258.

29 Day, *Glacier Pilot*, 182.

30 Reeve as quoted in ibid.

31 Ibid., 182.

32 Smith as quoted in Janson, *Mudhole Smith*, 85.

33   Gillam as quoted in Day, *Glacier Pilot*, 183–84.

34   Ibid., 149.

35   Civil Aeronautics Board, R. C. Reeve's "Statement before the Civil Aeronautics Board, in the Matter of the Application of Reeve Airways, Valdez, Alaska, for a Certificate of Public Convenience and Necessity, Exceptions to Examiners Reports, Docket No. 340," August, 1939.

36   The CAB held a new round of hearings in 1941, and it was not until October 1942 that temporary certificates were actually issued to Alaska carriers. Subsidies, in the form of mail rates, were not established for Alaska flyers for another five years. In all, it took nine years for the territory's flyers to receive the benefits of the protective legislation that the Lower 48 carriers enjoyed. Another nine years passed before Alaska carriers were finally granted permanent certificates. Day, *Glacier Pilot*, 178.

37   "List of Stockholders as of June 30, 1943, Yellow Band Gold Mines, Inc.," Asa C. Baldwin Papers, circa 1907–1982, MS 36-1-2-4, Alaska State Library, Juneau.

38   Smith as quoted in Janson, *Mudhole Smith*, 86.

6. WORLD WAR II, REEVE'S FIELD, AND THE NORTHERN AIR ROUTE

1   Cohen, *Flying Beats Work*, 37.

2   Lavell Wilson, "Northway and Tanacross: Airports for the War Effort," *Alaska Geographic, World War II in Alaska* (1995): 72–76.

3   Galen Roger Perras, *Stepping Stones to Nowhere: The Aleutian Islands, Alaska, and American Military Strategy, 1867–1945* (Annapolis, MD: Naval Institute Press, 2003), xi.

4   Ibid., 9.

5   "The Army's Role in Building Alaska," Pamphlet 360–5, U.S. Army Alaska (April 1969): 70.

6   Ibid., 70–71.

7   Anthony J. Dimond, "National Defense in Alaska," *National Aeronautics* (March 1940): 14–15.

8   Gruening, *State of Alaska*, 309–10.

9   Dimond, "National Defense in Alaska," 14–15.

10   Gruening, *State of Alaska*, 309.

11   Ibid., 310.

12   Dimond, "National Defense in Alaska," 14–15; and Alaska Territorial Chamber of Commerce, "Alaska: Its Need for National Defense and Airmail Service," Juneau (1934).

13   Perras, *Stepping Stones to Nowhere*, 30. John Hail Cloe also discusses Alaska's strategic position in his classic study *Top Cover for America: The Air Force in Alaska, 1920–1983* (Anchorage: Air Force Association and Pictorial Histories Publishing Company, 1984), 1.

14   Kennedy, "Arctic Flying Machines and Alaska Bush Pilots," 212–17.

15   Dimond, "National Defense in Alaska," 14–15.

16   Ibid.

17 Gruening, *State of Alaska*, 314.

18 "Army's Role in Building Alaska," 85.

19 Dimond as quoted in Gruening, *State of Alaska*, 313.

20 "The American Aerospace Industry during World War II," *U.S. Centennial of Flight Commission*, online at www.centennialofflight.gov.

21 The government first developed the Emergency Planet Facilities program in August 1940 and then established the Defense Plant Corporation (DPC) to help construct new plants.

22 "American Aerospace Industry during World War II."

23 "U.S. Aviation Research Helped Speed Victory," World War II and the National Advisory Committee for Aeronautics, FS-LaRC-95-07-01, July 1995, National Aeronautic and Space Administration (NASA), online at www.nasa.gov/centers/langley/news/factsheets/WWII_prt.htm.

24 "World War II Aviation," Smithsonian National Air and Space Museum, online at http://airandspace.si.edu/exhibitions/gal205/; and Stephen Sherman, "North American P-51: Generally Considered the Best Fighter of WWII," *Acepilots.com*, April 2002, online at http://acepilots.com/planes/aces_descr.html.

25 Everett A. Long and Ivan Y. Neganblya, *Cobras over the Tundra* (Fairbanks: Arktika Publishing, 1992).

26 Alaska Defense Command, report by Lt. Col. James D. Bush Jr., *Narrative Report of Alaska Construction 1941–1944*, Washington, D.C. (October 1943): 91.

27 Major General H. H. Arnold, "Our Air Frontier in Alaska," *National Geographic Magazine* (October 1940): 487–504.

28 Cohen, *Flying Beats Work*, 37.

29 Bush, *Narrative Report of Alaska Construction*, 91.

30 Arnold, "Our Air Frontier in Alaska," 487–504.

31 Cohen, *Flying Beats Work*, 37.

32 Franklin D. Roosevelt made his famous "garden hose" reference at a press conference on December 17, 1940.

33 Long and Neganblya, *Cobras over the Tundra*, 3.

34 "ALSIB—The Road of Courage," *Voice of Russia*, January 28, 2008, online at http://english.ruvr.ru/2008/01/28/174235.html.

35 "Army's Role in Building Alaska," 91.

36 Long and Neganblya, *Cobras over the Tundra*, 3.

37 Perras, *Stepping Stones to Nowhere*, 51.

38 See the inside cover map from 1942 in Long and Neganblya, *Cobras over the Tundra*.

39 "Army's Role in Building Alaska," 91.

40 Captain Richard L. Neuberger, "Airway to Russia," *Alaska Life* (October 1944): 3–14.

41 "ALSIB—The Road of Courage."

42 Dimond as quoted in "Army's Role in Building Alaska," 73.

43 In 1938 the Alaska International Highway Commission was appointed by

President Roosevelt. In 1940 the commission reported favorable on two routes. After the fall of France in 1940, government authorities of both the United States and Canada were seriously considering the road as a defense measure. On August 18, 1940, a Joint Board recommended that a highway be constructed and adopted plans for the construction of an airway across Canada and Alaska via the route from Edmonton to Grand Prairie, Fort Saint John, Fort Nelson, Watson Lake, and Whitehorse in Canada, and Northway, Tanacross, Big Delta, and Fairbanks in Alaska. This recommendation was approved by both governments for immediate execution. On February 2, 1942, the government concluded that a highway to Alaska must be commenced at once and recommended that it follow the route of the then-existing chain of airports. "Army's Role in Building Alaska," 80.

44   The corporate voice of Morrison-Knudsen, "Keep 'Em Flying," *The Em Kayan* (July 1942): 3.

45   Wilson, "Northway and Tanacross," 72.

46   "Alaska Community Database," Community Information Summaries, online at www.commerce.state.ak.us.

47   Wilson, "Northway and Tanacross," 72.

48   Patti Normile, "Giving Alaska Wings," Iowa Contractor Ralph Green's first-hand account of Alaska airfield construction in 1940, date unknown, in "Aviation History Files," Alaska Aviation Heritage Museum, Anchorage.

49   Stanley, *Nabesna Gold*, 123.

50   Jim Rearden, *In the Shadow of Eagles, Rudy Billberg's Story* (Anchorage: Alaska Northwest Books, 1992).

51   Stanley, *Nabesna Gold*, 124.

52   Reeve as quoted in Day, *Glacier Pilot*, 210.

53   Wilson, "Northway and Tanacross," 72.

54   "Cats over Alaska," *The Em Kayan* (April 1942): 8–11.

55   Wilson, "Northway and Tanacross," 72; and Day, *Glacier Pilot*, 211.

56   "Cats over Alaska," 8–11.

57   Reeve as quoted in Day, *Glacier Pilot*, 211.

58   Green as quoted in Normile, "Giving Alaska Wings."

59   Green as quoted in ibid.

60   Y. Yarber and C. Madison, *Walter Northway* (Fairbanks: Alaska Native Language Center College of Liberal Arts, 1987), 45.

61   Cohen, *Flying Beats Work*, 37; and Day, *Glacier Pilot*, 212–13.

62   Cohen, *Flying Beats Work*, 37.

63   Day, *Glacier Pilot*, 219.

64   Reeve Aleutian Airways ceased operation on December 5, 2000.

65   "Army's Role in Building Alaska," 86.

66   Ann Chandonnet, "Rudy Billberg: Civilian Flyboy 1942–1945," in *Alaskan Embers: Stories Tales, Anecdotes, Vignettes, Poems, and Other Such Stuff* (Anchorage, AK: MMUKC Publishers, 1995), 19–21.

1   Construction contractor Morrison-Knudsen, "Alaska Plane Crash: Tragedy and Rescue, An Epic of Faith and Heroism in the Frozen North," *The Em Kayan* (March 1943): 1–5.

2   Stephen Haycox, "Strengthening the Indian Voice: U.S. Military Relations with Natives at Two Sites in Alaska, 1942–44, and 1987–89," in *Borderlands: 1989 Heritage Conference, June 2nd–4th 1989*, Yukon College, Alaska Historical Society and the University of Victoria (Whitehorse, Canada: Yukon Historical and Museums Association, 1989), 202–26; and U.S. National Park Service, Anthropology and Historic Preservation, Cooperative Park Studies Unit, by Holly Reckord, *Where Raven Stood: Cultural Resources of the Ahtna Region*, Occasional Paper No. 35. (Fairbanks: University of Alaska–Fairbanks, 1977), 71–72.

3   Haycox, "Strengthening the Indian Voice."

4   The new road was later named the Glenn Highway after Captain Edwin F. Glenn, commander of several expeditions along routes that later became four of Alaska's highways. U.S. Congress, House, Committee on Roads, *An Interim Report*, House Report No. 1705, 79th Cong., 2nd session (1946), pp. xi–xiii.

5   Annie Ewen as quoted in Joseph Judge, "Alaska: Rising Northern Star," *National Geographic* (June 1975): 730–66.

6   Haycox, in "Strengthening the Indian Voice," cites Report, Highway Facilities, November 18, 1943, file Facilities (003.12), Box 89002, Records of the Bureau of Public Roads, RG 30, NA.

7   Haycox, "Strengthening the Indian Voice," 202–26.

8   U.S. National Park Service, Anthropology and Historic Preservation, Cooperative Park Studies Unit, by Holly Reckord, *That's the Way We Live: Subsistence in the Wrangell–St. Elias National Park and Preserve* (Fairbanks: University of Alaska–Fairbanks, 1977); and U.S. National Park Service, by Frank Norris, *Alaska Subsistence: A National Park Service Management History* (Anchorage: Alaska Regional Office, 2002).

9   Dean Kohlhoff, *When the Wind Was a River: Aleut Evacuation in World War II* (Seattle: University of Washington Press, 1995).

10 Merle Smith as quoted in Janson, *Mudhole Smith*, 89.

11 Griese, *Bush Pilot*, 271.

12 John M. Tippets, *Hearts of Courage: The Gillam Plane Crash and the Amazing True Story of Survival in the Frozen Wilderness of Alaska* (Anchorage: Publication Consultants, 2008), 2.

13 Janson, *Mudhole Smith*, 90.

14 Jim Rearden, *In the Shadow of Eagles: Rudy Billberg's Story* (Anchorage: Alaska Northwest Books, 1992), 123.

15 Billberg as quoted in Chandonnet, "Rudy Billberg," 19–21.

16 Billberg as quoted in Rearden, *In the Shadow of Eagles*, 123.

17 Janson, *Mudhole Smith*, 90.

18   Johanna Boucher, private journal, circa 1940.

19   Alaska Defense Command, *Narrative Report of Alaska Construction, 1941–1944,*
        report by Lt. Col. James D. Bush Jr. (Washington, D.C., 1943), 111–13.

20   Smith as quoted in Janson, *Mudhole Smith,* 91.

21   Neuberger, "Airway to Russia," 4.

22   Bush, *Narrative Report of Alaska Construction, 1941–1944,* 111–13.

23   Ibid.

24   "ALSIB—The Route of Courage."

25   "Lend Lease," Bravo 369, Flight Foundation, 1–6. Figures show Lend-Lease
        Aircraft Deliveries over the Alaska-Siberia Route 1942–1945, recorded at Ladd
        Field, Fairbanks, Alaska.

26   "ALSIB—The Route of Courage."

27   Brian Garfield, *Thousand-Mile War: World War II in Alaska and the Aleutians*
        (Fairbanks: University of Alaska Press, 1995).

28   Laurel J. Hummel, "The U.S. Military as Geographical Agent: The Case of Cold
        War Alaska," *Geographical Review* 95 (January 2005): 47–72.

29   Neuberger, "Airway to Russia," 9.

30   "Lend Lease," Bravo 369, Flight Foundation, 1–6.

31   Hummel, "U.S. Military as Geographical Agent," 47–72.

32   Smith as quoted in Janson, *Mudhole Smith,* 103.

33   "Alaska Airlines 60th Anniversary: Salute to the Bush Pilots," Cordova Air-
        lines File, Alaska Airlines Corporate Headquarters, Seattle, Washington.

34   Quoted in Janson, *Mudhole Smith,* 104.

35   After the war the 80A was stored and then discarded. It was recovered from
        a dump in 1960 and eventually brought to Seattle for restoration. It is the
        only surviving example of the Boeing Model 80 series and is currently on
        display at the Seattle Museum of Flight.

36   Ray Shinn as quoted in Janson, *Mudhole Smith,* 107.

37   Winchell as quoted in Wachel, "Alaskan Fearless Flier," 18–20.

38   Morrison-Knudsen, "Alaska Plane Crash: Tragedy and Rescue, An Epic of
        Faith and Heroism in the Frozen North," *The Em Kayan* (March 1943): 1–5.

39   Tippets, *Hearts of Courage,* 5.

40   "Report of the Civil Aeronautics Board on the Investigation of an Accident
        Involving Aircraft in a Cross-Country Commercial Flight," File No. 1299–43,
        Civil Aeronautics Authority, August 25, 1943.

41   Gebo as quoted in Griese, *Bush Pilot,* 287.

42   Gebo as quoted in Ethel Dassow, "The Gillam Plane Was Missing," *Alaska
        Sportsman* (July 1943): 16–18, 21–23.

43   Morrison-Knudsen, "Alaska Plane Crash."

44   Ibid.

45   Quoted in Dassow, "Gillam Plane Was Missing," 16.

46   Smith as quoted in Janson, *Mudhole Smith,* 102.

47   "Robert Gebo, Seattle, Five Others Aboard Missing Plane," *Seattle Times,*
        January 8, 1943.

48   Gebo as quoted in Dassow, "Gillam Plane Was Missing," 17.
49   Morrison-Knudsen, "Alaska Plane Crash."
50   Dassow, "Gillam Plane Was Missing," 18.
51   "Report of the Civil Aeronautics Board on the Investigation of an Accident
      Involving Aircraft in a Cross-Country Commercial Flight," File No. 1299–43,
      Civil Aeronautics Authority, August 25, 1943.
52   Morrison-Knudsen, "Alaska Plane Crash."

8. FROM AIR CARRIER TO CORDOVA AIRLINES

1   Rederick Graham, "Aviation in Alaska," *New York Times*, February 9, 1947.
2   "Jack and 'General' Take New Jobs," *Cordova Daily Times*, May 12, 1942.
3   "Star Purchases Local Flying Firm," *Cordova Daily Times*, March 30, 1943.
4   "Merle Smith Purchases Local Air Service," *Cordova Daily Times*, July 19, 1944.
5   Janson, *Mudhole Smith*, 108.
6   Judy Rumerman, "The Douglas DC-3," U.S. Centennial of Flight Commission,
      online at www.centennialofflight.net/essay/Aerospace/DC-3/Aero29.htm.
7   Smith as quoted in Janson, *Mudhole Smith*, 111.
8   Letter to Mr. Pollock from Department of the Air Force, February 24, 1969,
      Aviation Files, Cordova Historical Museum, Cordova, Alaska.
9   Janson, *Mudhole Smith*, 87.
10   Cordova Air Service brochure from circa 1950, Aviation Files, Cordova Histor-
      ical Museum, Cordova, Alaska.
11   The crash of Northwest Flight 4422 on March 12, 1948, is considered the
      deadliest disaster in Alaska aviation history but one shrouded in mystery.
      The Accident Investigation Report filed on July 28, 1948, noted that the
      pilots were experienced. There was no sufficient moisture in the air to
      cause aircraft icing. In fact, the air was stable, save light mechanical turbu-
      lence over the mountains. The moon set that Friday night at 8:12 p.m., an
      hour before the plane hit the mountain at its cruising altitude of eleven
      thousand feet. The Civil Aeronautics Administration concluded that Flight
      4422 had changed its intended route, flying south of the airway, to pursue
      a more direct line from Gulkana to Snag, Yukon, and on to Edmonton for
      a refueling stop. CAB investigators determined that the pilot failed to see
      Mount Sanford because it was obscured by a thin layer of clouds, the aurora
      borealis, or both while flying a course off the airway. Despite the loss of thirty
      people, the tragedy was instantly overshadowed by stories of buried gold that
      sparked a Sierra Madre–like treasure hunt to Mount Sanford beginning in
      1948. Rumors claimed that Chinese Nationalist leader Chiang Kai-shek, while
      losing a civil war to Communist leader Mao Tsetung, had slipped gold out of
      the country on board the Northwest aircraft. Although Northwest Airlines
      did its best to discount tales that a "vast amount of wealth in gold" was lost
      with the plane, rumors of buried treasure nevertheless sparked at least
      twenty expeditions to the crash site. Decades later, two commercial U.S.
      pilots, Kevin McGregor and Marc Millican, successfully reached the wreck-

age. Not only did their subsequent research undermine any validity to the rumors that gold remained at the site, but they brought out pieces of the plane, a table knife, a man's ring, and human body parts that were later identified as belonging to Francis Joseph Van Zandt, a thirty-six-year-old merchant marine from Roanoke, Virginia. The attempt by McGregor and Millican to shed light on the mysterious Northwest Airlines crash brought a modicum of peace to the victims' families. Still, the whispers and gossip of gold at the time only reinforced Alaska's image as a place of intrigue, ripe with opportunity, prosperity, and adventure. Even though World War II and the ensuing "age of the airlines" launched Alaska toward Kennedy's "new frontier," the contagious tales of gold found by men who conquered a strange and mysterious wilderness were not easily replaced.

12 Janson, *Mudhole Smith*, 115.

13 Ibid.

14 Ibid., 124.

15 The Alaska Development Board in 1946 listed "the last frontier" as a tourist attraction, among other tourist attractions, such as scenery, hunting, animals, mountains, Alaska Natives, and hot springs.

16 War Production Board Limitation Order L-208, 7 Federal Register 7992–7993, provided as follows: "The fulfillment of requirements for the defense of the United States has created a shortage in the supply of critical materials for defense, for private account and for export which are used in the maintenance and operation of gold mines; and the following order is deemed necessary and appropriate in the public interest and to promote the national defense."

17 Cole, "Golden Years," 65.

18 To Claude Stuart, from Carl Whitham, Signal Corps U.S. Army Telegram, Seattle March 20, 1942, Asa C. Baldwin Papers, circa 1907–1982, MS 36-1-2-4, Alaska State Library, Juneau.

19 Yellow Band Gold Mining, Inc., Board of Directors, "Report to the Stockholders," December 20, 1945, Chitina, Alaska, Asa C. Baldwin Papers, circa 1907–1982, MS 36-1-2-4, Alaska State Library, Juneau; and White, *Bremner Historic District*, 76.

20 To Taplin from O. A. Nelson, 1961, Asa C. Baldwin Papers, circa 1907–1982, MS 36-1-2-4, Alaska State Library, Juneau.

21 By way of explanation regarding the spelling of "Kennecott" versus "Kennicott," the geologist who studied the area was named Kennicott and the glacier is thusly named. The corporation and town are spelled Kennecott.

22 Cole, "Golden Years," 65.

23 Father Bernard Hubbard quoted in Barrett Willoughby, *Alaskans All* (Boston: Houghton Mifflin, 1933).

24 "Alaska's Recreational Riches," Alaska Development Board, Juneau, July 1946.

25 Cole, "Golden Years," 64. Janson, *Mudhole Smith*, 115–16. "Alaska's Recreational Riches" (1946).

26 Roderick Nash, "Tourism, Parks, and the Wilderness Idea in the History of Alaska," *Alaska in Perspective* 4, no. 1 (1981): 1–27.

27 After the death of Harold Gillam, Gillam Airways was incorporated under Northern Consolidated.

28 Petersen as quoted in Louis R. Huber, "Flight to Katmai," *Alaska Sportsman* (April 1951): 9; and U.S. National Park Service, by Frank Norris, *Tourism in Katmai* (McCarthy: Alaska Regional Office, 1993), 20.

29 Norris, *Tourism in Katmai*, 20.

30 *Christian Science Monitor*, September 22, 1950; Frank Dufresne, "Katmai Adventure," *Field and Stream* (May 1952); Enos Bradner, "Anglers' Eldorado," *Alaska Sportsman* (April 1952):18; and Norris, *Tourism in Katmai*, 19.

31 Norris, *Tourism in Katmai*, 32.

32 Douglas Brinkley has developed this theme in his book *The Quiet World: Saving Alaska's Wilderness Kingdom, 1879–1960* (New York: Harper, 2011).

33 By the 1970 census the West had become the most highly urbanized of the four American sections, with 83 percent of its population dwelling in urban areas. Also see John M. Findlay, *Magic Lands: Western Cityscapes and American Cultural after 1940* (Berkeley: University of California Press, 1992), 1.

34 King, *Bird in the Bush*, 58–60.

35 Gregory D. Ringer, *The Wilderness Begins at McCarthy: Perceptual Impacts of Tourism on Communities* (McCarthy: McCarthy-Kennicott Museum, 1993), 1.

36 William Cronon, "Kennecott Journey: The Paths in and out of Town," in *Under an Open Sky: Rethinking America's Western Past*, edited by William Cronon, George Miles, and Jay Gitlin (New York: W.W. Norton & Company, 1992), 32.

37 Cronon, "Kennecott Journey," 30

38 Findlay, *Magic Lands*, 52–105; and Patricia Nelson Limerick, "The Adventures of the Frontier in the Twentieth Century," in *The Frontier in America Culture*, edited by James R. Grossman (Berkley: University of California Press, 1994), 68.

39 Limerick, "Adventures of the Frontier in the Twentieth Century," 67–102.

40 Smith as quoted in Janson, *Mudhole Smith*, 130.

41 For example, "Tour Number One" went to McCarthy; "Tour Number Four" went to Chitina for a weekend of fishing; and "Tour Number Five" went to Chisana for a pack train trip into the Wrangell Mountains. Kathryn Winslow, *Alaska Bound* (New York: Dodd, Mead & Company, 1960), 212.

42 "Cordova Airlines Sourdough Tours brochure, ca, 1955," Cordova Air Service folder, Aviation Files, Cordova Historical Museum, Cordova, Alaska.

43 Ibid.

44 Ringer, *Wilderness Begins at McCarthy*, 33.

45 Ibid., 30.

46 Winslow, *Alaska Bound*, 108.

47 Ibid., 213.

48 Kirchhoff, *Historic McCarthy*, 94.

49 Alaska Division of Mines and Minerals, Annual Report 1959, by J. A. Williams, "Report of Division of Mines and Minerals, 1959,", 68.

50 Letter to Hon. Ernest Gruening from Merle Smith, July 29, 1959, Gruening Collection, Folder 406, box 197, "Aviation-Cordova Airlines," Alaska and Polar Regions Collections and Archives, University of Alaska–Fairbanks.

51 Western Union Telegram to Senator Gruening from Merle Smith, June 2, 1960, Gruening Collection, Folder 403, box 197, "General-Cordova," Alaska and Polar Regions Collections and Archives, University of Alaska–Fairbanks.

52 Letter to Ernest Gruening, from Ellis Armstrong, commissioner of public roads, August 16, 1960, Gruening Collection, Folder 403, box 197, "General-Cordova," Alaska and Polar Regions Collections and Archives, University of Alaska–Fairbanks.

53 To Richard A. Downing, commissioner of public works, from Norman L. Schwalb, assistant attorney general, September 23, 1960; Gruening Collection, Folder 403, box 197, "General-Cordova," Alaska and Polar Regions Collections and Archives, University of Alaska–Fairbanks.

54 To Ernest Gruening, from Richard A. Downing, Department of Public Works, October 6, 1960; Gruening Collection, Folder 403, box 197, "General-Cordova," Alaska and Polar Regions Collections and Archives, University of Alaska–Fairbanks.

55 To Richard A. Downing, commissioner of public works, Alaska Department of Public Work's, from Merle Smith, October 11, 1960; Gruening Collection, Folder 403, box 197, "General-Cordova," Alaska and Polar Regions Collections & Archives, University of Alaska–Fairbanks.

56 Ibid.

57 Ibid.

58 Ibid.

59 "Economic Characteristics of Individual Cities," appendix, page 6, in "Cordova Airlines Temporary Points Service Investigation," Civil Aeronautics Board, Docket 16325, (Washington, D.C., 1967); Gruening Collection, Folder 407, box 197, "Aviation-Cordova Docket," Alaska and Polar Regions Collections and Archives, University of Alaska–Fairbanks.

60 "Cordova Airlines Temporary Points Service Investigation," Civil Aeronautics Board, Docket 16325 (Washington, D.C., 1967), 57; Gruening Collection, Folder 407, box 197, "Aviation-Cordova Docket," Alaska and Polar Regions Collections and Archives, University of Alaska–Fairbanks.

9. SOARING SPIES, SURVEYORS, AND SCIENTISTS

1 William Hurd Hillyer, "Alaska as a New Frontier: Wartime Road and Skyways May Implement Post-War Boom," *Barron's National Business and Financial Weekly* (December 6, 1943): 23.

2 David Holloway, *Stalin and the Bomb: The Soviet Union and Atomic Energy* (New Haven: Yale University Press, 1994), 242; *Chicago Daily Tribune*, March 4, 1951;

and Terrence Cole, *Fighting for the Forty-Ninth Star* (Fairbanks: University of Alaska Foundation, 2010), 206–7.

3 Hanson W. Baldwin, "Alaska Rampart We Must Watch," *New York Times*, April 23, 1950.

4 Ernest Gruening, *Many Battles: The Autobiography of Ernest Gruening* (New York: Liveright, 1973), 360–64.

5 Kathy Price, *Northern Defenders: Cold War Context of Ladd Air Force Base, Fairbanks Alaska, 1947–1961*, CEMML TPS 01-2 (Fort Richardson, AL: U.S. Army, 2001), 7; and Hummel, "U.S. Military as Geographical Agent," 47–72.

6 Price, *Northern Defenders*, 7.

7 John E. Metcalf, "Alaska—Its Strategic Role in Our Defense," *Magazine of Wall Street* (January 3, 1957): 345.

8 Cloe, *Top Cover for America*, 154.

9 "Report of Investigation for Nabesna Bar / *Dehsoon' Cheeg*," AA-10714I, Bureau of Land Management, nd., WRST History Files, Copper Center, Alaska.

10 Stanley, *Nabesna Gold*, 123; and "The Nabesna Faction," *Great Lander*, August 2, 1978.

11 Bob K., "The Alaskan Project: Secret Plans for Agents to Defend Alaska," *Gung-Ho Annuals* (1986): 54–60; *The Air Force Office of Special Investigation: 1948–2000*, U.S. Air Force, Office of Special Investigations (2000): 118–24; U.S. Army Corps of Engineers, Alaska District, "The Cold War in Alaska: A Management Plan for Cultural Resources," by D. Colt Denfeld, Jennifer Abel, and Dale Slaughter (August 1994): 78; and U.S. Army Military History Institute, "Counter Intelligence Corps: History and Mission in World War II," Carlisle Barracks, PA (nd): 64.

12 *Air Force Office of Special Investigation: 1948–2000* , 118–24.

13 Reeve as quoted in Day, *Glacier Pilot?*, 64.

14 Denfeld, Abel, and Slaughter, "Cold War in Alaska," 17.

15 Ibid.

16 Merle Smith described his frustration with the military in a letter to Ernest Gruening in 1959. To Gruening from Smith, July 29, 1959, Gruening Collection, Folder 406, box 197, "Aviation-Cordova Airlines," Alaska and Polar Regions Collections and Archives, University of Alaska–Fairbanks.

17 To Base Commander, Middleton Island AFS, from Merle Smith, February 15, 1960, Gruening Collection, Folder 406, box 197, "Aviation-Cordova Airlines," Alaska and Polar Regions Collections and Archives, University of Alaska–Fairbanks.

18 On March 22, 1963, the Civil Aeronautics Board granted Smith his extension. CAB Application of Cordova Airlines for exception to provide air transportation of persons, property, and mail to Tok and Fort Greely–Delta Junction, Alaska, Docket 14228, November 21, 1962. Also see Bill Johnson's "Fort Greely's Remote Reactor: Alaska's Experiment with Nuclear Power," *Alaska History* 11, no. 1 (Spring 1996): 27–34.

19　Hillyer, "Alaska as a New Frontier," 23; and Hummel, "U.S. Military as Geographical Agent," 47–72.

20　Hillyer, "Alaska as a New Frontier," 23.

21　"Cordova, Alaska, the Friendly City," *Cordova Times* pamphlet, circa 1950; Aviation Files, Cordova Historical Museum, Cordova, Alaska.

22　Virgil Kauffman, "It's Rugged in Alaska!" *Aero Service Corp Newsletter* (December 1950).

23　Charles R. "Bob" Leitzel, personal communication, November 2011.

24　Rex Beach, *The Iron Trail* (New York: Harper & Brothers Publishers, 1913), 74.

25　Kauffman, "It's Rugged in Alaska!"

26　Ibid.

27　Ibid.

28　Ibid.

29　Ninneman as quoted in ibid.

30　Leitzell, personal communication.

31　In Kauffman, "It's Rugged in Alaska!"

32　Ninneman as quoted in ibid.

33　Leitzell, personal communication.

34　Kauffman, "It's Rugged in Alaska!."

35　Ibid.

36　Charlie Crangle, "The Copper River Highway," *Alaska Geographic Newsletter*, 97–101; copy on file at WRST Headquarters, Copper Center, Alaska.

37　Charles Siebert, "After the Spill," *Men's Journal* (April 1999).

38　Steve Edwards, "Cordova: No Road, No Problem: Cordova's Isolation Gives It a Real 'Alaska Feel,'" *Anchorage Daily News*, October 20, 2008.

39　Terrence Cole interviewed in the film *Building Alaska*, Great Projects Film Company Production, 2010.

40　Reckord, *That's the Way We Live*.

41　Daniel Solie, "Icing on the Fire: A Season on the Summit of Mount Wrangell," *Alaska Journal* (Fall 1984): 12; and Carl S. Benson and Roman J. Motyka, "Glacier-Volcano Interactions on Mt. Wrangell, Alaska," *Geophysical Institute* (University of Alaska–Fairbanks) (1978): 8.

42　Terrence Cole, *The Cornerstone on College Hill* (Fairbanks: University of Alaska Press, 1994); and Neil Davis, *The College Hill Chronicles: How the University of Alaska Came of Age* (Fairbanks: University of Alaska Foundation, 1992), 195.

43　Davis, *College Hill Chronicles*, 226.

44　Ibid., 230.

45　Ibid., 496.

46　Ibid., 495.

47　Charles Keim, "Otto W. Geist: A Legend in His Own Lifetime," *UA News Release*, August 6, 1963.

48　Davis, *College Hill Chronicles*, 506.

49　Ibid., 507.

50 Ibid., 509.

51 Ibid., 509–11.

52 Ned Rozell, "Forty Years and Counting on Mount Wrangell," *Alaska Science Forum*, Article #1711, August 12, 2004.

53 Benson and Motyka, "Glacier-Volcano Interactions on Mt. Wrangell, Alaska," 8.

54 Solie, "Icing on the Fire," 12.

55 The Jamesway huts were abandoned in 1953 and have since been destroyed by wind, ice, and corrosive fumes.

56 Benson and Motyka, "Glacier-Volcano Interactions on Mt. Wrangell, Alaska," 8.

57 Moore's resignation letter as quoted in Davis, *College Hill Chronicles*, 524.

58 Ibid., 536–37.

59 Benson and Motyka, "Glacier-Volcano Interactions on Mt. Wrangell, Alaska," 8.

60 Jack Wilson, *Glacier Wings and Tales* (Anchorage: Great Northwest Publishing and Distributing Company, Inc., 1988), 34.

61 Davis, *College Hill Chronicles*, 510.

62 Wood, "Icefield Ranges Research Project," 163–84.

63 Ibid.

64 Solie, "Icing on the Fire," 12.

65 Ibid., 12–13.

66 Ibid., 13.

67 Benson and Motyka, "Glacier-Volcano Interactions on Mt. Wrangell, Alaska," 9.

68 Solie, "Icing on the Fire," 15; and Carl Benson, personal communication, June 2011.

69 Gerry Bruder, *Heroes of the Horizon: Flying Adventures of Alaska's Legendary Bush Pilots* (Portland: Alaska Northwest Books, 1991), 115.

70 Wilson, *Glacier Wings and Tales*, 19.

71 Ibid., 26.

72 King, *Bird in the Bush*, 43.

73 "Jack Wilson—Glennallen," H95-71-10, Project Jukebox, University of Alaska–Fairbanks.

74 Wilson, *Glacier Wings and Tales*, 53.

75 Carl Benson's foreword to Wilson's *Glacier Wings and Tales*.

10. FLYING HUNTSMEN

1 King, *Bird in the Bush*, 44.

2 Ibid., 44.

3 Wilson, *Glacier Wings and Tales*, 36–37.

4 Ibid., 37.

5 "L. Jo King Obituary," *Anchorage Daily News*, November 13, 2013.

6 Kenny Smith, "Airplanes in the Wrangells—Jack Wilson," *Wrangell St. Elias News* (January and February 2002).

7 Wilson, *Glacier Wings and Tales*, 87–93.

8 George Plafker and Henry C. Berg, "The Geology of Alaska," vol. G-1 in *The Geology of North America* (Geological Society of America, 1994).

9 William L. Fox, "Helicopters Star in Alaska Development," *Alaska Industry* (July 1969): 40–44.

10 Wilson, *Glacier Wings and Tales*, 87–93.

11 Ibid.

12 By the late 1960s Federal Aviation Administration (FAA) "helicopter pads" was a single-item category on its Master Reports of airports.

13 William L. Fox, "Commercial Aviation: Marking Time," *Alaska Industry* (January 1972): 33.

14 On August 23, 1958, President Eisenhower signed the Federal Aviation Act, which transferred the Civil Aeronautics Authority's functions to a new independent Federal Aviation Agency responsible for civil aviation safety. In 1966, Congress authorized the creation of a cabinet department that would combine major federal transportation responsibilities. This new Department of Transportation (DOT) began full operations on April 1, 1967. On that day the Federal Aviation Agency became one of several modal organizations within the DOT and received a new name: the Federal Aviation Administration. At the same time, the Civil Aeronautics Board's accident investigation function was transferred to the new National Transportation Safety Board. For a brief history of the FAA, see the FAA website at www.faa.gov/about/history/brief_history/.

15 Wilson, *Glacier Wings and Tales*, 17.

16 John B. Burnham, "Hunting in the Nutzotins," in *Hunting and Conservation: The Book of the Boone and Crockett Club*, edited by George Bird Grinnell and Charles Sheldon (New Haven: Yale University Press, 1925), 412–37.

17 Burnham quoted in James A. McGuire, *In the Alaska-Yukon Gamelands* (Cincinnati: Stewart Kidd Company, 1921), 12.

18 Wilson, *Quest for Dall Sheep*, 27.

19 Ibid., 24.

20 McGuire, *In the Alaska-Yukon Gamelands*, 88 and 90–91.

21 Jim Rearden, *Hunting Alaska's Far Places* (Missoula: Pictorial Histories Publishing Company, 2008), 131.

22 Wilson, *Quest for Dall Sheep*, 77.

23 Ibid., 46–47.

24 Ibid., 50

25 Janson, *Mudhole Smith*, 126.

26 LeNora Conkle, *Bush Pilots' Wives* (Anchorage: Publication Consultations, 2000), 28.

27 Ibid., 68–69.

28 Howard Knutson, personal communication, August 15, 2013.

29 "Airplanes were used most often by sheep hunters. . . . Airplane-transported hunters harvested larger-horned rams than hunters using other access. . . . Hunters transported by airplane and particularly those transported by horse accounted for a disproportionately large share of the harvest. Seventy-five

percent of the hunters used these access modes and accounted for 90 percent of the harvest. Success rates of hunters using off road vehicles and highway vehicles were relatively low. Very little sheep habitat is easily accessible from the road systems, and such habitat probably was subjected to greater hunter destinations than areas accessible only by aircraft. Nonresidents used airplanes or horse transportation more often than did residents and rarely used mechanized ground transportation as primary access. Comparing only airplane transport hunters, Alaskans had lower success rates than did nonresidents. By law, nonresident sheep hunters must be accompanied by guides. As guides have usually worked in an area for several years, they certainly can provide surer hunting opportunities than resident Alaskans would have on their own." See U.S. National Park Service, *Hunting Activity and Harvest in the Wrangell–St. Elias Region, Alaska, 1973–1977*, report by Edward C. Murphy and Frederick C. Dean, Final Report for National Park Service, CX-9000-6-0154 (Fairbanks: University of Alaska, 1978), 27–34.

30 Memorandum, To Al Henson, project leader, from Rich Gordon on Wrangells air strips and guiding, September 5, 1974; WRST Park Files, Copper Center, Alaska.

31 "Sheep hunting emphasis within the Wrangells has shifted during the decade. Those individuals hunting north of the crest of the Wrangells constituted 78 percent of all sheep hunters in the Wrangells in 1968 but only 58 percent in 1976. Conversely the number of sheep hunters in the upper Chitina Valley increased from 34 in 1968 to 160 in 1976, constituting 9 and 21 percent, respectively, of the total number of hunters in the Wrangells." See Murphy and Dean, *Hunting Activity and Harvest in the Wrangell–St. Elias Region, Alaska, 1973–1977*, 27–34.

32 Memorandum, To Al Henson, project leader, from Rich Gordon on Wrangells air strips and guiding, September 5, 1974; WRST Park Files, Copper Center, Alaska.

33 Morgan Sherwood, *Big Game in Alaska* (New Haven: Yale University Press, 1981), 1.

34 Hummel, "U.S. Military as Geographical Agent," 47–72.

35 Jack John Justin Jr. as quoted in Alaska Department of Fish and Game, ANILCA Program, "Upper Tanana Ethnographic Overview and Assessment, Wrangell St. Elias National Park and Preserve," report by Terry L. Haynes and William E. Simeone, Technical Paper No. 3251, Division of Subsistence (July 2007): 21

36 Walter R. Goldschmidt, "Delimitation of Possessory Rights of the Athapascan Indian Natives of the Villages of Northway, Tanaross, and Tetlin in the Interior of Alaska," unpublished report submitted to the Commissioner of Indian Affairs, U.S. Office of Indian Affairs, Washington, D.C., 1948. Cited in Haynes and Simeone, "Upper Tanana Ethnographic Overview and Assessment, Wrangell St. Elias National Park and Preserve," July 2007.

37 Sherwood, *Big Game in Alaska*, 1–2.

38 William Hunt, *Mountain Wilderness: An Illustrated History of Wrangell–St. Elias National Park and Preserve, Alaska* (Anchorage: Alaska Natural History Association, 1996), 207.

39 Wilson, *Glacier Wings and Tales*, 128.

40 Hunt, *Mountain Wilderness*, 206.

41 Lappen, "Whose Promised Land," 114–15. In 1973 the state legislature created the Guide Licensing and Control Board, intended to protect fish and game management and to get competent people as guides in Alaska. In 1974 the board established an area system for limiting guides to operations within Exclusive Guide Areas (EGA). The EGA system was found unconstitutional by the Alaska Supreme Court in 1988, in what is commonly known as the Owsichek decision. See the website of the Alaska Department of Land and Water, http://dnr.alaska.gov/mlw/gcp/.

42 "Horse Hunts—the Sporting Way," *Alaska Sportsman* (November 1968): 27.

43 Lappen, "Whose Promised Land," 115.

44 Wilson, *Quest for Dall Sheep*, 52.

11. CREATING AN AIRPLANE CULTURE

1 Kathryn Winslow, *Alaska Bound* (New York: Dodd, Mead & Company, 1960), 209; "Cordova Airlines Temporary Points Service Investigation," Civil Aeronautics Board, Docket 16325, Washington, D.C., Gruening Collection, Folder 407, box 197, "Aviation-Cordova Docket," Alaska and Polar Regions Collections and Archives, University of Alaska–Fairbanks.

2 "Cordova Airlines Temporary Points Service Investigation," Civil Aeronautics Board, Docket 16325, Washington, D.C., pages 1 and 58, Gruening Collection, Folder 407, box 197, "Aviation-Cordova Docket," Alaska and Polar Regions Collections and Archives, University of Alaska–Fairbanks.

3 "Cordova Airlines Temporary Points Service Investigation," Civil Aeronautics Board, Docket 16325, Washington, D.C., pages 1, 17, and 59; Gruening Collection, Folder 407, box 197, "Aviation-Cordova Docket," Alaska and Polar Regions Collections and Archives, University of Alaska–Fairbanks.

4 Press Release, Civil Aeronautics Board, "The Civil Aeronautics Board Has Approved the Merger of Cordova Airlines, Inc. into Alaska Airlines, Inc.," December 7, 1967, CAB 67-165, 382–6031, Gruening Collection, Folder 409, box 197, Cordova Alaska Airline Merger," Alaska and Polar Regions Collections and Archives, University of Alaska–Fairbanks.

5 For more about Alaska Airlines history, see Serling's *Character and Characters*.

6 To Senator Ernest Gruening, from Page Crosland, Press Secretary, December, 7, 1967; Civil Aeronautics Board, "Immediate Release: The Civil Aeronautics Board Has Approved the Merger of Cordova Airlines, Inc. into Alaska Airlines, Inc.," December 7, 1967, CAB 67-165, 382–6031, Gruening Collection, Folder 409, box 197, Cordova Alaska Airline Merger," Alaska and Polar Regions Collections and Archives, University of Alaska–Fairbanks.

7 Serling, *Character and Characters*, 65–66.

8 Ken Smith, "First Crash on the New McCarthy Airstrip," *Wrangell St. Elias News* (March and April 2008).

9 Alaska Trunk Airport Bond, Proposition 3 (1962), Alaska 1962 Ballot Measures.

10 Smith, "First Crash on the New McCarthy Airstrip."

11 To Chief, Airport Division, from G. O. Kempton, Chief Air Traffic Division, March 18, 1963, Airstrip History Files, "McCarthy #2," Federal Aviation Administration, Alaska Region, Anchorage.

12 Howard Knutson, personal communication, August 15, 2013.

13 Ibid.

14 Ibid.

15 To Chief Airports Division, from Acting Chief Air Traffic Division, July 9, 1965, Airstrip History Files, "McCarthy #2," Federal Aviation Administration, Alaska Region, Anchorage.

16 Reckord, *That's the Way We Live*.

17 Ibid.

18 Alaska Department of Fish and Game, ANILCA Program, "Documenting Traditional and Subsistence Access in Wrangell–St. Elias National Park and Preserve," by Terry L. Haynes and Stan Walker (November 1995): 36.

19 Reckord, *That's the Way We Live*?

20 Ibid.

21 Ibid.

22 Donald C. Defenderfer and Robert B. Walkinshaw, *One Long Summer Day in Alaska: A Documentation of Perspectives in the Wrangell Mountains* (Santa Cruz: University of California–Santa Cruz, 1981), 45.

23 Reckord, *That's the Way We Live*, 1977.

24 Haynes and Walker, "Documenting Traditional and Subsistence Access in Wrangell–St. Elias National Park and Preserve," 36.

25 Paul Claus, personal communication, December 16, 2012.

26 Ibid.

27 Martin Harrais worked and developed the Darling M. no. 1 through 5 load claims and was finally granted a patent to his claims in 1936, the year he died. Ownership of the five Darling M. claims went to his wife, Margaret, who in coming years would become a high-ranking officer in the National Woman's Christian Temperance Union. She bequeathed unto the national organization the five patented lode-mining claims on her death in October 1964. In 1970 it granted the five claims to a Mr. Malcolm C. Frazier of Anchorage, Alaska, a relation of Margaret Harrais's niece, Helen Frazier. Nine years later, Malcolm passed the claims to Donna M. Frazier, a Seattleite who had never stepped foot in Alaska. In 1988, Donna Frazier sold the Darling M. claims to Paul Claus. Claus exchanged that land for the Hubert Landing site with the National Park Service in 1989. Deed #21, Retired File WRST 35-103 John Claus, Alaska Regional Office, Anchorage.

28 Margaret Keenan Harrais, "Alaska Periscope" (unpublished manuscript), 145, copy located at Alaska Regional Office, National Park Service files, Anchorage.

29 "Cole and Lorene Ellis," H95-71-02, interviewed by Bill Schneider and Dave Krupa, 1992; "Kirk Ellis," H95-71-01, interviewed by Bill Schneider and David Krupa, 1992. Both interviews part of Project Jukebox, University of Alaska–Fairbanks.

30 "Cole and Lorene Ellis," H95-71-02.

31 Joseph L. Sax, *Keeping Special Places Special: McCarthy Kennicott and the Wrangell–St. Elias Park, a Great Challenge, an Unique Opportunity* (McCarthy: McCarthy-Kennicott Historical Museum, 1990), 1.

12. SEEKERS OF THE INACCESSIBLE

1 "Kirk Ellis," part of Project Jukebox interviews, University of Alaska–Fairbanks, 1993.

2 Josephine Gordon Diaries, Archives and Special Collections, HMC-0407, University of Alaska–Anchorage.

3 A good source of information for the construction of the trans-Alaska pipeline and the ensuing controversy that pitted state and federal governments against environmentalists and Native groups is Coates, *Trans-Alaska Pipeline Controversy*.

4 Joseph Judge, "Alaska: Rising Northern Star," *National Geographic* 147, no. 6 (June 1975): 730–67.

5 Everhardt as quoted in Lappen, "Whose Promised Land?" 165.

6 Nash, "Aviation and Gates of the Arctic National Park," 5–13.

7 Ibid.

8 Robert Marshall, *Alaska Wilderness: Exploring the Central Brooks Range* (Berkeley: University of California Press, 1973), xxxiii.

9 Nash, "Aviation and Gates of the Arctic National Park."

10 Defenderfer and Walkinshaw, *One Long Summer Day in Alaska*, 36.

11 Nash, "Aviation and Gates of the Arctic National Park."

12 U.S. National Park Service, Alaska Regional Office, *"Do Things Right the First Time": Administrative History of the National Park Service and the Alaska National Interest Lands Conservation Act of 1980*, report by G. Frank Williss (Anchorage: Alaska Regional Office, 2005).

13 Gruening, *Many Battles*, 518–19.

14 Ibid.

15 Ibid.

16 "Alaska Task Force Report," National Park Service, January 1965.

17 Geoffrey Bleakley, *Contested Ground: An Administrative History of Wrangell–St. Elias National Park and Preserve, Alaska, 1978–2001* (Anchorage: Alaska Support Office, 2002), 18.

18 Memorandum, Project Leader, ATFO, from Team Captain, Wrangells–St. Elias, "Report on LUPC Hearing sat Copper Center, Cordova, Yakutat, and Northway," May 13–16, 1973, WRST Park Files, Copper Center, Alaska.

19   U.S. Congress, House, "A Bill to Designated Certain Lands in the State of Alaska as Units of the National Parks, National Wildlife Refuge, and Wild and Scenic Rivers and National Wilderness Preservation System, and for Other Purposes," H.R. 39, 95th Congress, 1st sess., 1977.

20   Bleakley, *Contested Ground*, 18–21.

21   Ibid., 21.

22   President Jimmy Carter, Presidential Proclamation 4625, December 1, 1978, Federal Register 43, no. 234 (December 5, 1978).

23   Lappen, "Whose Promised Land?," 171–72.

24   Bleakley, *Contested Ground*, 21.

25   Lappen, "Whose Promised Land?," 173,

26   *Anchorage Daily News*, December 13, 1978; and January 15, 1979. *Anchorage Times*, January 14, 1979; and January 15, 1979.

27   Lappen, "Whose Promised Land?," 175.

28   Norris, *Alaska Subsistence*, 91

29   Budge also was serving as acting superintendent at Denali National Monument.

30   Lappen, "Whose Promised Land?," 175.

31   Nash, "Aviation in Gates of the Arctic National Park."

32   WRST consists of an 8,147,000-acre park and 4,171,000-acre preserve.

33   Bleakley, *Contested Ground*, x; 22, 27.

34   Judge, "Alaska," 731.

35   Defenderfer and Walkinshaw, *One Long Summer Day in Alaska*, 57–58.

36   "Jim Hannah," H97105, UAF.

37   Reckord, *That's the Way We Live*.

38   Defenderfer and Walkinshaw, *One Long Summer Day in Alaska*, 40.

39   Bleakley, *Contested Ground*, 28; and U.S. National Park Service, "Hunting Activity and Harvest in the Wrangell–St. Elias Region, Alaska, 1973–1977," report by Edward C. Murphy and Frederick C. Dean, Final Report for National Park Service, CX-9000-6-0154 (University of Alaska–Fairbanks, 1978).

40   Memorandum: To Project Leader, ATFO from Park Planner regarding fair chase sport hunting, September 16, 1974, WRST Park Files, Copper Center, Alaska.

41   Defenderfer and Walkinshaw, *One Long Summer Day in Alaska*, 38.

42   Ibid.

43   LeNora Conkle, *Hunting the Way It Was in Our Changing Alaska* (Anchorage: Publication Consultants, 1998), 213.

44   "Jim Hannah," H97105, UAF.

45   H. 10541, *Congressional Record*, November 12, 1980.

46   The SRC is a management advisory group made of local subsistence uses whose main purpose is to recommend to the governor of Alaska and the secretary of the interior a program for subsistence hunting within the park and preserve. Norris, *Alaska Subsistence*, 135.

47 W. T. Ellis to Regional Director, NPS, August 2, 1985, SRC Folder, "WRST History Files," Wrangell–Saint Elias National Park and Preserve, Copper Center, Alaska.

48 Horn to Bill Ellis, October 29, 1985, SRC Folder, "WRST History Files," Wrangell–Saint Elias National Park and Preserve, Copper Center, Alaska.

49 Norris, *Alaska Subsistence*, 136.

50 "Cole and Lorene Ellis," H95-71-02, UAF.

51 Ibid.

52 James Edwards, interviewed by Katherine Ringsmuth and Dan Trepal on July 7, 2010.

53 Harrais, "Alaska Periscope," 64–65.

54 Paul Claus, personal communication with the author, December 16, 2012.

55 See the website of the Ultima Thule Lodge at www.ultimathulelodge.com.

CONCLUSION

1 "Death Claims the Glacier Pilot," *Anchorage Daily News*, August 26, 1980.

2 Stanton H. Patty, "Mudhole Smith, One of Alaska's Early Bush Pilots, Is Gone," *Seattle Times*, July 5, 1981.

3 Greg Witter, "Flying into Seventy Years of Service: Mudhole's the Name," *Alaska's World* (August 17, 2001).

4 "Merle K. 'Mudhole' Smith, 1920–1981," *Alaska Airlines Magazine* (August 1981).

5 "Terris Moore, Educator and an Adventurer, 85," *New York Times*, November 10, 1993.

6 "1949–1953 Terris Moore: University of Alaska's Second President," *UA Journey, UA Online* at www.alaska.edu/uajourney/presidents/1949–1953.

7 Kenny Smith, "Airplanes in the Wrangells—Jack Wilson," *Wrangell St. Elias News* (January and February 2002).

8 Café Supercub, discussion forum, online at www.supercub.org/forum/showthread.php?21580-Jack-Wilson.

9 Howard Knutson, personal communication with the author.

10 See Richard White, "Are You and Environmentalist or Do You Work for a Living? Work and Nature," in *Uncommon Ground: Rethinking the Human Place in Nature*, edited by William Cronon (New York: W. W. Norton & Company, 1996), 171–85.

11 Conkle, *Hunting the Way It Was*, 210.

12 Nash, "Aviation and Gates of the Arctic National Park."

13 Williss, *"Do Things Right the First Time."*

14 As Richard White points out in *The Organic Machine: The Remaking of the Columbia River* (New York: Hill and Wang, 1996), "human work and the work of nature" are different, but "it is our work that ultimately links us, for better or worse, to nature" (ix, x). Nash, "Aviation and Gates of the Arctic National Park."

15 Stephen Haycox, "Early Aviation in Anchorage: Ambivalent Fascination with the Air Age," *Alaska History* (Fall 1988): 1–20.

16   Collen Mondor, *The Map of My Dead Pilots: The Dangerous Game of Flying in Alaska* (Lyons Press, 2012), 158.

17   Byron Acohido, "Did Alaska Airlines' 'Can-Do' Ethic Go Too Far?" *Seattle Times*, July 2, 2000; and Christine Clarridge, "Tenth Anniversary of Alaska's Flight 261," *Seattle Times*, January 28, 2010.

18   Haycox, "Early Aviation in Anchorage," 4.

19   Ibid., 4.

20   Ibid., 3.

21   Richard West Sellers, *Preserving Nature in the National Parks: A History* (New Haven: Yale University Press, 1997), 1–5.

22   Theodore Catton, *Inhabited Wilderness: Indians, Eskimos, and National Parks in Alaska* (Albuquerque: University of New Mexico Press, 1997), 2.

23   "Economic Impact of the Ted Stevens Anchorage International Airport," Alaska Economic Development Council and McDowell Group Research Based Consulting, February 2012.

24   Susan Bramsteadt, interviewed by Katherine Ringsmuth, June 2011.

BIBLIOGRAPHY

ARCHIVAL COLLECTIONS

Airstrip History Files. Federal Aviation Administration, Alaska Region. Anchorage, Alaska.

Alaska Aviation Heritage Museum Files. Anchorage, Alaska.

Alaska Road Commission. Bureau of Public Roads—Project Correspondence, 1916–1959, RG 30. National Archives at Seattle.

Aviation Files. Cordova Historical Museum. Cordova, Alaska.

Aviation Files. Wrangell–Saint Elias National Park and Preserve Headquarters. Copper Center, Alaska.

Asa C. Baldwin Papers, circa 1907–1982. MS 36-1-2-4. Alaska State Library. Juneau, Alaska.

Bertha Ramer Album. McCarthy-Kennicott Historical Museum. McCarthy, Alaska.

Bremner Gold Mining Company. Alaska State Archives. Juneau, Alaska.

Cordova Airlines File. Alaska Airlines Corporate Headquarters. Seattle, Washington.

Cordova Air Service. Alaska State Archives. Juneau, Alaska

Gruening Collection. Alaska and Polar Regions Collections and Archives. University of Alaska–Fairbanks.

"Historical Sketch of Chitina Historic Books." Index General, 1915–44. Film Roll 745, Book 24, page 401–3. Glennallen, Library. Glennallen, Alaska.

Johanna Boucher. Private journal, circa 1940–1942. Dillingham, Alaska.

Josephine Gordon Diaries. Archives and Special Collections. University of Alaska–Anchorage.

Margaret Keenan Harrais. "Alaska Periscope" (unpublished manuscript), 162–63. Copy located at Alaska Regional Office. Anchorage, Alaska.

McCarthy-Kennicott Historical Museum. McCarthy, Alaska.

Nabesna Mining Corporation. Alaska State Archives. Juneau, Alaska. Ramer Scrapbook.

Records of the Bureau of Public Roads. RG 30. National Archives at Seattle.

Russell Dow Papers (1917–1992). Archives and Special Collections, Consortium Library, University of Alaska–Anchorage.

WRST Park Files. Wrangell–Saint Elias National Park and Preserve Headquarters. Copper Center, Alaska.

GOVERNMENT DOCUMENTS

Alaska Defense Command. *Narrative Report of Alaska Construction 1941–1944.* By Lt. Col. James D. Bush Jr. Washington, D.C., 1943.

Alaska Department of Fish and Game. ANILCA Program. "Documenting Traditional and Subsistence Access in Wrangell–St. Elias National Park and Preserve." Report by Terry L. Haynes and Stan Walker. Juneau, Alaska. 1995.

———. Division of Subsistence. "Upper Tanana Ethnographic Overview and Assessment, Wrangell St. Elias National Park and Preserve." Report by Terry L. Haynes and William E. Simeone. Technical Paper No. 3251. Juneau, Alaska. 2007.

Alaska Department of Transportation and Public Facilities. "Alaska Roads Historic Overview: Applied Historic Contexts for Alaska Roads." Alaska Department of Natural Resources. Anchorage. 2014.

Alaska Development Board. "Alaska's Recreational Riches." Juneau, Alaska. 1946.

Alaska Division of Mines and Minerals Annual Report. "Report of Division of Mines and Minerals." By J. A. Williams. Juneau, Alaska. 1959.

Alaska Historical Commission. *Paving Alaska's Trails: The Work of the Alaska Road Commission.* By Claus-M. Naske. Studies in History No. 152. 1986.

Alaska Territorial Chamber of Commerce. "Alaska: Its Need for National Defense and Airmail Service." Juneau, Alaska. 1934.

Alaska Territorial Report. "Upper Nabesna, Chisana and Snag River Area." By Earl Pilgrim. MR-078-02. 1930.

Board of Road Commissioners for Alaska. "Alaska Road Commission, Annual Report 1929, Vol. II." Juneau, Alaska. 1929.

———. "Alaska Road Commission. Annual Report 1930, Vol. II." Juneau, Alaska. 1930.

———. "Alaska Road Commission. Annual Report 1932, Vol. II." Juneau, Alaska. 1932.

———. "Annual Report of the Alaska Road Commission, Fiscal Year 1923, Part II." Juneau, Alaska. 1923.

Bureau of Land Management. "Report of Investigation for Nabesna Bar / *Dehsoon' Cheeg.*" AA-10714I. Nd.

Civil Aeronautics Authority "Report of the Civil Aeronautics Board on the Investigation of an Accident Involving Aircraft in a Cross-Country Commercial Flight." File No. 1299-43. August 25, 1943.

Civil Aeronautics Board. R. C. Reeve's "Statement before the Civil Aeronautics Board, in the Matter of the Application of Reeve Airways, Valdez, Alaska, for a Certificate of Public Convenience and Necessity, Exceptions to Examiners Reports, Docket No. 340." Washington, D.C. 1939.

Congressional Record. H. 10541. November 12, 1980.

Denfeld, D. Colt, Jennifer Abel, and Dale Slaughter. "The Cold War in Alaska: A Management Plan for Cultural Resources." U.S. Army Corps of Engineers, Alaska District. August 1994.

Division of Legislative Finance for the House Finance Committee. "Air Service to Rural Alaska: A Study in Inadequacy." Report by Walter B. Parker, Patricia I. Parker, and G. Michael Harmon. 1979.

Else, Daniel H. "Defense Production Act: Purpose and Scope." Congressional Research Service. Report for Congress, RS20587. May 14, 2009.

Federal Register. "President Jimmy Carter, Presidential Proclamation 4625, December 1, 1978." 43, no. 234. December 5, 1978.

Gatchell, L. B., William R. Alley, and J. G. Johnson, editors. "Alaska Pioneer Flights." In *American Air Mail Catalogue: Reference Listing of the Air Posts of the World*. American Air Mail Society. 1940.

"Great Anchorage Today: Air Crossroad of the World." Anchorage Chamber of Commerce. Anchorage, Alaska. 1965.

"History and Mission in World War II." Counter Intelligence Corps. U.S. Army Military History Institute. Carlisle Barracks, Pennsylvania.

Parker, Walter B., Patricia I. Parker, and G. Michael Harmon. "Air Service to Rural Alaska A Study in Inadequacy." Division of Legislative Finance for the House Finance Committee. October 20, 1979.

Pilgrim, Earl. "Upper Nabesna, Chisana and Snag River Area." MR-078-02. Alaska Territorial Report. 1930.

Presidential Proclamation 4625. President Jimmy Carter. December 1, 1978. Federal Register 43, no. 234 (December 5, 1978).

"Public Hearing." Alaska Redistricting Board. April 21, 2011.

"Recollections of an Electrician at Kennecott by Wesley O. Bloom." National Park Service files. Alaska Regional Office, Anchorage.

"Reconnaissance for Radioactive Deposits in Eastern Alaska." Circular 348. U.S. Geological Survey. 1952.

"Report to the Second Assistant Postmaster General on the First Trip of the Alaska Air Mail Service." Report by C. B. Eielson. 1924.

"The Significance of the Frontier in American History." By Frederick Jackson Turner. In *Annual Report of the American Historical Association for the Year 1893*. Washington, D.C.: Government Printing Office, 1984.

Territorial Mining Report. "Mining Investigations and Mine Inspection in Alaska, Including Assistance to Prospectors." Report by B. D. Stewart. 1933.

U.S. Air Force. Office of Special Investigations. *The Air Force Office of Special Investigation: 1948–2000*. 2000.

U.S. Army. *Northern Defenders: Cold War Context of Ladd Air Force Base, Fairbanks, Alaska, 1947–1961*. By Kathy Price. CEMML TPS 01-2. Anchorage: Fort Richardson, Alaska, 2001.

U.S. Army Alaska. "The Army's Role in Building Alaska." Pamphlet 360–5. Washington, D.C. 1969.

U.S. Army Corps of Engineers. Alaska District. "The Cold War in Alaska: A Management Plan for Cultural Resources." Report by D. Colt Denfeld, Jennifer Abel, and Dale Slaughter. 1994.

U.S. Army Military History Institute. "Counter Intelligence Corps: History and Mission in World War II." Carlisle Barracks. Philadelphia. Nd.

U.S. Congress, House. *A Bill to Designated Certain Lands in the State of Alaska as Units of the National Parks, National Wildlife Refuge, and Wild and Scenic Rivers and National Wilderness Preservation System, and for Other Purposes*. HR 39, 95th Congress, 1st sess. 1977.

U.S. Congress, House Committee on Roads. *An Interim Report*. House Report No. 1705, 79th Cong., 2 sess. 1946. Pp. xi–xiii.

U.S. Geological Survey. "A Geological Guide to Wrangell–Saint Elias National Park and Preserve, Alaska; a Tectonic Collage of Northbound Terranes." By Gary Winkler et al. Professional Papers 1616. 2000.

———. "Geology of the Hanagita-Bremner Region Alaska." By Fred Moffit. Bulletin 57617. 1915.

———. *Mineral Industry of Alaska in 1931 Administrative Report*. Report by P. S. Smith. Bulletin 844-A. 1933.

U.S. Office of Indian Affairs. "Delimitation of Possessory Rights of the Athapascan Indian Natives of the Villages of Northway, Tanaross, and Tetlin in the Interior of Alaska." Report by Walter R. Goldschmidt. Unpublished report submitted to the Commissioner of Indian Affairs, Washington, D.C. 1948.

U.S. National Park Service. Alaska Regional Office. "Historic Structures Inventory, WRST." Anchorage, Alaska. 1991.

———. *Alaska Subsistence: A National Park Service Management History*. By Frank Norris. Anchorage: Alaska Regional Office, 2002.

———. "Alaska Task Force Report." January 1965.

———. Anthropology and Historic Preservation, Cooperative Park Studies Unit. *That's the Way We Live: Subsistence in the Wrangell–St. Elias National Park and Preserve*. By Holly Reckord. University of Alaska–Fairbanks, 1977.

———. Anthropology and Historic Preservation and Historic Preservation, Cooperative Park Studies Unit. *Where Raven Stood: Cultural Resources of the Ahtna Region*. By Holly Reckord. Occasional Paper No. 35. University of Alaska–Fairbanks.

———. *Bremner Historic District, Cultural Landscape Report Wrangell–St. Elias National Park and Preserve, Alaska*. By Paul J. White. Anchorage: Alaska Regional Office, 2000.

———. *Contested Ground: An Administrative History of Wrangell–St. Elias National Park and Preserve, Alaska, 1978–2001*. By Geoffrey Bleakley. Anchorage: Alaska Support Office, 2002.

———. Deed #21, Retired File WRST 35–103 John Claus. Alaska Regional Office. Anchorage, Alaska.

———. "The Development of Air Transportation, 1929–1955." By Geoffrey Bleakley. Copper Center, Alaska. Nd.

———. *"Do Things Right the First Time": Administrative History of the National Park Service and the Alaska National Interest Lands Conservation Act of 1980.* By G. Frank Williss. Anchorage: Alaska Regional Office, 2005.

———. "Hunting Activity and Harvest in the Wrangell–St. Elias Region, Alaska, 1973–1977." By Edward C. Murphy and Frederick C. Dean. CX-9000-6-0154. University of Alaska– Fairbanks, 1978.

———. *Kennecott Kids: Interviews with the Children of Kennecott,* vol. 2. Anchorage: Alaska Support Office, 2001.

———. *Mountain Wilderness: An Illustrated History of Wrangell–St. Elias National Park and Preserve, Alaska.* By William Hunt. Anchorage: Alaska Natural History Association, 1996.

———. "Nabesna Bar (Reeve Field) History." In *Historic Structures Inventory, WRST.* Anchorage: Alaska Regional Office, ca. 1991.

———. "Nizina Bridge." In *Historic Structures Inventory, WRST.* Anchorage: Alaska Regional Office, ca. 1991.

———. "Pioneer Pilots of the Wrangell-St. Elias." By Margie Steigerwald. Copper Center, Alaska. 1996

———. "Selected Residents of and Visitors to the Wrangell–St. Elias National Park Region, 1796–1950." By Geoffrey Bleakley. May 2006.

———. *Tourism in Katmai.* By Frank Norris. Anchorage: Alaska Regional Office, 1993.

———. *Whose Promised Land: A History of Conservation and Development Management Plan for the Wrangell and Saint Elias Mountains Regions Alaska (1938–1980), WRST Administrative History.* Report by Michael Lappen. Wrangell–St. Elias National Park and Preserve and UC–Santa Barbara. 1984.

———. Wrangell–Saint Elias National Park and Preserve. "A History of the Chisana Mining District, Alaska, 1890–1990." By Geoffrey T. Bleakley. Copper Center, Alaska. 1996.

BOOKS AND ARTICLES

Acepilots.com. Online at http://acepilots.com/planes/aces_descr.html.

"Alaska Community Database." Community Information Summaries. Online at www.commerce.state.ak.us.

Alaska Department of Land and Water. Online at http://dnr.alaska.gov/mlw/gcp/.

"Alaska Plane Crash: Tragedy and Rescue, an Epic of Faith and Heroism in the Frozen North." *Em Kayan* (March 1943): 1–5.

"Alaska Trunk Airport Bond, Proposition 3 (1962)." Alaska 1962 Ballot Measures. Online at www.Ballotpedia.com.

Alford, M. E. "The St. Elias." *Alaska Sportsman* (January 1965): 13–15.

Allen, June. "Harold Gillam: A Tragic Final Flight." *Sitenews.us.org.* August 17, 2004. Online at www.sitnews.us/JuneAllen/HaroldGillam/081704_final_flight.html.

"ALSIB—The Road of Courage." *Voice of Russia.* January 28, 2008. Online at http://english.ruvr.ru/2008/01/28/174235.html.

"The American Aerospace Industry during World War II." *U.S. Centennial of Flight Commission.* Online at www.centennialofflight.gov.

Arnold, Major General H. H. "Our Air Frontier in Alaska." *National Geographic Magazine* (October 1940): 487–504.

Bates, Robert. *The Love of Mountains Is Best.* Portsmouth: Peter E. Randall Publisher, 1994.

Beach, Rex. "Alaska's Flying Frontiersmen." *American Magazine* (April 1936): 42–43, 96–101.

———. *The Iron Trail.* New York: Harper & Brothers Publishers, 1913.

———. "The Place Is Alaska—the Business Is Mining." *Cosmopolitan* (January 1936).

———. *Valley of Thunder.* New York: Grosset & Dunlap, 1939.

Benson, Carl S., and Roman J. Motyka. "Glacier-Volcano Interactions on Mt. Wrangell, Alaska." *Geophysical Institute* (University of Alaska–Fairbanks) (1978): 1–25.

Berton, Pierre. *The Klondike Fever: The Life and Death of the Last Great Gold Rush.* New York: Carroll & Graf Publishers, Inc., 1958.

"Beth Day, 1924–present." *Something about the Author* 33 (1983): 55.

Bleakley, *Contested Ground: An Administrative History of Wrangell–St. Elias National Park and Preserve, Alaska, 1978–2001.* Anchorage: Alaska Support Office, 2002.

Brinkley, Douglas. *The Quiet World: Saving Alaska's Wilderness Kingdom, 1879–1960.* New York: Harper, 2011.

Bruder, Gerry. *Heroes of the Horizon: Flying Adventures of Alaska's Legendary Bush Pilots* Portland: Alaska Northwest Books, 1991.

Burnham, John B. "Hunting in the Nutzotins." *Hunting and Conservation: The Book of the Boone and Crockett Club.* Edited by George Bird Grinnell and Charles Sheldon. New Haven: Yale University Press, 1925.

Button, Kenneth John, and Roger Stough. *Air Transport Networks: Theory and Policy Implications.* Northampton: Edward Elgar Publishing, 2000.

"CAB Examiner Warns of 'Destructive Competition' in Alaskan Aviation." *American Aviation* (January 1941).

Camp, Willis. "Alaska-the World's New Crossroad." *Alaska Life* (May 1943): 19–23.

"Cats over Alaska." *The Em Kayan* (April 1942): 8–11.

Catton, Theodore. *Inhabited Wilderness: Indians, Eskimos, and National Parks in Alaska.* Albuquerque: University of New Mexico Press, 1997.

Chandonnet, Ann. "Rudy Billberg: Civilian Flyboy 1942–1945." In *Alaskan Embers: Stories Tales, Anecdotes, Vignettes, Poems, and Other Such Stuff*, 19–21. Anchorage: MMUKC Publishers, 1995.

Cloe, John Hail. *Top Cover for America: The Air Force in Alaska, 1920–1983.* Anchorage: Air Force Association and Pictorial Histories Publishing Company, 1984.

Coates, Peter A. *The Trans-Alaska Pipeline Controversy: Technology, Conservation, and the Frontier.* Fairbanks: University of Alaska Press, 1993.

Cohen, Stan. *Flying Beats Work: The Story of Reeve Aleutian Airways.* Missoula: Pictorial Histories Publishing Company, 1988.

Cole, Dermot. *Frank Barr: Bush Pilot and Alaska and the Yukon.* Edmonds: Alaska Northwest Publishing Company, 1986.

Cole, Terrence. *The Cornerstone on College Hill*. Fairbanks: University of Alaska Press, 1994.

———. *Fighting for the Forty-Ninth Star*. Fairbanks: University of Alaska Foundation, 2010.

———. "Golden Years: The Decline of Gold Mining in Alaska." *Pacific Northwest Quarterly* 80, no. 2 (April 1989): 62–71.

Collins, Reba Neighbors. *Will Rogers and Wiley Post in Alaska: The Crash Felt "Round the World."* Claremore, Oklahoma: Will Rogers Heritage Press, 1984.

Conkle, LeNora. *Bush Pilots' Wives*. Anchorage: Publication Consultations, 2000.

———. *Hunting the Way It Was in Our Changing Alaska*. Anchorage: Publication Consultants, 1998.

Courtwright, David T. *Sky as Frontier: Adventure, Aviation, and Empire*. College Station: Texas A&M University Press, 2005.

Cronon, William. "Kennecott Journey: The Paths in and out of Town." In *Under an Open Sky: Rethinking America's Western Past*. Edited by William Cronon, George Miles, and Jay Gitlin. New York: W.W. Norton & Company, 1992.

Dassow, Ethel. "The Gillam Plane Was Missing." *Alaska Sportsman* (July 1943): 16–18, 21–23.

Davis, Neil. *The College Hill Chronicles: How the University of Alaska Came of Age*. Fairbanks: University of Alaska Foundation, 1992.

Day, Beth. *Glacier Pilot: The Story of Bob Reeve and the Flyers Who Pushed Back Alaska's Air Frontiers*. New York: Henry Holt and Co., 1957.

———. "He Looked Like a Tramp." In *Early Air Pioneers: 1862–1935*. Edited by Major James F. Sunderman. New Work: Franklin Watts, Inc., 1961.

Defenderfer, Donald C., and Robert B. Walkinshaw. *One Long Summer Day in Alaska: A Documentation of Perspectives in the Wrangell Mountains*. University of California– Santa Cruz, 1981.

Dimond, Anthony J. "National Defense in Alaska." *National Aeronautics* (March 1940): 14–15.

Douglas, Dick. *In the Land of Thunder Mountain: Adventuring with Father Hubbard among the Volcanoes of Alaska*. New York: Brewer, Warren and Putnam, 1932.

Dunn, Joseph M. "Problems of Alaskan Aviation." *Farthest-North Collegian* (June 1929): 15–17.

"Economic Impact of the Ted Stevens Anchorage International Airport." *Alaska Economic Development Council and McDowell Group Research Based Consulting* (February 2012).

Etulain, Richard W. "Origins of the Western." *Journal of Popular Culture* 5 (Spring 1972): 799–805.

Findlay, John M. *Magic Lands: Western Cityscapes and American Cultural after 1940*. Berkeley: University of California Press, 1992.

Fox, William L. "Commercial Aviation: Marking Time." *Alaska Industry* (January 1972): 33. Online at www.faa.gov/about/history/brief_history/.

"From a Mountain Climber's Album: Bradford Washburn Is First to Scale Mt. Lucania." *Life* (September 27, 1937).

"Frontier Flight." *Alaska Geographic* 25, no. 4 (1998): 8.

Gallaher, Samme, and Aileen Gallaher. *Sisters: Coming of Age and Living Dangerously in the Wild Copper River Valley*. Kenmore, WA: Epicenter Press, 2004.

Garfield, Brian. *Thousand-Mile War: World War II in Alaska and the Aleutians*. Fairbanks: University of Alaska Press, 1995.

Gatchell, L. B., William R. Alley, and J. G. Johnson, eds. "Alaska Pioneer Flights." In *American Air Mail Catalogue: Reference Listing of the Air Posts of the World*. American Air Mail Society, 1940.

"Great Anchorage Today: Air Crossroad of the World." Anchorage Chamber of Commerce, Alaska, 1965.

Griese, Arnold. *Bush Pilot: Early Alaska Aviator Harold Gillam, Sr. Lucky or Legend?* Anchorage: Publication Consultants, 2005.Gruening, Ernest. *Many Battles: The Autobiography of Ernest Gruening*. Liveright Publishing, 1973.

———. *The State of Alaska*. New York: Random House, 1954.

Hartsfield, Karen. "Reeve's Unique Family Airline." *Alaska Industry* (January 1973): 34–35.

Hawley, Charles C., and T. K. Bundtzen. "William Sulzer." Alaska Mining Hall of Fame. Online at http://alaskamininghalloffame.org/inductees/sulzer.php.

Haycox, Stephen. "Early Aviation in Anchorage: Ambivalent Fascination with the Air Age." *Alaska History* (Fall 1988): 1–20.

———. *Frigid Embrace: Politics, Economics, and Environment in Alaska*. Corvallis: Oregon State University Press, 2002.

———. "Strengthening the Indian Voice: U.S. Military Relations with Natives at Two Sites in Alaska, 1942–44, and 1987–89." In *Borderlands: 1989 Heritage Conference, June 2nd–4th 1989*. Yukon Historical and Museums Association, Yukon College, Alaska Historical Society and the University of Victoria, 1989. Pp. 202–26.

Heacox, Kim. "Bold Pilots and the Great Beyond." *Alaska Magazine* 55 (July 1989): 30–35.

Helmericks, Harmon. *The Last of the Bush Pilots*. New York: Alfred A. Knopf, Inc. 1969.

Hillyer, William Hurd. "Alaska as a New Frontier: Wartime Road and Skyways May Implement Post-War Boom." *Barron's National Business and Financial Weekly* (December 6, 1943): 23.

Holloway, David. *Stalin and the Bomb: The Soviet Union and Atomic Energy*. New Haven: Yale University Press, 1994.

"Horse Hunts—the Sporting Way." *Alaska Sportsman* (November 1968): 27.

Huber, Louis R. "Flight to Katmai." *Alaska Sportsman* (April 1951): 9.

Hummel, Laurel J. "The U.S. Military as Geographical Agent: The Case of Cold War Alaska." *Geographical Review* 95 (January 2005): 47–72.

Inouye, Ronald. "Harry Sotaro Kawabe: Issei Businessman of Seward and Seattle." *Alaska History* (1990).

"Jack Wilson." Thread on Café Supercub forum. Online at www.supercub.org/forum/showthread.php?21580–Jack-Wilson.

Janson, Lone E. *Mudhole Smith: Alaska Flier.* Anchorage: Alaska Northwest Publishing Company, 1981.

Jessen, Gene Nora. *The Powder Puff Derby of 1929: The True Story of the First Women's Cross-Country Air Race.* Naperville, Illinois: SourceBooks, Inc., 2002.

Johnson, Bill. "Fort Greely's Remote Reactor: Alaska's Experiment with Nuclear Power." *Alaska History* 11, no. 1 (Spring 1996): 27–34.

Judge, Joseph. "Alaska: Rising Northern Star." *National Geographic* 147, no. 6 (June 1975): 730–67.

K., Bob. "The Alaskan Project: Secret Plans for Agents to Defend Alaska." *Gung-Ho Annuals* (1986): 54–60.

Kauffman, Virgil. "It's Rugged in Alaska!" *Aero Service Corp Newsletter* (December 1950).

"Keep 'Em Flying." *The Em Kayan* (July 1942): 3.

"Keeping the Engine Oil Warm at 60 below." *Aircraft Maintenance Technology* (April 2007).

Keim, Charles. "Otto W. Geist: A Legend in His Own Lifetime." *UA News Release* (August 6, 1963).

Kennedy, Michael S. "Arctic Flying Machines and Alaskan Bush Pilots: A Synopsis of Early Aviation History." In *Transportation in Alaska's Past,* 183–238. Office of History and Archaeology Publication No. 30. (Anchorage: Alaska Historical Society, 1982).

Kesselman, Steven. "The Frontier Thesis and the Great Depression." *Journal of the History of Ideas* 29, no. 2 (April–June 1968): 253–68.

King, L. Jo. *Bird in the Bush.* Anchorage: KwiE Publishing, Ltd., 2008.

Kirchhoff, M. J. *Historic McCarthy: The Town That Copper Built.* Juneau: Alaska Cedar Press, 1993.

Kohlhoff, Dean. *When the Wind Was a River: Aleut Evacuation in World War II.* Seattle: University of Washington Press, 1995.

Kollin, Susan. *Nature's State: Imagining Alaska as the Last Frontier.* Chapel Hill: University of North Carolina Press, 2001.

Komons, Nick A. *Bonfires to Beacons: Federal Civil Aviation Policy under the Air Commerce Act, 1926–1938.* Washington, D.C.: Smithsonian Institution Press, 1989.

Koontz, G. Bradley. "Alaska's 1930s Bush Pilots: Remarkable Fliers and Creative Mechanics Keeping the Engine Oil Warm at 60 below." *Aircraft Maintenance Technology* (April 2007): 36–41.

Lappen, Michael. *Whose Promised Land? A History of Conservation and Development Management Plans for the Wrangell and Saint Elias Mountain Region, Alaska, 1938–1980.* Report commissioned by National Park Service. 1984.

Lauzen, Elizabeth. "Marketing the Image of the Las Frontier." *Alaska Journal* (Spring 1982): 13–19.

Levi, Steven C. *Cowboys of the Sky: The Story of the Alaska's Bush Pilots.* Anchorage: Publications Consultants, 2008.

Lien, Paul. "Angels in Furs: A Cavalcade of Alaska Aviation" *Alaska Life* (1940).

Long, Everett A., and Ivan Y. Neganblya. *Cobras over the Tundra*. Fairbanks: Arktika Publishing, 1992.

Marshall, Robert. *Alaska Wilderness: Exploring the Central Brooks Range*. Berkeley: University of California Press, 1973.

Maschmeyer, Gloria J. "Merle 'Mudhole' Smith." *Alaska Business Monthly* (January 1993): 42–43.

Metcalf, John E. "Alaska – Its Strategic Role in Our Defense." *Magazine of Wall Street* (January 3, 1957).

"Merle K. 'Mudhole' Smith, 1920–1981." *Alaska Airlines Magazine* (August 1981).

"Merle K. 'Mudhole' Smith, 1908–1981." *Alaskafest* (August 1981): 4.

Miller, Orlando W. *The Frontier in Alaska and the Matanuska Colony*. New Haven: Yale University Press, 1975.

Mills, Stephen E., and James W. Phillips. *Sourdough Sky*. New York: Bonanza Books, 1969.

Mondor, Colleen. *The Map of My Dead Pilots: The Dangerous Game of Flying in Alaska*. Gillford, Connecticut: Lyons Press, 2012.

Nash, Roderick. "Aviation and Gates of the Arctic National Park." *Orion Nature Quarterly* 2 (Spring 1993): 5–13.

———. "Tourism, Parks, and the Wilderness Idea in the History of Alaska." *Alaska in Perspective* 4, no. 1 (1981): 1–27.

———. *Wilderness and the American Mind*. New Haven: Yale University Press, 1982.

Naske, Claus-M. *Alaska Road Commission Historical Narrative*. Anchorage: Alaska Department of Transportation and Public Facilities, 1983.

———. *Paving Alaska's Trails: The Work of the Alaska Road Commission*. Studies in History no. 152. Anchorage: Alaska Historical Commission, 1986.

Neuberger, Captain Richard L. "Airway to Russia." *Alaska Life* (October 1944): 3–14.

"1949–1953 Terris Moore: University of Alaska's Second President." *UA Journey, UA Online* at www.alaska.edu/uajourney/presidents/1949–1953.

Page, Dorothy. *Polar Pilot: The Carl Ben Eielson Story*. Danville, Illinois: Interstate Publishers, Inc. 1992.

Parrington, Vernon L. *Main Currents in American Thought*, vol. 3. New York, 1930.

Patty, Ernest N. "The Airplane's Aid to Alaskan Mining." *Mining and Metallurgy* (February 1937): 92–94.

Perras, Galen Roger. *Stepping Stones to Nowhere: The Aleutian Islands, Alaska, and American Military Strategy, 1867–1945*. Annapolis, Maryland: Naval Institute Press, 2003.

Plafker, George, and Henry C. Berg. "The Geology of Alaska." In *The Geology of North America*. Boulder, Colorado: Geological Society of America, 1994.

Potter, Jean. *Flying Frontiersmen*. New York: Macmillan Company, 1956.

———. *The Flying North*. New York: Macmillan Company, 1945.

Rearden, Jim. *Alaska's First Bush Pilots, 1923–30: And the Winter Search in Siberia for Eielson and Borland*. Missoula: Pictorial Histories Publishing Company, Inc., 2009.

———. *Hunting Alaska's Far Places*. Missoula: Pictorial Histories Publishing Company, 2008.

———. *In the Shadow of Eagles: Rudy Billberg's Story*. Anchorage: Alaska Northwest Books, 1992.

Redding, Robert H. *The Young Eagles: The Story of the Alaska Road Commission*. Valdez: Camprobber Publishers, 1977.

Reeder, Pat. "Remember When or As I Recollect." *WillRogers.com*. Online at www .willrogers.com/writers/stories/recollections/remember.html.

Riegel, Robert E., and Robert G. Athearn. *America Moves West*. 4th edition. New York: Holt, Rinehart and Winston, Inc., 1964.

Ringer, Gregory D. "The Wilderness Begins at McCarthy: Perceptual Impacts of Tourism on Communities." PhD dissertation for the Department of Geography, University of Oregon. June 1993. McCarthy-Kennicott Museum.

Roberts, David. *Escape from Lucania: An Epic Story of Survival*. New York: Simon & Schuster, 2002.

Roosevelt, Theodore. *Winning of the West*. 4 volumes. Charleston, South Carolina: BiblioLife, 2010.

Ross, LeahDean Kirkpatrick. *Some of My Experiences in Alaska*. Newton, Kansas: Mennonite Press, 1998.

Rozell, Ned. "Forty Years and Counting on Mount Wrangell." *Alaska Science Forum* (August 12, 2004).

Rumerman, Judy. "The Douglas DC-3." U.S. Centennial of Flight Commission. Online at www.centennialofflight.gov/essay/Aerospace/DC-3/Aero29.htm.

Salisbury, Gay, and Laney Salisbury. *The Cruelest Miles: The Heroic Story of Dogs and Men in a Race against an Epidemic*. New York: W. W. Norton & Company.

Savage Jr., William W. *Cowboy Life: Constructing an American Myth*. 2nd edition. Niwot: Colorado Press, 1993.

Sax, Joseph L. *Keeping Special Places Special: McCarthy Kennicott and the Wrangell–St. Elias Park, a Great Challenge, an Unique Opportunity*. McCarthy, Alaska: McCarthy-Kennicott Historical Museum, 1990.

Sellers, Richard West. *Preserving Nature in the National Parks: A History*. New Haven: Yale University Press, 1997.

Serling, Robert J. *Character and Characters: The Spirit of Alaska Airlines*. Seattle: Documentary Media LLC, 2008.

Sheldon, Charles, Clinton Hart Merriam, and Edward William Nelson. *Wilderness of Denali*. New York: C. Scribner's Sons, 1930.

Sherman, Stephen. "North American P-51: Generally Considered the Best Fighter of WWII." April 2002.

Sherwood, Morgan. *Big Game in Alaska*. New Haven: Yale University Press, 1981.

Siebert Charles. "After the Spill." *Men's Journal* (April 1999).

"Sky King TV Show." *Crazy about TV.com*. Online at www.crazyabouttv.com/skyking .html.

Smith, Kenny. "Airplanes in the Wrangells." *Wrangell St. Elias News* (January and February 2000).

———. "Airplanes in the Wrangells." *Wrangell St. Elias News* (March and April 2000).

———. "Airplanes in the Wrangells, Harold Gillam Update." *Wrangell St. Elias News* (May and June 2001).

———. "Airplanes in the Wrangells—Jack Wilson." *Wrangell St. Elias News* (January and February 2002).

———. "First Crash on the New McCarthy Airstrip." *Wrangell St. Elias News* (March and April 2008).

Solie, Daniel. "Icing on the Fire: A Season on the Summit of Mount Wrangell." *Alaska Journal* (Fall 1984): 12.

Spenser, Ted. "Stearman Saga." *Alaska Flying*. Nd.

Stanley, Kirk. *Nabesna Gold and the Making of the Historic Nabesna Gold Mine and Town on the Frontier of Alaska Territory*. Anchorage: Todd Communications, 2005.

Sterling, Bryan B., and Frances N. Sterling. *Will Rogers and Wiley Post: Death at Barrow*. New York: M. Evans and Company, Inc., 1993.

Stevens, Robert W. *Alaskan Aviation History*. Des Moines, Washington: Polynyas Press, 1990.

———. "*Spirit of Valdez*, Owen Meals, and the First Airplane in Valdez." *Alaska Journal* (Spring 1985): 46–48.

"They Died Flying the Mail." National Postal Museum. Online at www.postalmuseum .si.edu/airmail/pilot/pilot_old/pilot_flying.html.

Tippets, John M. *Hearts of Courage: The Gillam Plane Crash and the Amazing True Story of Survival in the Frozen Wilderness of Alaska*. Anchorage: Publication Consultants, 2008.

Tordoff, Dirk. *Mercy Pilot: The Joe Crosson Story*. Kenmore, Washington: Epicenter Press, 2002.

Tower, Elizabeth. *Alaska's First Homegrown Millionaire: Life and Times of Cap Lathrop*. Anchorage: Publication Consultants, 2006.

Turner, Frederick Jackson. "The Significance of the Frontier in American History." *Annual Report of the American Historical Association for the Year 1893*. Washington, D.C.: Government Printing Office, 1984.

"U.S. Aviation Research Helped Speed Victory." World War II and the National Advisory Committee for Aeronautics, FS-LaRC-95-07-01, July 1995. National Aeronautic and Space Administration (NASA). Online at www.nasa.gov/centers/ langley/news/factsheets/WWII_prt.htm.

Wachel, Pat. "An Alaskan Fearless Flier: Harold Gillam." *Alaska Northern Lights* 1, no. 2 (1966): 18–20.

———. *Oscar Winchell: Alaska's Flying Cowboy*. Minneapolis: T. S. Denison & Company, Inc., 1967.

Walsh, John Evangelist. *When the Laughing Stopped: The Strange, Sad Death of Will Rogers*. Fairbanks: University of Alaska Press, 2008.

"Walter Wood's First Ascent of Mount Steele." *Life* (November 30, 1936).

Washburn, Bradford. "Aerial Exploration of the Great Glaciers of the Alaskan Coast and Interior (abstract)." *American Geological Society Bulletin* 52, no. 12 (December 1, 1941): 1937.

———. "A Preliminary Report on Studies of the Mountains and Glaciers of Alaska." *Geographical Journal* 98, no. 5/6 (November–December 1941): 219–27.

Webb, W. P. *Divided We Stand: The Crisis of a Frontierless Democracy.* New York: Farrar & Rinehart, 1937.

White, Richard. "Are You and Environmentalist or Do You Work for a Living? Work and Nature." In *Uncommon Ground: Rethinking the Human Place in Nature.* Edited by William Cronon. New York: W. W. Norton & Company, 1996.

———. *The Organic Machine: The Remaking of the Columbia River.* New York: Hill and Wang, 1996.

White, Richard, and Patricia Nelson Limerick. *The Frontier in American Culture.* Edited by James R. Grossman. Berkley: University of California Press, 1994.

Willoughby, Barrett. *Alaskans All.* Boston: Houghton Mifflin, 1933.

Wilson, Jack. *Glacier Wings and Tales.* Anchorage: Great Northwest Publishing and Distributing Company, Inc., 1988.

———. *The Quest for Dall Sheep.* Wasilla, Alaska: Northern Publishing, 1997.

Wilson, Lavell. "Northway and Tanacross: Airports for the War Effort." *Alaska Geographic, World War II in Alaska* (1995): 72–76.

Wilson, John R. M. *Turbulence Aloft: The Civil Aeronautics Administration amid Wars and Rumors of Wars, 1938–1953.* Washington, D.C.: U.S. Department of Transportation, 1979.

Winslow, Kathryn. *Alaska Bound.* New York: Dodd, Mead & Company, 1960.

Witter, Greg. "Flying into 70 Years of Service: Mudhole's the Name." *Alaska's World* (August 17, 2001).

Wood, Walter A. "The Icefield Ranges Research Project." *Geographical Review* 53, no. 2 (1963): 163–84.

"World War II Aviation." Smithsonian National Air and Space Museum. Online at http://airandspace.si.edu/exhibitions/gal205/.

Yarber, Y., and C. Madison. *Walter Northway.* Fairbanks: Alaska Native Language Center College of Liberal Arts, 1987.

INTERVIEWS AND PERSONAL COMMUNICATION

Benson, Carl. Personal communication with author. June 2011. Fairbanks, Alaska.

Bramsteadt, Susan. Interviewed by author. June 2011. Anchorage, Alaska.

Claus, Paul. Personal communication with author. December 16, 2012. Eagle River, Alaska.

"Cole and Lorene Ellis." *Project Jukebox*, H95-71-02. By Bill Schneider and Dave Krupa. University of Alaska–Fairbanks. June 11, 1993.

Cole, Terrence. *Building Alaska, Great Projects.* Film Company Production, 2010.

Edwards, James. Interviewed by author and Dan Trepal. July 7, 2010. McCarthy, Alaska.

"Hannah, Jim." *Project Jukebox,* H97105. University of Alaska–Fairbanks. June 14, 1993.

"Jack Wilson—Glennallen." *Project Jukebox*, H95-71-10. University of Alaska–Fairbanks. 1992.

"Kirk Ellis." *Project Jukebox*, H95-71-01. Interviewed by Bill Schneider and David Krupa. University of Alaska–Fairbanks. June 11, 1992.

Knutson, Howard. Personal communication with author. August 15, 2013. Anchorage, Alaska.

Leitzel, Charles R. "Bob." Telephone communication with author. November 2011. Anchorage and California.

INDEX

Woods, Earl, 44
World Heritage Park, 179
World War I, 21
World War II, Alaska's role: airfield construction, 100, 101–6, 110–16, 124;
civilian conditions, 110–12, 114–15,
118; congressional debates/actions,
98, 99–100; gold mining, 118, 125–
27, 224n16; isolationism's influence,
97–98; Japanese occupation, 5, 109,
114, 116–17; pre-war military concerns, 98–99; road construction,
219n43; as transport bridge to Soviet
Union, 101, 102–3; weather hazards,
115–16
Wrangell Mountain Air, 187
Wrangell Mountain Observatory, 146–
53, 154, photo section B

Wrangell Mountains, overview, 2, 11–12
Wrangell-Saint Elias National Monument, 179
Wrangell-Saint Elias National Park and
Preserve, 145, 180–81, 186–87, 192,
199
Wright, Gerald, 178, 182
writers, portrayals of bush pilots, 5–7,
19–20, 22–23, 60–62, 67

Yakataga Beach, 42, 73, 74, 124, 165,
photo section A
Yakutat, 74, 165, 178, 184
Yellow Band Gold Mines, Inc., 82, 94,
126, 127
Yukon tourism, Canada's support, 136

Zenith biplanes, 38, 44, 208n75